MAXIMIZING INTELLIGENCE

MAXIMIZING INTELLIGENCE

DAVID J. ARMOR
WITH THE ASSISTANCE OF SUSAN L. AUD

TRANSACTION PUBLISHERS
NEW BRUNSWICK (U.S.A.) AND LONDON (U.K.)

Second printing 2005
Copyright © 2003 by Transaction Publishers, New Brunswick, New Jersey.

Library of Congress Catalog Number: 2002075087
ISBN: 0-7658-0185-X
Printed in the United States of America

Library of Congress Cataloging-in-Publication Data

Armor, David J.
  Maximizing intelligence / David J. Armor.
    p. cm.
  Includes bibliographical references and index.
  ISBN 0-7658-0185-X (cloth)
    1. Intellect. 2. Intelligence levels. I. Title.

BF431 .A5775 2003
153.9—dc21   2002075087

Contents

Preface

I first became interested in the factors that influence intelligence and academic achievement in 1965. That was the year I joined a large team doing a study required by the Civil Rights Act of 1964. The team was led by the late sociologist James Coleman, and it produced the now classic report, Equality of Educational Opportunity (EEO). Like Coleman and the rest of the team, I believed we were going to explain why African American students had lower test scores than white students. I believed we were going to demonstrate that black students attended segregated schools with inadequate resources and programs, and that these school deficiencies would explain most of the achievement gap.

I was as surprised as any team member when we could not document significant school resource differences between predominately black and predominately white schools, at least when we divided schools by region (at that time Southern school districts generally had fewer resources than Northern districts). I was even more surprised when we found very small achievement effects for most school and teacher characteristics after controlling for family socioeconomic (SES) characteristics. Even without formal controls for SES, the simple correlations between achievement and school resources were much smaller than the correlations between achievement and family background. My first essay on this issue appeared in *On the Equality of Educational Opportunity,* edited by Harvard Professors Frederick Mosteller and Patrick Daniel Moynihan (1972).

The EEO report had one set of findings that seemed to support the notion that desegregated schools benefited the academic achievement of African American students. The seminal Supreme Court decision, *Brown v. Board of Education,* had also implied this benefit, and therefore many civil rights advocates immediately concluded that the Coleman report supported the desegregation benefit thesis. I was not so sure, because in the EEO data most school characteristics had fared poorly as predictors of academic achievement. Moreover, at the time of the EEO study, most desegregated schools existed because of housing patterns, which meant that desegregated schools had higher SES black students than segregated schools.

Given my concerns about how the Coleman report was being interpreted, I welcomed the opportunity to participate in a study of a voluntary busing program in the Boston area (called METCO). The METCO program bused Boston

African American students to suburban school districts in order to experience integrated education in some of the finest school systems in the nation. Because of my work with the Coleman data, I was not too surprised to find that desegregation did not improve the academic achievement of black students. Moreover, I discovered that other busing programs were also documenting the lack of educational benefits, and I published these findings in *The Public Interest* in 1972 ("The Evidence on Busing").

Over the next twenty-five years I served as an expert witness in dozens of school districts that were involved in some type of litigation, and I conducted special case studies as a basis for my testimony. In many of these cases a major question was whether the lower achievement of minority students (or minority school districts) was caused by policies of the school district or whether it was due to factors beyond control of school officials, such as the socioeconomic conditions of minority families.

There were two consistent findings in these case studies that are relevant to the propositions advanced by this book. First, lower minority achievement could be explained by a combination of family socioeconomic factors (usually poverty) and low achievement scores at the beginning of schooling—before school policies and programs could have much effect. Second, the achievement levels of minority students were generally not correlated (or correlated only weakly) with school characteristics such as expenditures, teacher experience, teacher education levels, teacher certification, class size, and the racial composition of schools. In other words, like the original Coleman report, student achievement was strongly related to family characteristics but only weakly, if at all, to school resources and programs.

A major limitation in all these case studies was that the number of family background measures was usually limited to poverty, limited English proficiency, and (sometimes) family structure (one versus two parent families). As important as these factors were, they did not comprise the totality of family characteristics that might be related to achievement. In an effort to expand my study of family factors that influence academic achievement, in 1994 I began analyzing data from the National Longitudinal Study of Youth (NLSY), which was tracking the development of children born to women in the original study. This study had many more family measures than most national studies, including mother's IQ and parenting behaviors, and it also administered a full array of cognitive tests to children both before and after they started formal schooling.

Just as I started analyzing this data, Herrnstein and Murray published *The Bell Curve*, in which they argued that parent IQ was the dominant cause of a child's intelligence through genetic transmission, and environmental factors played only a very small role. They relied heavily on data from the NLSY to support their conclusions. Although I was finding parent IQ to be the strongest single correlate of a child's IQ, I found that other family variables were also correlated with children's IQ and achievement scores even after removing the effect of mother's IQ. Moreover, when these other factors were combined in a multivariate analysis, I found that family environment factors had a combined effect on a child's achievement greater than parent IQ. This led me to reject the Herrnstein and Murray thesis that a child's intelligence was largely determined by genetic factors at birth.

There was still one vexing problem: if a child's intelligence is influenced by so many family environment factors, why do most special school and preschool programs (and school resources in general) fail to improve the achievement of low-achieving students? As I was pondering this question, the Zero to Three movement came to my attention with its controversial focus on brain development. While I do not base any of my propositions on theories of brain development, this new movement did lead me to investigate whether the malleability of intelligence might be time-dependent. Based on several different bodies of research (reviewed in chapters 2, 3, and 5), I concluded that intelligence was malleable but that malleability decreases over time. I believe this conclusion is the only reasonable explanation for two sets of well-documented results that appear inconsistent on their face. These are (1) the very strong correlations between a child's intelligence and family environmental factors (after controlling for parent IQ), and (2) the very weak correlations between a child's academic achievement and school resource or program variables.

Finally, having concluded that family environment plays a key and possibly irreversible role in shaping a child's intelligence, I was not sure what the policy implications should be. It is one thing to know that parent behaviors influence a child's intelligence; it is quite another to try to change them. Parent behavior—such dropping out of school, deciding when to have children and whether to marry first, how many children to have, how to raise children—has many deep roots and causes imbedded in our modern culture. It is notoriously difficult to change basic values about family and children.

As I was pondering the policy implications of all this, I became aware of the major pro-family initiatives being undertaken as part of the welfare reform that began in 1996. Although the welfare reform movement is concerned about children's welfare in general, it is probably not motivated primarily by improving children's intelligence levels. Yet, if the welfare reform movement succeeds in restoring the value of two-parent families and good parenting behavior to low income families, that might be its greatest legacy. It was not much of a leap to conclude, in chapter 6, that since the family has the greatest potential for maximizing the intelligence of all children, a whole family policy would be an excellent subject for a national campaign to improve the family risk factors that impact on a child's intelligence.

Acknowledgments

I would first like to thank three organizations that made this book possible. A grant from the Smith Richardson Foundation (Phoebe Cottingham, Program Director) provided support for doing the research and much of the time it took to write it. An earlier grant from the National Center for Educational Statistics, "Measuring Socioeconomic Effects on Academic Performance" (Grant no. R999B50011), also helped in the preparations for this book by supporting analyses of data collected by the National Assessment of Educational Progress. The School of Public Policy at George Mason University, and its Dean Kingsley Haynes and Senior Associate Dean Jim Finkelstein, provided important research assistant support as well as a highly conducive setting for carrying out the research and writing.

Of the many individuals who made contributions during the writing of this book, I am especially indebted to the work of Susan Aud, my research assistant for this project. She did much of the library research on the risk factors, the timing of IQ change, and early childhood interventions. Susan also wrote summaries of the literature and wrote a "technical" report, some of which has been incorporated into this book.

Several persons read the entire manuscript or major chapters and offered numerous helpful suggestions and corrections. These include Frank Fukuyama of Johns Hopkins University, Ellen Frankel Paul of Bowling Green State University, Larry Feinberg of the National Assessment Governing Board, Stephan Thernstrom of Harvard University, Belle Sawhill of the Brookings Institution, Al Lindseth of Sutherland Asbill and Brennan, and Bill Dickens of the Brookings Institution.

I owe a special intellectual debt to the late James Coleman, who gave me the opportunity to participate in the Equality of Education Opportunity project, the results of which generated some of my earliest insights about the relationship between families, schools, and cognitive ability.

I owe a very special personal debt to my wife, Marilyn Armor, who read portions of the manuscript and provided very helpful editing suggestions, but most of all because she tolerated the many inconveniences and privations that accompany the many agonies of writing a book.

1

Maximizing Intelligence

The principal aim of this book is to investigate whether children's intelligence can be raised by the intentional actions of parents and other caregivers during the developmental years. To answer this question, several other questions must also be answered: Can intelligence be changed, and if so by how much? Does the timing of actions make a difference on how much intelligence can be raised? What types of caregivers can have the greatest impact, and in particular how important are impacts of parents versus the impacts of formal educational programs, such as Head Start or Title 1? Are there specific programs or policies that would enhance the process of raising children's intelligence?

I am using the term "intelligence" broadly to represent those types of mental or cognitive abilities a child needs to succeed in school, including the mastery of such skills as language, reading, and mathematics, and that adults need to master complex knowledge and skills. To distinguish it from other types of intelligence, such as common sense or emotional and social skills, the term "academic intelligence" might be more precise. Many psychologists use the term IQ (short for "Intelligence Quotient") for this purpose, that is, the general mental abilities that lie behind specific academic skills. Many educators and social scientists use the terms "academic ability" or "academic achievement" instead. I will use these terms interchangeably in this chapter, and it should be understood that "IQ" and "academic achievement" are being used as general terms here and not as specific types of tests.

I want to state unequivocally that intelligence or IQ should not be thought of as simply a genetic or inherited mental characteristic, a common misunderstanding in our society. Some portion of intelligence may have a genetic origin, but the whole point of this book is to examine the ways in which intelligence can be changed by environmental influences. There is still much dispute about how to measure intelligence and the meaning of IQ scores, but I will save a more detailed discussion of the nature and measurement of intelligence for the next chapter.

1

To decide whether a child's IQ can be maximized, this book proposes and evaluates four basic propositions about mental ability. None of these propositions are completely original. They have been formulated and tested in the fields of education, psychology, and sociology, and they are accepted by many experts and lay persons although not necessarily a majority in each case. But these propositions have not yet been merged into a unified framework for understanding mental ability, nor one that can be used to build specific strategies for maximizing IQ.

This framework provides an alternative to the perspective offered in *The Bell Curve*, which emphasized genetic rather than environmental causes in the development of intelligence, and offered a rather pessimistic view about the feasibility of changing IQ levels.[1] In particular, this book postulates that a number of environmental conditions play a significant role in the development of intelligence, and that these environmental conditions can be molded and mobilized to help maximize a child's intelligence.

Four Propositions about Intelligence

The four propositions move successively from the nature and importance of intelligence to the external factors that influence its development. The four propositions concern the importance of intelligence, the malleability of intelligence, the risk factors for intelligence, and the ways to optimize these risk factors to maximize intelligence and achievement.

Proposition 1: The Importance of Intelligence

The first proposition is that a person's intelligence is important because it exerts a significant influence on a person's ultimate educational and occupational success. This influence follows a chronological sequence. First, a child's intelligence is manifested by basic cognitive skills that develop prior to the start of formal schooling. These include knowledge of the alphabet, vocabulary and word skills that prepare children for reading, and familiarity with numbers and counting that prepare children for mathematics.

These basic skills, which can be measured when children are three or four years old, strongly influence a student's academic success first in elementary school and then in junior and senior high. How well they master basic skills strongly affects their proficiency in more complex subject matters in reading, language, math, and science. In turn, academic success during the K-12 grades strongly influences whether a student will drop out of school, graduate without further education, or enter college and graduate successfully. Needless to say, a college graduate has many more job and career choices than a high school dropout, and these choices will in turn influence ultimate job and career success. Although factors other than IQ are important for career success, a child's IQ at the beginning of this developmental process is one of the most important determinants of later outcomes.

This proposition may sound like belaboring the obvious, but there has been much debate about the importance of academic intelligence, both within the scientific community and among the broader intellectual community. While many behavioral scientists believe that mental ability as measured by IQ tests is important, much has been written in both popular and academic media that criticizes or diminishes the importance of IQ. Some of these critiques attack the concept of IQ itself and associate it with racism and early attempts to prove that certain groups were genetically inferior to whites.[2] Others criticize the way it is measured, its reliability, that it is culturally biased, that it is not predictive of career success, or all of the above. Still others downplay the importance of traditional IQ measures by arguing that there are really multiple intelligences, and that other intelligences such as emotional intelligence or social intelligence are more important than academic IQ in determining one's life accomplishments.[3]

There is nothing wrong with the notion of multiple intelligences. Few would take issue with the fact that individuals are bestowed with (and develop) many different gifts and talents, such as athletic skill, musical or artistic ability, spiritual expression, or social skills, all of which influence a person's ultimate success in life, particularly in the occupational world of work and careers. But the existence of other valuable human characteristics should not diminish the importance of IQ as traditionally defined, given its major impacts on educational attainment, which in turn determines the range of occupations open to a person after the completion of school.

Proposition 2: Malleability of Intelligence

The second proposition is that a child's intelligence can be modified. Most behavioral scientists believe that IQ, as traditionally defined, is influenced by both "nature" and "nurture." That is, intelligence is influenced both by inherited genes and a child's environment. But there is much less consensus on exactly how much of a child's IQ comes from genes and how much from the environment, and whether environmental interventions can have an impact. At this time the genetic or "nature" component of a child's IQ—whatever its size—cannot be modified, since it is inherited from the child's biological parents. Developments in the biological sciences may someday offer a way to maximize IQ by means of genetic engineering, but that prospect is beyond technical capability at the present.

The "nurture" component of IQ has to do with a child's environment, and it covers a host of social and behavioral circumstances both within the home and in the broader community that might affect IQ. It includes the parents' socio-economic level and other family characteristics, parenting behaviors, the influences of neighborhoods and peers, and a child's involvement with other institutions such as schools and churches. It even includes the different ways in which a parent may interact with each of their children in families with more than one child, and the ways in which a child interacts with his or her environment.

Regarding the amount of IQ that comes from genes and the amount that comes from the environment, psychologists who specialize in IQ research estimate that genetic background determines anywhere from 40 to 80 percent of a person's IQ. Many social scientists believe that more than half is determined by a child's environment, and some social scientists believe that IQ is determined mostly by environmental factors. There is even new research that argues for a much more complex model, where genetic and environmental factors are highly correlated due to reciprocal causation.[4] This approach concludes that environmental factors can have strong effects on IQ even if genetic heritability is high.

This book will not take a position on exactly how much of IQ is determined by genetic versus environmental factors. Rather, it will argue and present evidence that IQ depends sufficiently on environmental influences to make it worthwhile for parents and others involved in child care and schooling to optimize these conditions in order to maximize their children's IQs.

A more important issue for this book is what aspects of the environment can be changed, and when they can be changed. I will argue that if a child's environment is changed optimally, some before birth and some after birth, a child's IQ can be raised on the order of 10 IQ points or more. While a change of this magnitude will not convert an unskilled laborer into an electronic engineer, it can make the difference between being a high school dropout and having a high school diploma, or being a high school graduate and having a two-year college degree.[5]

Proposition 3: Risk Factors for a Child's IQ

Since some portion of a child's IQ is determined by genetic factors that cannot be changed, maximizing a child's IQ requires optimizing those environmental risk factors that can be changed. The third proposition is that the most important environmental influences on a child's IQ take place in the family, and most of them occur before a child reaches school or even preschool. I call these early influences "risk factors" in the development of a child's mental ability and achievement.[6]

Optimizing some of these environmental risk factors involve parental decisions and behaviors that occur before a child is born, and others occur fairly early in a child's life but at least after birth. These risk factors include the socioeconomic status of a child's family such as education and income, various family characteristics such as family structure and family size, and parenting behaviors. Two chapters in this book are devoted to describing and explaining these risk factors and showing their impact on children's IQs.

A corollary to this third proposition is that formal schooling and even pre-school training play a secondary role in maximizing IQ and achievement. This is not to say that schools are not important, or do not make a difference. Schools are essential for learning, and in fact schools are where most children learn the specific skills of reading, writing, math, and science. But the formal education programs in America at this time are quite similar for all children, especially in the elementary grades, and therefore the effects of schooling are approximately *uniform* for most children. This means that individual differences in IQ and academic skills that exist when children start their formal schooling tend to be perpetuated from the early elementary years to the later high school years. Most children who start school with low IQs will go through school with below-average performance and will be less likely to enter and graduate from college, and consequently will have fewer opportunities for professional, technical, and managerial careers.

This phenomenon is best illustrated by the well-known achievement gap between white and certain minority children (see chapter 4). This gap can be measured in kindergarten, and even in the pre-school years. It is well documented that the achievement gap between black and white children, taken as two groups, persists from the early elementary grades to the later secondary grades despite the best efforts of special school programs to counteract the difference.

Proposition 4: Families are the Best Agents of Change

The fourth proposition is that the most likely and most promising agents for maximizing a child's IQ are the child's parents and family, who are in the best position for optimizing environmental risk factors. In fact, parents are the only people who can reduce the risk of some environmental factors with decisions made before a child is born, and they have a better opportunity than anyone else for maximizing other environmental factors.

For example, considering the risk factors before conception, only a woman can control the age at which she gets pregnant, or the decision to have and raise a child out of wedlock, or the number of children she will have. With regards to risk factors after birth, parents are not the only potential agents of change. Trained staff at an early childhood center can also engage in "parenting" behaviors. But since a young child spends most of the time with its family, parents are in the best position for optimizing those parenting behaviors that influencing a child's environment and development.

The importance of this fourth proposition cannot be overemphasized. Today's focus on government programs for improving the academic achievement of at-risk children—remedial programs in schools, preschool training like Head Start, and special child care programs—may have convinced many parents that the best opportunity for improving their child's academic achievement is in school rather than at home. Parents with at-risk children who fail to understand the critical importance of the early childhood environment and early parenting behaviors, and who wait for school programs to help their children, are probably increasing the likelihood that their children will experience academic failure.

To sum up, these four propositions about intelligence can be stated simply. IQ is important because it influences success in school and careers. IQ can be changed by environmental influences (risk factors) providing they occur early enough. The most important risk factors reside in the family, and therefore the family is in the best position to maximize intelligence.

The Ten Most Important Risk Factors

There is much agreement among researchers about the conditions or behaviors that have the greatest influence on a child's IQ, what I call "risk factors." I am using the term "risk factor" in a way similar to its use in medical research, that is, to identify conditions or behaviors that increase or decrease the risk (or probability) of getting various illnesses. In the case of intelligence, a risk factor is a condition or behavior that tends to increase or decrease a child's intelligence. A risk factor can be either genetic or environmental in origin.

I will briefly describe the ten most important risk factors for a child's IQ here, but they will be explained and discussed in more detail in chapter 3. A child's IQ is affected by the following conditions:

1.   Parents' IQ;

2.   Parents' educational attainment;

3.   Family income and poverty status;

4.   Family structure (marriage and parents at home);

5.   Age of mother when child is born;

6.   The number of siblings;

7.   The child's nutrition;

8.   The child's birth weight;

9.   Parental instruction (cognitive stimulation); and

10.   Parental nurturing (emotional support).

With the exception of risk factor 1, parents' IQ, and factor 8, birth weight, the other eight factors in this list are environmental, meaning they can be modified by parents or prospective parents, at least to some extent. Parents' IQ, and particularly a mother's IQ, cannot be easily changed after a prospective parent has reached the late teen years. Parents' IQ includes genetic or biological effects, but parents' intelligence may also lead to environmental effects. That is, more intelligent parents might create a better home environment that optimizes other factors such as parenting. For the purpose of this book, however, it does not matter whether the effect of parental IQ is genetic or environmental; the important thing is that a new or prospective mother, whether a teenager or a young adult, cannot easily increase her IQ. Moreover, a mother might not be able to control a child's birth weight, since it may be due to medical conditions or other circumstances beyond a mother's control. To the extent that other risk factors influence low birth weight, such as adolescence or poor nutrition, this risk factor might also be classified as partially determined by other environmental factors.

Risk factors 7, 9, and 10—nutrition, cognitive stimulation, and emotional support—can be changed or optimized after a child is born, and to some extent they can be provided or supplemented by non-parents inside or outside the home. Theoretically, parents are in the best position to provide instruction and nurturing, since most young children spend most of their time with parents. Cognitive stimulation, at least, can be enhanced in child care settings by professional caregivers, providing the caregivers know what they are supposed to do and how to do it. It is less clear whether a parent's nurture can be replaced by a caregiver outside the home; absence of love and nurturing by a parent may create emotional problems that cannot be overcome by outside intervention. Factor 3, income, can also be supplemented by government welfare programs.

Factors 2 through 6 are controlled primarily by the decisions and behaviors of prospective parents before conception. Prospective mothers who decide to drop out of high school, who decide to have a child without a father at home, or who decide to have a large family in spite of limited financial resources, may increase the risk that their child will have a low IQ. While non-parents can counsel prospective parents about these adverse influences, the decisions themselves are solely in the hands of prospective parents.

By introducing the notion of risk, I want to stress that the conditions or behaviors in question are not *guaranteed* to have a certain effect on IQ for a particular child, but that each of them has a significant *probability* of affecting IQ on the average. For example, smoking and being overweight are known to increase the risk of certain illnesses such as cancer or heart disease, but no single smoker or obese person is certain to get cancer or heart disease. One stops smoking or loses weight because it lowers the risk or probability of getting various illnesses.

Likewise, each of the ten risk factors outlined above are associated with increases or decreases in a child's IQ, but no single factor determines what a child's IQ will be, nor will maximizing all ten factors guarantee a result for a given child. When I speak of maximizing a child's IQ, I mean that children who have optimal levels for all ten factors are *most likely* to have the highest IQ's and the best academic records in school. Children who have lower levels of all factors generally start school far behind their peers and seldom catch up.

In order to maximize a child's IQ, it is also important to understand some of the conditions or factors that are less important for a child's IQ. Parent's energies should be put into those activities that matter, rather than those that do not. For example, once the risk factors above are taken into account, there is little evidence of negative influences on a child's IQ from a mother who smokes or uses alcohol moderately during pregnancy, or by a mother who works while her children are growing up.

Perhaps the most overrated environmental factors are those special educational programs designed to raise the achievement of low-IQ children during the pre-school and elementary school years, such as Head Start or the remedial school programs offered under the federal Title 1 program. If a child has reached the age of four or five and has a low IQ, research shows that these programs rarely raise a child's IQ or academic achievement by a significant degree. More will be said about these less important factors in chapter 5.

As in the case of preventive medicine, it is one thing to identify risk factors for a given illness and something else to alter these risk factors. For example, it is well documented that smoking substantially increases the risk of lung cancer and emphysema, but many people still smoke. It is well known that being overweight contributes to a variety of health problems, but people still overeat.

Likewise, while there is much evidence that the ten risk factors identified above influence a child's IQ, there is less agreement about how to change some of these factors. One conclusion, however, is uppermost and is a major theme of this book. All but two of these factors (parent IQ and birth weight) *can* be changed by people who are planning to become parents, providing the right decisions are made prior to conception or early in a child's life. It may not be easy to change these conditions, and not everyone can attain the highest levels for each of the factors, but it is important for prospective parents, and their parents, to know that these risk factors *can* be changed in a positive direction, and if changed, they are likely to make an important contribution to their child's IQ.

The Basis for the Book

The advice offered in this book is based on an extensive research literature about the relationships between a child's IQ or academic achievement and a large number of potential influences. These influences include family background, parental behaviors, characteristics of the child, and factors outside the family such as childcare and school programs. This research literature is in general (but not total) agreement about the ten risk factors that directly influence a child's IQ. There is less agreement among experts, however, about the factors or conditions that have little or no influence on a child's IQ, and especially on the question of whether special pre-school programs and school remedial programs can have a significant impact on a child's IQ or achievement.

One study of risk factors that will be relied on heavily in this book is called Children of the National Longitudinal Study of Youth. This study will be abbreviated as Youth Study or simply CNLSY. This is the most comprehensive study of child development ever undertaken in the United States. It follows a large group of 9,000 children born to a representative sample of 5,000 women who were first surveyed in 1979 when they were fifteen to twenty-one years old. Aside from the large number of children, and the fact that children are followed over time, this study assesses a greater number of potential risk factors than most other national studies of child development.

Most research on IQ and academic achievement is in agreement about the important role played by such characteristics as parent education, poverty, marital status, and the parenting behaviors of cognitive stimulation. That is, few researchers would disagree that a child whose family consists of a single mother, who is a high school dropout, and who is below the poverty line is at a high risk of having academic problems in school. In fact, the U.S. Census defines such children as being at "high risk" for academic problems.

There has been more debate, however, about the extent to which special educational programs, especially those provided by government-funded Head Start or Title 1 compensatory programs, can raise the low IQ of a child who comes from an impoverished, uneducated, single-parent family. In spite of many comprehensive research studies that show few lasting effects from these programs on a child's academic achievement, many education experts maintain that these programs could have a significant effect if they were better-implemented, which usually means more intensity and more time (and greater cost). It remains to be seen if the government will put substantially greater money into these programs, and even then it will have to be proven that more intense programs are more effective than the current programs. In the meantime, given the number of risk factors under the control of parents, it makes little sense to wait and see if a government program can overcome negative influences from the family, rather than attacking the problem at the source.

Because of the traditional importance of formal school programs in overcoming the adverse effects of poverty and disadvantage on academic achievement, a major portion of chapter 5 will be devoted to presenting and discussing the role of formal schooling as an agent of change, and particularly evaluations of compensatory programs. Several major evaluations of compensatory programs will be discussed, as well as some original analyses of national data and a number of case studies that have bearing on the issue.

Organization of the Book

Chapter 2, "The Nature and Importance of Intelligence," presents evidence and arguments concerning both propositions 1 and 2. Regarding the proposition that IQ is an important predictor of school and occupational success, evidence is presented to show the chronological sequence of influence. First, a child's pre-schooling IQ influences academic achievement in the early school years. Second, academic achievement in the early school years has a very strong influence on academic achievement in the later school years, during which time key educational choices are made, including dropping out of high school and going on to higher education. Finally, academic achievement at the end of high school is a strong predictor of final educational attainment and occupational status. While IQ is not the only personal characteristic that determines educational and occupational outcomes, it is one of the strongest predictors at each stage of development.

Regarding the proposition that IQ is malleable, evidence is discussed at two different levels of change. At the societal level, IQ has changed for total populations or large subpopulations over relatively short time intervals, suggesting environmental rather than genetic causes. At the individual level, both IQ and academic achievement are relatively stable at older ages, with little reliable change, but the younger the child, the more likely it is that both IQ and academic achievement can change by meaningful degrees. This also opens the door for possible environmental effects, albeit at younger ages. This chapter suggests environmental effects on IQ but does not attempt to specify exactly what these environmental effects might be.

Chapter 3, "The Risk Factors for Intelligence," will evaluate Proposition 3 by describing each of the most important risk factors for a child's IQ, showing the effect each factor has on IQ and any important conditions that might modify the effect. In some cases, the risk factor itself has to be explained, because it is made up of many separate components. Explanation is especially important for the parenting behaviors of cognitive stimulation and emotional support. The major studies that have documented the effect of each risk factor will also be mentioned. This chapter is perhaps the most important in the book, because it establishes the basis for arguing that changes in a risk factor can influence a child's IQ and subsequent academic achievement.

Chapter 4, "Race, Family, and Intelligence," continues the discussion of risk factors, but in the context of helping to explain the IQ and achievement gaps between white children and the children of certain minority groups, especially African American children. The size of the achievement gap is documented, as well as some of the reductions in the achievement gap that have been observed in national studies. The discussion goes on to show how the risk factors can explain a good portion of existing achievement and IQ gaps, as well as some of the earlier reductions in achievement gaps. Chapter 4 also shows that very little of the existing gaps can be explained by existing deficiencies in school programs. An important goal of this chapter is to show that the IQ and achievement gaps between white children and black or Hispanic children are not due to race or ethnicity per se, and that the best strategy for closing these gaps is by changing certain family risk factors that have the greatest impact on minority children's IQ.

Chapter 5, "Agents of Change for Intelligence," will start with the corollary of Proposition 3 that risk factors operate early in a child's development, and that the ability to change a child's IQ and achievement diminish substantially by the time a child is seven or eight. It then moves on to discuss another corollary of Proposition 3, which is that most special schooling and pre-school interventions come too late to have a large impact on raising IQ or academic achievement of high-risk children. These interventions include pre-school programs such as Head Start, and school programs such as compensatory education (e.g., Title 1 programs). The evidence introduced here represents some of the best arguments for the early-childhood theory of IQ modification.

Chapter 5 will then discuss Proposition 4, that the best agent of change for optimizing risk factors and maximizing IQ is the family. Evidence and discussion will focus on the problem of changing the risk factors themselves, including the extent to which each risk factor can be changed, when the factor should or can be changed, and who is in the best position to bring about change. The role of parents, parents-to-be, and non-family persons or agencies such as childcare workers and centers are evaluated as potential agents of change. While the family is proposed as the best and most "cost effective" place for change, evidence will be introduced that intensive early-infant childcare interventions is another possible avenue for maximizing a child's IQ, but is an avenue that is probably limited by considerations of cost and the ethics of intervening when children are still in their infancy.

Finally, chapter 6 discusses some of the broader public policy implications of the findings and conclusions of the preceding chapters. Assuming that the family is the best locus for maximizing IQ, the major policy issue becomes what sort of public policies might be able to change the most important risk factors. Special attention will be given to policies that might affect such family characteristics, such as teen pregnancy, single parent families, family size, and key parenting behaviors, in order to equip parents with better tools to influence their child's intellectual development and therefore to provide greater opportunities for maximizing IQ.

Notes

1. R. J. Herrnstein and C. Murray, *The Bell Curve*, New York: The Free Press, 1994.
2. For a thorough critique of the concept and measurement of IQ, see Stephen Jay Gould, *The Mismeasure of Man*, New York: W.W. Norton, 1996.
3. For a popularized version of multiple intelligences, see Thomas Armstrong, *7 Kinds of Smart: Identifying and Developing Your Multiple Intelligences*, New York: Plume, 1999. See also Daniel Goleman, *Emotional Intelligence*, New York: Bantum, 1995.
4. W. T. Dickens and J. R. Flynn, "Heritability Estimates Versus Large Environmental Effects: The IQ Paradox Resolved," *Psychological Review*, 108: 346-369, 2001.
5. The large national sample used in this book (NLSY) shows that high school drop-outs have an average IQ of 87, high school grads 98, two years of college 106, and college graduates 118.
6. I am not the first to use the term "risk factors" for these influences; that privilege belongs to other behavioral scientists who have done major work in this field. For example, see Eric F. Dubow and Tom Luster, "Adjustment of Children Born to Teenage Mothers: The Contribution of Risk and Protective Factors," *Journal of Marriage and the Family*, 52:393-404, 1990.

2

The Nature and Importance of Intelligence

In addressing the importance of intelligence and whether it can be changed, one cannot avoid the very complex topic concerning the nature of intelligence and how it is measured. This is a very large and often controversial topic, with contributions and commentary from expert and nonexpert alike. Literally thousands of books, monographs, research articles, and popular essays on intelligence and IQ testing have been published in the nearly 100 years since the seminal works of the French psychologist Alfred Binet. It is beyond the scope of this book to produce a thorough treatise on the nature of intelligence, and fortunately it is not necessary for my purposes. It is necessary, however, to inform the reader about how I define the related concepts of intelligence, IQ, and academic achievement; what sorts of measurements I will use; and to show that goal of maximizing a child's IQ is both possible and worthwhile.

First, given the many different conceptions of intelligence or IQ and the many ways to measure it, what definitions and measurements are used in this book? In answering this first question, the difference between IQ and academic achievement is addressed. Second, what is the nature of IQ, and does this nature include the possibility of changing IQ over time? Are there time constrains on when IQ can be changed? If IQ is a fixed characteristic of a person, then there is no point in trying to maximize it. Finally, why is IQ or academic achievement important, or more accurately, in what specific ways is it important? Obviously, if the concept of intelligence is so poorly defined or so hard to measure that it has no practical value, then there is no need to worry about maximizing it.

Definition and Measurement of Intelligence

In chapter 1, the terms IQ and intelligence were used in a fairly general sense, defined loosely as those mental abilities and cognitive skills that influence how well a child does in school or how well adults can acquire complex knowledge and skills. Before discussing whether or how IQ can be changed or maximized, it is necessary to describe in more detail the definitions of intelligence and IQ used in this book, the assumptions made about the nature of intelligence, and the way in which IQ is measured. Each of these issues has been debated vigorously in the social and behavioral sciences for the past century.

Definitions

The words "intelligence" and "intelligent" are widely used with a variety of meanings in ordinary discourse. In its broadest sense, intelligence means simply the existence of rational thought, as in "human beings are intelligent life-forms." This usage is close to the original Latin, *intellegere*, which means "to understand." Perhaps more often the word is used to distinguish people who have more understanding than others, such as "she is a very intelligent student." This second usage has various synonyms such as bright, clever, shrewd, and so forth. For centuries, ordinary discourse and common sense have recognized that some people have greater understanding (of certain things) than others, and people who are described as "more intelligent" than others are generally thought to have greater understanding of a variety of topics (although not necessarily all topics).

It is not such a radical leap to try to quantify this second usage, which is precisely what Alfred Binet did when he developed the first intelligence test for the purpose of distinguishing "subnormal" children in Paris. The early Binet tests were basically a series of "thought" problems of varying complexity: a "mental" age was assigned to each problem representing the age at which a "normal" child should be able to solve it. The intelligence scale, as it was called, was derived by comparing the average mental age for the problems solved to a child's actual chronological age (scoring details are discussed below).

Most IQ tests devised since Binet's original work are variations on this theme: a person is asked to solve a variety of thought problems, such as symbol analogies; completing a sequence of numbers or objects; finding something missing in a picture; and so forth. Binet avoided explicit reliance on reading and arithmetic skills, since he was testing young children before they started school. Many later IQ tests—particularly paper-and-pencil tests for older children or adults—rely more heavily on word or arithmetic knowledge in order to pose more complex reasoning or thought problems. The earliest and most widely used written IQ test was the Army Alpha test, developed by Robert Yerkes for the Army during World War I. The Alpha test was used to some extent to place conscripts in various occupational categories, but primarily to select men for officer training.

As IQ testing developed, two other types of standardized testing evolved: aptitude testing and achievement testing. Achievement tests were developed to measure specific academic skills such as reading and mathematics as a child moves through school, as well as more specialized academic knowledge in such areas as science, history, civics, and other topics. Achievement tests can be used by teachers to evaluate the progress of individual students or by education researchers to evaluate the academic performance of groups of students—classrooms, schools, or entire school districts. Traditionally, most of these tests have been developed and maintained by test publishers, such as McGraw-Hill or the Psychological Corporation. There are also some national achievement tests developed by the Department of Education which are used to monitor state and national academic progress, the best example of which is the National Assessment of Educational Progress (NAEP).

The most prominent aptitude test is the Scholastic Aptitude Test (SAT), developed by the College Board for testing academic aptitudes of high school students who are planning to attend college. The SAT assesses verbal, quantitative, and nonverbal aptitudes (such as spatial visualization) thought to be important for college-level work. The SAT also has an achievement series for more specialized knowledge in specific subject matters, such as chemistry, various languages, history, and so forth. During the 1960s and 70s, the SAT and the ACT, another aptitude test similar to the SAT, became widely used by colleges and universities as part of their admissions requirements. In recent years, however, admissions tests have become controversial due to affirmative action concerns (since minority students tend to score lower than white students). Another widely used aptitude test is the Armed Forces Qualification Test (AFQT), which is used by the military to screen new recruits. Those with very low aptitudes (lower than the tenth percentile) are not eligible to enlist; those with higher-than-average aptitudes are offered various enlistment incentives, because they tend to perform better in certain military jobs.

From the very earliest intelligence tests, a debate emerged about the dimensionality of intelligence and IQ test scores. Since the content of IQ problems falls into various categories, especially problems with more verbal content (like word analogies) and those with more quantitative content (like completing a sequence of numbers), it is reasonable to ask whether intelligence is a single mental ability or a composite of multiple mental abilities.

The single dimension view was first argued most forcefully by Charles Spearman, who used factor analysis to support this view. He showed that when a variety of cognitive subtests are analyzed, each stressing somewhat different abilities, a single strong factor emerges—called "g" for general intelligence— with most subtests having relatively strong correlations with the single g factor.[1] The single dimension view, advocated more recently by Arthur Jenson, sees IQ scores as reflecting a single, comprehensive dimension of intelligence that underlies all other cognitive skills, and people can be ranked or scored along this dimension according to the quantity of intelligence they possess.[2]

The multidimensional theory of intelligence was given its greatest boost by Leo Thurstone, who also used factor analysis to argue that more than one factor can be interpreted from correlations among a battery of cognitive tests.[3] Most contemporary psychologists have followed Thurstone's lead and believe that intelligence is more usefully defined as a complex, multidimensional cluster of differing cognitive abilities. This allows for people to be weaker or stronger on specific abilities, so that a person's intelligence cannot be reduced to a single score; instead, one could have differing scores on a variety of cognitive abilities.

There is not complete consensus, however, on exactly what cognitive abilities should go into the list. Thurstone's original list includes seven primary abilities: verbal ability, numeric ability, spatial visualization, word fluency, associative memory, perceptual speed, and reasoning. The number of dimensions was exacerbated by the plethora of standardized aptitude and achievement tests that emerged after World War II. One recent review identified seventy different abilities measured by present-day cognitive tests.[4]

A useful distinction made by some psychologists divides cognitive abilities (and their respective tests) into two broad groupings: fluid ability (or intelligence) and crystallized abilities.[5] Fluid ability corresponds to pure reasoning ability, perhaps closest to what Spearman meant by the "g" factor. Crystallized ability is somewhat derivative, corresponding to the amount of specific knowledge that one acquires and retains over time, such as the learning that occurs in school. They are related, of course, in that persons with highly developed knowledge in various areas undoubtedly have relatively high fluid ability, and persons with low fluid ability would not be able to absorb and retain complex bodies of knowledge. On the other hand, people with low to moderate fluid ability might be able to memorize a lot of facts and do fairly well on certain types of knowledge tests (vocabulary, arithmetic, history), and others with high fluid ability could be deprived of formal education and might score poorly on knowledge tests.

Although existing tests can be classified as assessing more or less of these two types of abilities, most tests embody a combination of the two. Most youth and adult IQ tests include word meaning (such as word analogies) and number meaning (completing numeric sequences), and most achievement tests include components that reflect more reasoning skill, such as reading comprehension and math concepts. A direct measure of fluid intelligence might be Raven's Progressive Matrices, a test involving completing sequences of abstract patterns or figures that do not have any intrinsic meaning. Relatively pure measures of crystallized intelligence might be a vocabulary test, a simple arithmetic test, or a test of history facts.

Some psychologists have broadened the definition of intelligence considerably to include human abilities and talents that are not usually considered to be cognitive reasoning skills. For example, Howard Gardner has formulated a theory of "multiple intelligences" that includes not only the linguistic, logical-mathematical, and spatial abilities measured by most IQ tests, but also such abilities as musical, body/kinesthetic, and personal qualities that are not measured by IQ tests.[6] Building on Gardner's work, Daniel Goleman has proposed the concept of "emotional intelligence," which involves such abilities as empathy, control of emotions, and various types of interpersonal skills.[7] Robert Sternberg has proposed a "triarchic" theory that recognizes three types of intelligence: analytic (what most IQ and aptitude tests measure), creative, and practical.[8] Practical intelligence includes what Sternberg calls "tacit knowledge," which is knowledge gained from one's personal experiences and actions in various pursuits; it could range from the specialized knowledge and skill of a trout fisherman to that of a successful burglar. Being based in personal experience, tacit knowledge is usually not correlated very highly with traditional IQ scores.

At least part of the motivation for developing these broader theories of intelligence is a concern that traditional intelligence and achievement tests are too narrow, that they measure only those cognitive skills that are important to academic success. As such, conventional IQ scores have been misinterpreted or misrepresented, often by nonexperts, as the *only* important attribute for educational and occupational success. Some psychologists may even place excessive emphasis on IQ, as though it is the only human ability important for success.

IQ scores do not measure the full range of human talents and skills that contribute to successful careers and lives. Thus kinesthetic skill, musical and creative talent, interpersonal and emotional skills, and practical intelligence in the form of tacit knowledge can also contribute to success in a wide range of careers including dramatic and performing arts, fine arts, athletics, many types of businesses, and even criminal careers.

I agree that IQ and achievement tests do not assess the full range of human talents and skills, but that fact does not justify diminishing or derogating the value of general reasoning and academic skills measured by IQ, aptitude, and achievement tests. As shown later in this chapter, IQ and aptitude tests are not only strong predictors of academic success, but they also correlate with other life outcomes that most people would view as important for success, such as income and family status. The reason is that persons with low IQs tend to perform poorly in school and have higher dropout rates, while those with high IQs tend to do much better in school. School success influences the decision to attend college, and both IQ and high school success predict the likelihood of completing college. High school graduation and college graduation are not only stepping stones to better paying jobs, but college graduation and higher degrees are prerequisites to many high-paying professional and business jobs.

In conclusion, I side with those psychologists who believe that the most useful definition of general intelligence is the degree of a person's general reasoning skills. I also agree that specific academic skills such as verbal and quantitative ability are not identical to general intelligence, but general intelligence strongly influences these academic skills as well as intellectual creativity. Some people can have exceptional verbal skills but mediocre quantitative skills, and vice versa. While verbal and mathematics skills are clearly different, one's proficiency in these skills can be an indicator of general intelligence. Therefore, general intelligence can usually be inferred from achievement test results, in the sense that students with high achievement in both verbal and quantitative skills usually have high general intelligence. Likewise, persons with the highest levels of intelligence usually have excellent verbal, quantitative, and creative talents (e.g., Albert Einstein).

Measurement of IQ and Achievement

Having defined intelligence and academic achievement, it remains to discuss several measurement issues. How is IQ measured, and does its measurement depend on deciding whether it is unitary or multidimensional? How should one interpret IQ tests as opposed to achievement tests? What measures are used in this book?

Initially, the Binet intelligence scales were scored by first averaging the mental ages assigned to a child's correct answers, and then subtracting the child's chronological age. Ultimately the average mental age was divided by the chronological age and multiplied by 100 to get rid of the decimal, hence the term "intelligence quotient" or IQ for short. If a child's average mental age was equal to his or her chronological age, then the child would have an IQ of 100, which would be average for that age.

An early technical problem was that the mental age assigned to a question (the age at which a "normal" child should be able to answer correctly) was arrived at by judgement of the psychologist making up the test. As psychometric methods became more sophisticated and rigorous, this judgmental method was replaced by "norming" studies. In a norming study, test questions are administered to large representative samples of various age groups, and then average performance on a given question (the "norm") can be calculated from the sample rather than relying on judgement. By convention, the average number of correct answers on a normed IQ test is set to 100, and the standard deviation (sd) is usually set to 15.[9] A test scored in this way is both normed and "standardized." By setting the sd to 15, nearly all scores would range from 55 to 145 (plus or minus three sd's), 95 percent would range between 70 and 130 (two sd's), and about two-thirds would range from 85 to 115 (one sd).[10]

Most standardized aptitude and achievement tests are scored in similar ways, using nationally representative samples to determine the norms for each item or question. However, the standardizing parameters of many aptitude and achievement tests are different than IQ tests. For example, the SAT is standardized using a national mean or average of 500 and a standard deviation of 100, and many achievement test scores are standardized using "normal curve equivalents," where the national average is set at 50 and the standard deviation is 20. It should be clear that the standardized metrics are arbitrary, and all tests could be scaled so that the national average was 100 with a standard deviation of 15.

The issue of single versus multiple intelligence domains does not affect the way an IQ or achievement test is scored, but it may affect how scores are presented and interpreted. For example, many IQ tests and most aptitude and achievement tests have subtest scores for different types of mental skills. The SAT offers an overall score and also separate scores for verbal and quantitative aptitudes. Likewise, the military AFQT has both verbal and math subscores. Many standardized achievement tests used in K-12 schools have vocabulary, reading comprehension, math concepts, and math computation scores; the first two and last two are usually combined into total reading and math scores, respectively. The NAEP program administers tests in reading, math, science, and several other skill areas. For all of these aptitude and achievement tests, it is likely that a total test score that combines verbal and quantitative components would be similar to an overall IQ test score, since most IQ tests assess both of these areas.

Another group of IQ and achievement tests that will be used in this book are those from the Children of the National Longitudinal Study of Youth (CNLSY). The tests include verbal IQ (the Peabody Picture Vocabulary Test, or PPVT) and two academic achievement tests, one in reading comprehension and one in math concepts and computation (Peabody Individual Achievement Tests or PIAT). In some cases, the reading and math scores are averaged to yield an overall academic achievement score.

Like adults, some children have higher verbal skills compared to their quantitative skills, and others have higher quantitative skills compared to their verbal skills. Therefore, when test scores are being used to evaluate individual children, it is prudent to examine subtest scores to determine whether a child is stronger or weaker in a particular cognitive skill. But when analyzing aptitude or achievement test scores for a large national sample, there is usually a high correlation between verbal/reading or quantitative/math scores on the order of .6 to .7, which means that students who are high on one ability tend to be high on the other.

For example, in 1992 the Department of Education sponsored the "Prospects" study, which was an evaluation of the Title 1 compensatory education program. The study administered reading and math achievement tests to a large national sample of 10,000 first graders. The simple correlation between total reading and math concepts was .68, which means that nearly half of the variation in individual reading scores is explained by math scores, and vice versa.

Figure 2.1
Average Math Scores by Grouped Reading Scores
(Prospects First Graders, 1992)

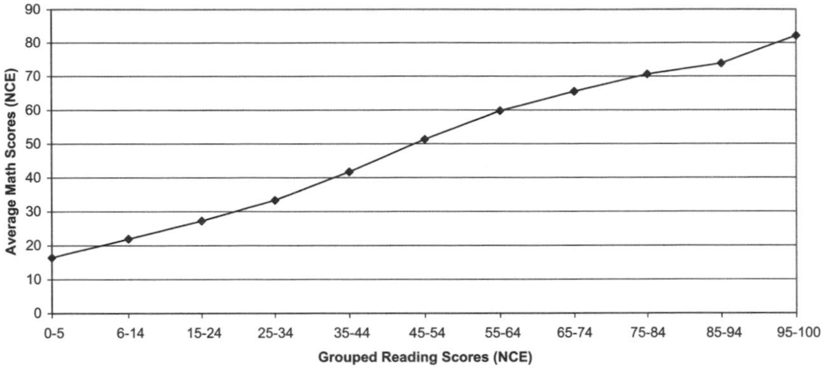

The correlation between reading and math scores is even higher when one looks at groups of students. Figure 2.1 shows the average math scores for students whose reading score have been grouped into ten point intervals. All scores are NCE units, in which the national mean is 50 and the standard deviation is 20. At this aggregated level, the relationship between reading and math is nearly perfect; the correlation coefficient for the grouped data is .996. Groups of students whose reading averages are 30, 40, 50, 60, and 70 have math scores of 33, 42, 51, 60, and 66, respectively. The relationship is more attenuated at the tails, meaning that students who averaged less than 6 points or more than 94 points in reading have 16 and 82 points in math, respectively, but these are still very low or very high scores.

A similar strong relationship exists between the PIAT reading and math achievement scores in the CNLSY. The correlation between reading and math for ages eleven and twelve was .62 in 1994, which is slightly weaker than the reading and math correlation for the Prospects study. Nonetheless, this is a relatively strong relationship, and it is within the range observed for many types of reading and math achievement tests. When the PIAT math and reading achievement scores are averaged into a single composite score, the correlation between composite achievement and verbal IQ is .72.

This latter correlation is displayed graphically in Figure 2.2. For this sample of children, the standardized achievement scores range from 65 to 135 with a mean of about 100 and a sd of 15, and the verbal IQ scores range from 20 to 160 with a mean of about 90. The vast majority of children fall close to a diagonal running through this cluster of points. That is, if we rounded off the IQ scores and computed average achievement scores, a very strong straight-line relationship would emerge similar to that depicted in Fig. 2.1. Children with IQs between 86 and 94 would have average achievement of about 100, those with IQs of about 110 would have average achievement of about 110, and so forth.

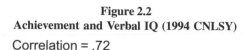

Figure 2.2
Achievement and Verbal IQ (1994 CNLSY)

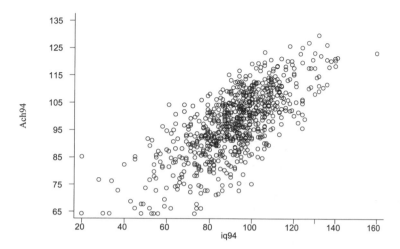

No child with a verbal IQ over 130 scores less than 105 on achievement, and most are above 115; no child scoring 60 or lower on verbal IQ scores higher than 95 on achievement.

Clearly, there is a lot of overlap between IQ and achievement scores, suggesting that they are both measuring something in common, undoubtedly general reasoning skills. Another indication that IQ and achievement tests are measuring something in common is to consider the relationships between various predictors of IQ and achievement, such as the risk factors discussed in chapter 1. For example, in the CNLSY data, the correlation between a child's verbal IQ and mother's IQ is about .52 and the correlation between a child's composite achievement and mother's IQ is .46. The correlation between verbal IQ and parent cognitive stimulation is .44 compared to .40 between composite achievement and parent cognitive stimulation. Similar patterns emerge for other risk factors, so that overall there is not a great difference between using IQ or achievement tests when studying factors that influence general intelligence.

Although general intelligence may be made up of multiple cognitive abilities, the strong relationships among these abilities may render the issue of single vs. multiple intelligences moot for many statistical studies. It may be important to distinguish these component abilities when evaluating an individual child or student, but the issue is less important when assessing groups of students or when studying the various factors that influences IQ and achievement.[11] Nevertheless, when assessing the influence of risk factors on IQ in chapter 3, both IQ and achievement tests will be utilized.

The Nature and Malleability of Intelligence

The nature and malleability of intelligence are intrinsically related issues, because some theories of intelligence have very definite implications about whether it can be changed. Theories that IQ is determined mostly by inherited genes imply that IQ cannot be changed for individual children. In contrast, theories that IQ is a product of the environment clearly leave room for changing it through manipulation of environmental factors. Thus the question of change and malleability is very much bound up with theories about the source and causes of IQ.

While there is considerable consensus that children inherit at least some of their intellectual ability from their parents, the size and significance of this inheritance has long been a controversial issue. At one end are those scientists who believe a child's IQ is genetically determined to a degree that it cannot be altered significantly by changes in social and environmental forces. *The Bell Curve* by Herrnstein and Murray is one of the more recent, and perhaps the most comprehensive, defenses of this viewpoint. The author's argue that a child's DNA largely determines their intelligence level, placing them at some point on a normal curve at birth where they remain for the rest of their life.

At the other end are those who believe that children are shaped almost entirely by their family and cultural environments, and, given the proper environmental conditions, there are few conditions that limit intellectual attainment. Some of the social scientists who wrote critical responses to *The Bell Curve* would fall into this category, especially *Inequality by Design* by a group of sociologists at the University of California at Berkeley.[12]

There is another category of criticism of *The Bell Curve,* which might be called the anti-IQ group. These scientists are critical of the very concept of IQ because of its historical ties to various racist and hereditarian philosophies, so that for them the debate over nature vs. nurture is practically irrelevant. Stephen Jay Gould is the best representative of this group, and especially his oft-quoted criticism of IQ and IQ testing in *The Mismeasure of Man*.[13]

As is often the case in a scientific dispute, it is unlikely that any of these more extreme viewpoints is correct. Rather, biological parents undoubtedly exert some degree of genetic influence on a child's intellect, but the environment into which the child is born also has a significant influence. One impressive new work by Dickens and Flynn attempts to integrate the hereditarian and environmentalist views by proposing a complex model of reciprocal causation between initial genetic endowment and subsequent environmental conditions.[14] In this model, a child's genetic inheritance interacts with the environment to create conditions that either enhance or retard further IQ growth. This model is used to explain the apparent paradox between the high heritability of IQ and the very large societal gains in IQ that have been documented in many countries (discussed below).

The Genetic Viewpoint

Some of the most compelling—but not necessarily the most rigorous—research on genetic influences are the identical twin studies, where the correlations for the IQs of identical twin raised together are compared to the correlations for identical twins raised apart. IQ correlations are also compared for fraternal twins, biological siblings, and unrelated adoptive siblings. Since identical twins have the same genetic makeup while fraternal twins share only 50 percent of their genes and unrelated siblings share none, the twin and sibling studies allow researchers to estimate the portion of children's IQ scores due to shared genes and the portion due to shared family environment. They do not, however, allow estimates of unique environmental effects not due to cultural transmission by parents.

One important sibling study was performed as part of the Colorado Adoption Project.[15] The Colorado Adoption Project (CAP) is an ongoing study of 245 adoptive families in the Denver area. In this study, the adoptive families were matched to 245 non-adoptive families according to age, education and occupational status of the father, gender of the adopted child, and number of children in the family. Within the adoptive families are 116 pairs of unrelated siblings and within the non-adoptive families are 122 pairs of related siblings. By examining academic achievement scores of these children on a variety of verbal and math tests in the summer following first grade, it was concluded that there was substantial genetic influence in the children's scores. Specifically, the *heritability*, or inherited portion of a child's IQ, was estimated to be 60 percent for perceptual organization and 21 percent for mathematics achievement. Accordingly, these researchers conclude that attempts at environmental influence should be directed at those achievement measures that do not appear to be as strongly genetic.

Another study on the genetic influence of a child's IQ was performed in Holland and involved 209 pairs of five-year-old Dutch twins.[16] The twin sets were given intelligence tests at the age of five and again at the age of seven. By comparing the intelligence test scores of the fraternal twin pairs to the biological twin pairs, the researchers were able to isolate the shared family environment influences from the biological influences. What is interesting in their findings is that the genetic influence increased from 27 percent at age five to 62 percent at age seven. Similarly, the influence of the shared family environment decreased from over 50 percent at age five to only 10 percent at age seven. In other words, as a child gets older, the family environment may become less important and genetic influence (or perhaps non-family environmental factors) may become stronger. This has important implications for the importance of a high quality family environment in the earliest years of a child's life.

The very high IQ correlations for identical twins raised together and raised apart is a compelling piece of evidence, but it does not tell the whole story. Identical twins by definition are a highly unique group of persons who represent a very tiny fraction of the total population; it is possible that their genetic makeup is not representative of the total population. Other methodologies using large representative samples of related and unrelated persons must also be considered.

Despite the identical twin studies, there is still a lack of consensus about the exact degree of heritability of IQ. A recent review by one experienced team of psychologists arrived at a heritability rate for adults of between 70 and 80 percent.[17] Another experienced team of scientists came up with a heritability rate of less than 50 percent.[18] In a recent review article in the *American Psychologist*, a distinguished panel of psychologists concluded that "If one simply combines all the available correlations in a single analysis, the heritability works out to about 50 [percent] and the between-family [environmental effects]…to about 25 [percent]."[19]

Apart from disagreements about heritability estimates in psychological research, there are even larger conceptual and empirical differences between psychologists and geneticists on the heritability of IQ. Most psychologists have relied heavily on twin studies and models of IQ that posit only genetic and environmental effects. More complex IQ models have been developed by biologists and geneticists as demonstrated in the work by Feldman, Otto, and Christianson. They postulate three components of IQ: a genetic component, an environmental component due to cultural transmission such as parenting, and a component due to the unique environmental experience of a person (similar to the environmental-genetic interaction assumed by Dickens and Flynn).[20] The transmission models then make various additional assumptions about covariance among the three components, mechanisms of cultural transmission, and assortative mating conditions. This last assumption recognizes the tendency of mates to resemble one another on various traits including IQ. Applying three different models to a set of sixteen IQ correlations among related and adopted family members, both living together and living apart, they find heritability estimates ranging from 29 to 42 percent, depending on the specific assumptions made about cultural transmission modes and assortative mating. In two of the three models the two environmental components explained about 30 percent each of the variability in IQ. In this more complex empirical approach, then, the potential contribution of the environment is seen as much greater than by a lot of psychological research.

In summary, genetics account for some but certainly not all of a child's IQ. It is quite possible that all environmental conditions and experiences of a child account for more of the variation in IQ scores than genetic conditions, and that the unique environmental experiences of a child may be as important as the environmental conditions established by the family.

While this nature-nurture debate reflects important scientific questions, at this point it is not necessary to decide on a particular degree of genetic or environmental influence. Indeed, the purpose in chapter 3 is to explore the influence of various environmental risk factors while controlling for parent IQ in order to exclude the potential effects of heredity. Thus the relationship between nurture and IQ will be further examined by analyses presented in the next chapter.

The Malleability of IQ

A more important question for this book is the malleability of IQ, that is, whether IQ is a relatively permanent characteristic of an individual or whether it can change over time in response to intentional, directed changes in the environment. Even if IQ is determined primarily by a person's genetic makeup, that does not mean it will not or cannot be changed. Many physical diseases are largely inherited, such as diabetes, but they can be controlled to some extent through medical interventions. A person's height, or at least potential for height, is largely genetic in origin, yet it is known that attained height can be affected by a variety of environmental conditions, such as illness and nutrition.[21] Of course, there are other physical characteristics, like skin color, which are determined at birth and that change very little during a person's lifetime. There is no intrinsic reason, however, to assume that IQ falls into one or the other category.

There are two types of studies that bear on the overall the malleability of IQ, both of which involve the measurement of IQ over time. At the societal level, there are a number of studies that document increases in the average IQ or academic achievement of large populations over time spans less than a generation. The other type of study tracks IQ or achievement scores of individual children over time, as they develop from pre-school ages to the later school years. Both types of studies indicate that IQ can improve over time, and the study of changes in individual IQ over time strongly suggest that this change comes relatively early in a child's life.

Before evaluating the specific studies of IQ change, additional clarification is necessary about the meaning of changes in IQ or achievement test scores. Changes in test scores can be interpreted in two different ways depending on the type of the test score. Although this point was mentioned briefly in the previous section on measurement, it is especially important when interpreting the meaning of group versus individual changes in IQ scores. These interpretations are also important in chapters 3 and 5 when discussing the impact of family and school factors on IQ.

The Meaning of Test Score Changes

Except in rare instances of severe deprivation, all children acquire substantial amounts of knowledge and many intellectual skills from birth to age three or four, well before they start formal schooling (or even preschool). This knowledge and these skills are transmitted to children primarily by parents and other caregivers during infancy. When a child starts school or preschool, this transmission of knowledge continues, some coming from the family but now more coming from school. The transfer of basic knowledge and skills continues at least though the high school years and even beyond for students going on to college. Thus, from birth to adulthood a person acquires a variety of cognitive skills such as reading, math, and general reasoning, as well as factual knowledge in fields like history, science, and literature.

If identical tests of basic skills are administered to an average group of elementary school children twice, say two years apart, the raw scores would reveal substantial gains in *absolute* skills and knowledge between the two times. But IQ tests and most standardized achievement tests are not absolute measures of knowledge or cognitive skill acquired from birth to adulthood. They are, rather, *relative* measures of knowledge or cognitive skill, where each child is measured relative to his or her peers. Therefore a child with the same IQ scores at age five and at age nine has acquired considerable cognitive skills just to stay even with his or her peers. If no cognitive skills were acquired, and the child's absolute levels of cognitive skill (as measured by raw scores) remained constant during this four-year period, then the IQ score would actually fall. Likewise, if a child shows a gain in standardized IQ scores, it means that the child has acquired more knowledge and skills than his or her peers during that time period.

Because children learn so much in one year, and because testing time is limited, most standardized achievement and IQ tests have different content for each grade or age level tested; sometimes the same content is used for a short time span of one or two years. For this reason, raw scores for a child usually cannot be compared from one grade to another, and instead "normed" standardized scores are used. As mentioned earlier, normed standardized scores are usually set to 50 or 100 for each age group (and the standard deviation is 20 or 15, respectively), and then each child's score is compared to the norm. IQ scores, percentile scores, and normal curve equivalent scores (NCEs) are of this form. It is critical to understand that, when a child's standardized IQ scores are compared at two different points in time, *the difference is not the change in absolute knowledge or skill, but rather the change in the child's position relative to the population mean (or norm).*

Some achievement test developers provide a type of standardized scores called "scale scores." A scale score is calculated to reflect the level of absolute knowledge, and, unlike raw scores, scale scores can be compared from one grade or year to another grade or year to assess absolute growth during that period. The National Assessment of Educational Progress (NAEP) uses scale scores like this for its achievement trend studies, so that differences in test scores among grades 4, 8, and 12 can be interpreted as gains or losses in absolute levels of knowledge.

In some experimental studies conducted in schools, researchers will administer the same IQ or achievement tests over relatively short time spans, in which case raw scores can be used to assess absolute change from one year to the next.[22] Since most children in school are learning continuously, the researcher has to be careful to compare test score gains among students in the experimental condition to those in a control group in order to make inferences about gains in the experimental condition.

In contrast, if a researcher uses aged-normed standardized tests to study the effects of a special intervention over time, and the test differs according to the age of the child, then conclusions about relative gains can be made without a comparison group. In this case gains (or lack of gains) will reflect changes in that group's scores relative to national norms. For example, if a group has an average IQ of 95 before an intervention, and it remains at 95 three years into the intervention, then one would conclude that intervention did not raise IQ relative to national norms. But students might have experienced considerable gains in absolute knowledge and skill between the two testings.[23]

To recap, individual or subgroup changes in normed, standardized scores over time mean changes in the level of skill relative to national norms. Lack of *relative* change on a normed test does not imply there is no learning or that there is no change in absolute skills. Changes in scale scores or raw scores do imply changes in absolute levels of knowledge and skills, but care must be exercised when interpreting these changes. Changes in raw scores do not necessarily imply improvement relative to national norms. When examining the changes in IQ or achievement scores, or the correlation between IQ and some potential causal factor, it is necessary to examine the nature of the test scores in order to interpret whether the changes or correlations reflect absolute improvement or improvement relative to national norms.

The purpose of this book is to evaluate ways to maximize intelligence by considering the role of family, school, and other environmental influences. To decide whether a potential environmental factor can raise IQ scores for individual children or groups of children, the factor must increase IQ or achievement relative to national norms. An environmental condition that raises IQ for all children may be beneficial to society as a whole, but it would be of little relevance for this book. For example, it is self-evident that virtually all families and all schools impart some degree of knowledge and cognitive skills to their children, and hence they contribute significantly to the absolute levels of human intelligence.

The key question in this book is whether particular family behaviors or school programs can raise IQ or other normed test scores for individual children, or groups of children. This means improving these children's cognitive skills relative to national norms. A broad environmental condition that produces gains in absolute knowledge for everyone is of less interest in this book because its does not produce differential improvement. Rather, to be effective in maximizing intelligence, a family behavior or a school program must produce *greater* gains than other behaviors or programs beyond the normal amount of learning expected for that age group.

Change in Aggregate IQ Levels

At the societal level, James Flynn has documented substantial increases in IQ in many countries.[24] The gains tend to be largest for measures of fluid intelligence, such as that measured by Raven's Progressive Matrices, and weakest for crystallized intelligence, such as achievement tests. The most rigorous evidence is found in studies of the Netherlands, Belgium, Israel, and Norway, where IQ data (Raven's test) is gathered for nearly all youth as part of military conscription. IQ gains average about six IQ points every decade, or twenty points over a thirty-year period. Similarly, in the United States the Wechsler-Binet IQ scores have risen twenty-five points between 1918 and 1995, assuming no renorming. This is a gain of just over three IQ points per decade, or about half that of the Raven's test. The Wechsler-Binet includes subtests of more crystallized intelligence, including vocabulary and math concepts. If the Wechsler gains are translated into standard deviation units, they indicate a gain of about .2 standard deviations every ten years, or .02 sds a year.

Modest gains in U.S. academic achievement have also been documented by the National Assessment of Educational Progress (NAEP) over a period of about three decades.[25] Although overall reading achievement has changed very little for the three age groups assessed, math scores have risen by 12-13 points for nine and thirteen year olds between 1973 and 1999, as shown in Figure 2.3. Since the standard deviation of NAEP math scores is about 30, this represents a total gain of about .4 sds, or about .16 sds every ten years. This is only slightly less than the Wechsler changes reported by Flynn and Horgan. The greater gains in math compared to reading are consistent with the observation that fluid abilities change more than crystallized abilities, since reading and word skills are generally more crystallized than math skills.

How are these society-wide changes to be explained? Unfortunately, there is no consensus on the precise causes of these changes, except that the time frame is too short for a genetic explanation. In the most comprehensive review of this phenomenon to date, various authors posited such factors as increased environmental complexity (which can improve test-taking skills), improved schooling, higher educational attainment of parents, better parenting skills, and improved nutrition.[26] Indeed, all of these may be happening simultaneously, each having an incremental effect on IQ.

The fact that IQ gains have occurred in whole societies may prove that environmental forces are at work, but it is not helpful for sorting out the particular type of environmental intervention most likely to help maximize IQ for individual children. Society-wide gains could be caused primarily by family

Figure 2.3
National Trends in Math Achievement

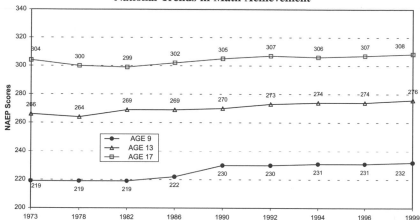

influences, with parenting behavior being the main mechanism, or by improved school resources and programs across the board, or even by broad cultural influences that might be transmitted through television, computer games, news media, and the like.

As mentioned earlier, a recent model proposed by Dickson and Flynn posits that IQ is influenced by a combination of reciprocal causation between genetic and environmental influences and social "multiplier" effects, and this model can explain substantial societal IQ gains as a result of fairly small environmental changes. Although precise environmental effects are not identified by the study, they suggest that the environmental changes could be any number of cultural and technological changes, such as introduction of television, greater use of technology by most citizens, improvement in schooling, and so forth. Again, the Dickson and Flynn model does not help rank the specific factors most likely to affect IQ scores for individual children.

A very different type of aggregate change has been documented for certain subgroups of American children. Since 1970 African American students have registered larger gains than white students in both reading and math. The math gains for black students in the NAEP assessment are shown in Figure 2.4. Some of these gains are truly remarkable, especially the gains of 21 and 23 points in math at ages nine and thirteen, respectively, in a thirteen-year period, which translates into two-thirds of a standard deviation. Blacks aged seventeen also gained 18 points in math between 1973 and 1990, but then they started declining again so the gain over the total period is only 13 points (about one-third of a sd). In reading, black students also out-gained white students for all three age groups. For both reading and math, nearly all of the gains occurred between 1970 and 1990, and then they leveled off or declined slightly between 1990 and 1999. Since the black gains were larger than white gains, the black-white

Figure 2.4
National Trends in Black Math Achievement

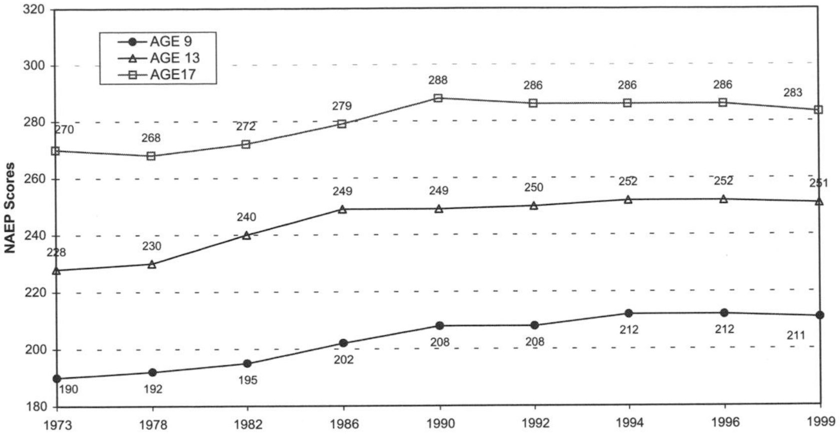

achievement gap in reading and math declined for all age groups during the earlier period. Similar but not quite as large achievement gains have also occurred for Hispanic students. The phenomenon of minority student gains has been discussed extensively in the education research literature.[27]

Again, there is no complete consensus about the causes of black student gains compared to white student gains, but the fact that the changes were much greater for one subgroup in America, and one that is economically disadvantaged, might narrow the list of potential environmental explanations. Additionally, the changes for black students are much larger than the Flynn effect for the nation as a whole, and they occurred over a very short time. As compared to the Flynn effect of .02 sds per year on national Wechsler test scores, the change for age thirteen black students on the NAEP math test is about .05 sds per year between 1973 and 1986. Not only does this rapid rate of gain eliminate genetic explanations, it also tends to rule out cultural, technological, or social changes that were occurring throughout society, because those changes should improve IQ for everyone and not just for black students.

Rather, these gains must be explained by changes in environmental conditions or experiences unique to the African American or Hispanic populations. There are a number of environmental changes unique to black families that might be candidates for explanations. One is the improved socioeconomic status of black families, especially gains in education and income during the 1960s and 1970s. A second is the growth in special school programs for disadvantaged students such as Head Start or federal Title 1 programs, which impact a much higher proportion of black than white children. A third is improved quality of educational programs and resources resulting from school desegregation starting in the early 1970s.[28] To the extent that school desegregation might be a factor, it is unlikely that interracial contact itself caused black performance gains. A more likely explanation was the increased equity in the allocation of educational programs and resources that took place after desegregation, including teachers. The viability of these various explanations for the reduced the black-white gap is taken up in more detail in chapter 4.

Whatever the ultimate explanation of aggregate IQ and achievement gains, the most important point to make here is that both IQ and achievement scores have increased by significant amounts over time, thereby supporting the thesis that they are malleable. Because some of the changes have taken place over relatively short time spans, less than a generation, it is highly unlikely that the primary cause of these IQ and achievement gains is genetic changes in the populations studied. While there is no consensus on exactly which environmental factors or combinations of factors are the most likely causes, it is significant that most experts who have studied these changes endorse environmental causes of some type. Hopefully, the discussions in chapters 3 to 5 will help sort out the relative importance of different types of environmental influences on IQ.

Changes in Individual IQ

Another way to evaluate the malleability of IQ and achievement is to consider changes in individual test scores over time. Two complexities must be addressed before taking up the issue of individual change: the issues of test reliability and test norming.

If a child takes an IQ test at two different times and the scores differ, there are two possible explanations. One reason may be that the person has truly changed by learning (or forgetting) more correct answers at the time of the second testing. The other possibility is pure chance, whereby a person gives a different answer either by mistake or by guessing differently. This latter possibility is considered random error, and it is a phenomenon present in all testing situations. The amount of random error is assessed by a "reliability" coefficient. The correlation between the same test given at relatively close intervals (e.g., a week or so) is one definition of the reliability of a test, since true change is unlikely over such a short time span.

The correlation between test scores measured at two times must be interpreted in the light of the reliability of the test, which usually is .9 or better for most published IQ and achievement tests. If an IQ test is administered to a group of children at two reasonably distant points in time (say, a year or more), and the correlation equals .9, then this correlation reflects mostly error and the "true" correlation is very close to 1.0. In this case, the true IQ scores would be perfectly stable, and any changes in actual scores would indistinguishable from random error. To estimate the true correlation (stability) of an IQ test over time, the actual correlation between two IQ or achievement tests should be divided by .9 (approximately).[29] If this adjusted correlation is appreciably less than one, then one might reasonably assume that real changes have occurred.

With regards to the norming issue, as mentioned earlier most IQ and achievement tests for children contain different content at different ages, so that tests for older children will have different and more complex content than tests for younger children. When comparing test scores at two widely spaced times, therefore, one is comparing a child's position relative to the national norm for that age group, rather than change in the number of questions answered correctly.

Most studies of changes in IQ scores show two patterns of correlations between test scores from two testings. First, for a fixed time interval between testing (e.g., four years), correlations tend to increase as children get older. Second, holding age constant, correlations tend to decrease as time intervals between testing get longer. After about age seven or eight, however, correlations between any two IQ test scores tend to be very high, approaching unity after reliability correction, regardless of the length of time between testings. Similar patterns of correlations are observed for most achievement test batteries administered over time. These results strongly suggest that IQ and academic achievement are highly stable and change very little after a child reaches a certain age. Again, this does not mean no learning has occurred, but only that there has been no change in a child's IQ relative to the IQs of others.

For example, a classic study of IQ stability found a correlation of .77 between IQ tested at age six and again at age eighteen, but for the same group of children the correlation between IQ at age twelve and eighteen was .89.[30] This second correlation is nearly 1.0 when corrected for reliability, which means there was no change in relative IQ rankings between age twelve and eighteen. The corrected correlation between ages six and eighteen, however, was .85. Thus, there might have been some true change between ages six and twelve, although not a large amount.

A study of IQ change among New Zealand children also demonstrates the increasing stability of IQ scores as children get older. Table 2.1 shows the cross-age correlations of Wechsler IQ scores for approximately 900 New Zealand children born between 1972-73 as they progressed from age seven to age thirteen (adapted from Moffit, et al.).[31] For seven-year-olds, the correlations decline from .78 at age nine to .74 at age thirteen. But for nine-year-olds the correlation with age eleven is much higher at .84, and the correlation with age thirteen declines only to .82. The age eleven to age thirteen correlation is also very high at .84. Another study by Humphreys showed increasing stability of IQ correlations over longer time spans.[32] The IQ correlations between ages two through nine and age fifteen were .47, .58, .60, .67, .69, .69, .78, and .80, respectively. The Humphreys' study also shows increasing stability with age after holding the interval between tests constant: the age two to six, three to seven, four to eight, and five to nine correlations are .61, .68, .72, and .79, respectively. Like the New Zealand data, the Humphrey's study suggests very little true change in IQ after the age of eight or nine.

Table 2.1
Cross-age Correlations of IQ Scores in New Zealand

	Age 7	Age 9	Age 11
Age 9	0.78		
Age 11	0.75	0.84	
Age 13	0.74	0.82	0.84

(N>900+)

Table 2.2
Cross-grade Correlations of Achievement Tests in NYC, 1992-1998

	COMBINED READING AND MATH					
	Grade 2	Grade 3	Grade 4	Grade 5	Grade 6	Grade 7
Grade 3	.83					
Grade 4	.82	.89				
Grade 5	.80	.86	.91			
Grade 6	.77	.83	.87	.89		
Grade 7	.75	.83	.87	.88	.89	
Grade 8	.73	.80	.84	.86	.87	.89

(N=33,342 taking all tests)

A similar degree of increasing stability over time is observed for combined reading and math achievement scores for New York City students, as shown in Table 2.2. Over 33,000 students took all reading and math achievement tests in grades two through eight between 1992 and 1998 (corresponding to ages seven through thirteen). For second graders in 1992, the correlations are .83, .82, .80, .77, .75, and .73 at grades three through eight, respectively. When these children reached grade three in 1993, the correlations rose to .89, .86, .83, .83, and .80 for grades four through eight, respectively.

After grade two the stability of the combined achievement scores is so high that very little true change occurs (after correcting for reliability), even though a great deal of new reading and math material is learned during the five years between grades three and eight. For example, the average number of correct answers on the NYC reading test increased from thirty-two to fifty-seven between grades three and eight (maximum score 77), indicating that much learning has taken place over this five year period. Yet the achievement correlation between grade three and grade eight is .80, which becomes .90 after reliability correction. This very high correlation means that the relative ranking of the students changed very little over this time span.

Figure 2.5
Grades 2 and 8 Achievement in NYC

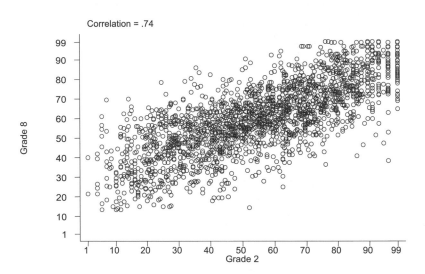

Even the correlation of .73 between grades two and eight (corrected to .80) reflects considerable stability over this six-year period, with opportunities for only modest levels of real change. In order to gauge the magnitude of changes over this time period, Figure 2.5 shows the actual distribution of achievement scores for the NYC grades two and eight achievement correlation (in NCE units).[33] Of course, only the actual scores can be plotted in the figure, and one should assume that at least some of the outliers are random errors, particularly at the low ends of the continuum where more guessing is expected.

First, it is apparent that the vast majority of scores are clustered fairly tightly around the linear regression line (not shown), which runs from the lower left-hand corner to the upper right-hand corner. Second, given the high association, about two-thirds of the cases are distributed within plus or minus ten points from the predicted score at grade eight (which runs from about 30 for the lowest grade twp scores to about 85 for the highest grade two scores).[34] Finally, most of the second graders who scored around 20-30 scored below 60 at grade eight, and most of those who scored 90 or above at grade two scored over 80 at grade eight (the overall mean at grade two is 54, while the overall mean at grade eight is 59). So change is occurring for some of these students, but the magnitude of change is strongly constrained by their second grade achievement levels.

Another illustration of stability and change in cognitive ability is from the CNLSY study, where correlations for IQ and achievement tests can be calcu-

Figure 2.6
IQ Correlations by Ages at Two Testings (CNLSY, 1996)

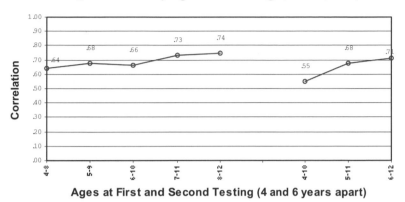

Ages at First and Second Testing (4 and 6 years apart)

lated for a large sample of over 4000 children as they develop from the pre-school years through adolescence and early teens. Verbal IQ tests are available in sufficient numbers from the ages of four to twelve, and achievement scores (averages of reading and math scores) are available from ages six to fourteen.

The correlations between verbal IQ at four and six year intervals as children develop from ages four to twelve are shown in Figure 2.6. The first line shows IQ correlations at four year intervals for children who are between four to eight years old at the first test; the number of cases for each correlation range from 360 to 522 (the different age groups have little overlap). The second line shows correlations at six-year intervals for children who are between four to six years old at the first test. Despite the long intervals, verbal IQ shows considerable stability by the time a child is five or six years old. The lowest correlations are observed for four-year-olds, where the age four and eight correlation is .64 and the age four and ten correlation is .55. In other words, by the time a child has reached the age of five, there is very little real change in verbal IQ scores even when the measurement intervals are as much as six years apart.

A similar pattern of increasing stability is observed for achievement test scores as children develop from ages six to twelve, as shown in Figure 2.7. The first line represents achievement correlations two years apart starting with ages six to eight (the first age group with a sufficient number of test scores) to ages twelve to fourteen; the Ns range from 463 to 1267. The second line represents achievement correlations four years apart starting with ages six to ten and ending with ages ten to fourteen. In the case of achievement scores, a high degree of stability is observed starting at age eight, or third grade, and it remains high after that. Compared to verbal IQ, there is more true change occurring between the ages of six to eight, or between first and third grades. This makes some sense in that a great deal of actual cognitive

Figure 2.7
Achievement Correlations by Ages at Two Testings (CNLSY, 1996)

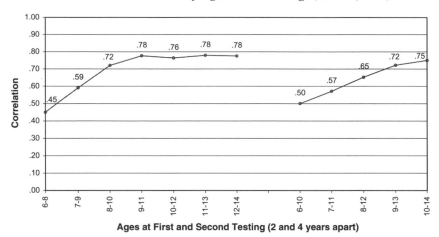

Ages at First and Second Testing (2 and 4 years apart)

content is learned during these early elementary years, and there may be greater possibility for change.

In conclusion, there is ample evidence that, whatever role genes might play in a person's initial intellectual capacity, both IQ and academic achievement are malleable, at least to some degree. The evidence on aggregate change, especially the dramatic improvement in black academic achievement in the 1970s and 1980s in comparison to white students, strongly suggests environmental effects of some type. The evidence on individual change suggests that, while individual IQ and achievement are fairly stable overall, the stability depends on the age of the child. In particular, by the age of five or six—about the time that most children enter school—IQ scores are quite stable. By the ages of seven or eight, achievement test scores are also quite stable.

The very important implication of these findings is that, to the extent that IQ or achievement can be changed, the potential for change appears to be at its maximum at younger ages. By the time a child reaches the age when formal schooling begins, or at the latest by the first year or two of formal schooling, both IQ and achievement scores are highly stable for most children relative to their peers. While considerable learning takes place during the formal school years, in that nearly all children amass large amounts of knowledge and information, the relative ranking of children's cognitive proficiency remain highly stable after the preschool or early elementary years.

The fact that stability correlations are lowest at the youngest ages of measurement suggests that the potential for changing IQ may be greatest at these very young ages, even before IQ can be reliably measured. Since the question of timing has important implications for policies that aim to maximize intelligence, it deserves some further discussion.

The Timing of IQ Changes

The timing of interventions aimed at improving a child's IQ and academic achievement has been a long-standing concern among practitioners and researchers in the fields of education and child development. On the one hand, many educators and social scientists—perhaps a large majority—believe that a child's cognitive ability is quite plastic. That is, intelligence can be enhanced during a student's academic career, although many would agree that the elementary years are more critical than the secondary years, simply because the early school years provide the foundation for the later years. Having visited more than thirty school systems with below-average test scores, I have never met a school administrator or teacher who did not believe this. While I do not have any formal polling data, perhaps the best evidence for this observation is the pervasiveness of compensatory programs (like Title 1) in low-achieving elementary schools throughout the nation.

On the other hand, there are a growing number of psychologists, social scientists, and child advocates who question the efficacy of academic interventions during the school years. Some of these professionals question the feasibility of intervention at any age, on the grounds that intelligence is largely genetically determined, and therefore there is little prospect for changing it at any time. This is the viewpoint espoused by Herrnstein and Murray in *The Bell Curve*. Moreover, many psychologists who believe that both genes and environment make a difference, such as Dicksen and Flynn, are skeptical that there are specific environmental interventions that would make a substantial and permanent increase in IQ.

There has emerged yet a third viewpoint, espoused by a group of scientists and policymakers backed by the Rob Reiner Foundation and U.S. Senator Hilary Clinton, who explains it in her book, *It Takes a Village*.[35] This group takes the position that interventions can change a child's intelligence, but opportunities are lost by waiting until the school years. In order to be most effective, interventions to improve a child's IQ should occur during the first three years of life. This claim is based in part on the neurological development of the brain. This biological argument itself has become controversial, with some neuroscientists challenging the scientific basis of this belief.

The Brain Science Debate

Rapid advances in scientific methods and technology have allowed neuroscientists to accumulate much knowledge about the human brain and brain development. Yet much remains unknown regarding the specific relationship between brain neurology and human cognitive functioning. While advocates on both sides of the *nature vs. nurture* controversy generally agree that some combination of both biology and environment determines a child's IQ, the specific mechanisms connecting genes, brain development, and cognitive growth are yet to be discovered.

National attention has become focused on the importance of the zero to age three period through a campaign by the I Am Your Child network, sponsored by the Rob Reiner Foundation, and interest groups such as Zero to Three: The National Center for Infants, Toddlers and Families. Both of these groups base their claims in part on recent developments in brain research as well as other research in education and child development. Much of the brain research is summarized in *Rethinking the Brain,* while some brain research but mostly behavioral science research is summarized in a 1994 Carnegie Corporation study titled *Starting Points: Meeting the Needs of Our Youngest Children.*[36] The campaign received a major boost and extensive publicity as the result of a White House Conference in April, 1997, titled "Early Development and Learning: What New Research on the Brain Tells Us About Our Youngest Children." The basic message of this conference was that if public policy hopes to have a real impact on children's academic success and other social and emotional outcomes, efforts must be focused on the infancy period (zero to three years), because neuroscience has determined that this is the critical time for brain development.

The Zero to Three theory has been challenged by John Bruer, a cognitive scientist and president of the James S. McDonnell Foundation in St. Louis. In his book, *The Myth of the First Three Years*, Bruer asserts that neither *Starting Points* nor *Rethinking the Brain* introduced much new evidence or provided sufficient basis for the claims being made by proponents of the Zero to Three theory. He argues that the description of the first three years of life as a period of critical brain development, which directly determines irreversible cognitive development (or lack of such) during this time period, is a myth that is unsupported by neuroscience research.[37]

Bruer suggests three strands in this myth. The first strand involves the concept of maximizing synaptic density. During the period from two months before birth to age three, a baby's brain develops trillions of neural synapses. These synapses are microscopic gaps that connect the millions of neurons laid down during fetal brain development. Synapses carry messages through the brain and create "pathways" which will eventually give the child the ability to acquire knowledge. Following this period of rapid synapse formation is a stage that extends to about age ten in which children's brains have 60 percent more synaptic density than adult brains. Beginning around puberty, the brain begins to eliminate synapses. This is considered a "pruning" phase that results in a mature human brain.

According to Bruer, proponents of the myth focus only on the synaptic formation period, claiming that learning during this time will result in greater cognitive functioning. The connection between more synapses and higher intelligence, however, has not been proven. In fact, there are cases of severely mentally impaired people having very high synaptic density, possibly resulting from arrested development during the synapse pruning phase. Secondly, significant learning also takes place during the synapse pruning period, suggesting a more complex relationship between synapse development and cognition. The main point, however, is that there is no hard proof from brain science that links the process of synapse formation and pruning to IQ levels or to any other cognitive functioning.

A second strand of the myth is that the first three years is a "critical period" of brain development, meaning that once it has ended it is too late to improve a person's IQ. Bruer acknowledges than neuroscience has discovered critical periods in brain development for both animals and humans, but he believes that they cannot be generalized to a Zero to Three critical period for intelligence. Critical periods are generally restricted to general species-specific skills, such as visual acuity and language acquisition, rather than culturally defined skills such as reading or playing music. Moreover, while there appears to be a critical period for learning a first language, this period extends at least to middle-childhood and perhaps later. For many other types of skills, there is evidence that the human brain remains relatively plastic at all ages. An example would be the ability of an adult amputee to "re-learn" physical skills using other limbs.

Finally, the third strand of the myth is that providing children with an "enriched" or "complex" environment during the first three years will lead to optimal neurological development. He criticizes early childhood advocates for describing synapses as neural circuitry that form in response to various stimuli, when there is no physical evidence that synapse formation in humans can be externally manipulated, or that it can be induced better in the first three years than at older ages. He acknowledges that some neuroscience research on rats, especially that by William Greenough, supports the theory that complex environments increase the density of synapses in rat brains, but he states these findings have been improperly generalized to support the myth. Aside from the problem of generalizing from rats to humans (no analogous findings exist for human beings), the rat research shows that synaptic density can be increased when rats are well beyond infancy and even into adult periods. Greenough himself has stated that his research on rat brain development does not support the Zero to Three theory.[38]

From the perspective of neuroscience, then, there is little hard evidence from brain research that supports the notion that the first three years of a child's development is more critical to IQ or other attributes than any other period in a child's development. Bruer believes that the brain remains relatively plastic and able to absorb knowledge and cognitive skills throughout life, and especially through early adolescence (in the case of language).

While I have no basis to dispute Bruer's views about what neuroscience research says or does not say about cognitive development, I would raise several questions about his review of other behavioral science research and theories concerning the development of IQ in early childhood. His review of behavioral research is quite selective and fairly general, and he replicates one mistake made by those he criticizes, which is a failure to distinguish among many different human attributes (especially IQ) and their presumably differing etiologies.

Bruer does distinguish the human attribute of language, and he acknowledges that effective language acquisition is subject to a critical learning period, but the critical period extends far beyond the age of three (perhaps into adolescence). But he fails to discuss the likelihood that other human attributes such as IQ, knowledge acquisition, emotional stability and control, creativity and artistic ability, and acquisition of behavioral skills all have different developmental sequences and, possibly, differing critical periods. For example, there is no reason to assume that the development of general reasoning ability (IQ) has the same causes and timing as control of emotional impulses (e.g., aggressiveness). Therefore, they might have different critical periods, and in fact some attributes may have no or very limited critical periods (e.g., learning a new physical skill).

Since this book is about intelligence, I do not want to digress into a discussion of other human attributes. Suffice it to say, Breur does not make a fully convincing case, based on behavioral research in general and IQ research in particular, that the development of IQ is not time dependent. He reviews two infant intervention studies that he claims failed to raise IQ scores significantly, briefly mentions several other studies showing that formal schooling can raise IQ, and a study of adult intervention in the military he claims raised IQ significantly. These studies will be discussed in greater detail in subsequent sections, but the main point to be made here is that there is a much larger literature on the issue of critical periods for IQ development than discussed by Bruer. This literature, some of which was discussed in this chapter, supports a conclusion that intellectual development is more rapid during the early years of a child's development, although it does not necessarily stop completely after the first three years of life.

Behavioral Research on Timing Issues

A fundamental problem in the developmental study of intelligence is that, as previously noted, IQ cannot be reliably measured before ages three or four. Accordingly, there is very little quantitative data on changes in IQ during the first three years of life (but see Hart and Risler study below).[39] There are, however, substantial bodies of data and research on the stability and change of both IQ and academic achievement from the ages of four or five to the mid-teens; some of the more important studies, along with some original data, were discussed earlier.

The research on the stability and change in IQ scores, reviewed in this chapter, makes it quite clear that there is little meaningful change in normalized IQ or achievement test scores after the ages of eight or nine. After correcting for

reliability of measurement, correlations between IQ scores taken at two different ages (after age eight or so) approach or exceed .9, even for tests taken five
years apart. Even at ages six or seven, just after children start formal schooling,
corrected correlations with tests taken during early teens are in the .8s, which
means that earlier IQ explains most of the variation in later IQ. Finally, IQ scores
taken as early as age four or five have very high correlations with IQ scores
taken four to six years later, after correcting for reliability. This makes preschool IQ a very strong predictor of later IQ, explaining on the order of one-half
the true variation.

While these findings do not support a strict version of the Zero to Three
theory, they do support a theory of reduced plasticity of IQ as a child ages.
Contrary to Bruer's view, plasticity seems to diminish linearly until the mid-
elementary ages, where it remains near zero throughout the rest of a child's
school career. It was also noted earlier that the malleability of IQ contradicts the
genetic determinism theory, such as that expressed in *The Bell Curve*, which
sees IQ largely fixed from birth onwards. That theory implies high and constant
correlations (correcting for reliability) as soon as IQ and achievement can be
measured, which contrasts with the pattern of increasing correlations as child
ages from four to the mid-teens. If one could extrapolate these correlation trends
back to age six months or so, correlations might diminish until they reach the
theoretical correlation between intelligence at birth and at later ages, which
should reflect just the genetic contribution to IQ. While the size of this correlation is unknown, the trend lines shown in this chapter suggest that it would
probably be greater than 0 but less than .5.

It cannot be emphasized enough that the high stability of IQ after age eight
or nine does not mean no learning is occurring. Obviously, throughout the
school and college years students continue to accumulate knowledge and skills
in many specific topics, such as vocabulary, history, second languages, higher
math, and science. But for standardized and normed IQ or achievement tests,
test scores reflect a student's mastery of content in relation to his or her peers.
Stable correlations do not mean that students stop learning at age eight or nine,
but rather that the rate of learning is relatively uniform from one student to
another, so that the relative rankings of mastery remain relatively invariant after
those ages.

Since there is little quantitative data on IQ before age three, one must turn to
other types of studies on child development, particularly observational studies, for clues about the growth of intelligence during infancy. While this type of
evidence is not as rigorous as brain science, it can offer important insights
about the origins and patterns of cognitive development and the importance of
early childhood.

The study of the mental development of babies and young children began
about 100 years ago when the end of the industrial revolution allowed children time to grow and learn before being put to work.[40] As research and statis-

tical methods became more sophisticated, so did cognitive science. In the post-World War II era Jean Piaget's theory of normal cognitive development became popular, as did the new mother-child attachment theories, the most famous being done on rhesus monkeys. As early as the 1960s, researchers such as J. McVicker Hunt and Benjamin Bloom had become convinced that a child's environment for the first three or four years of life had a significant impact on their intellectual development.[41]

The most influential theory of early cognitive development was that of Jean Piaget, who postulated multiple stages of mental development beginning in infancy and progressing into early adolescence.[42] Although he characterized the first two years of infancy as the "sensorimotor" period, it is clear that intellectual or "thinking" operations were part of the child's early development. The last stage of the sensorimotor period is "representation," which is the ability to remember mental images and to use those images to think out how to accomplish new tasks. This is clearly a manifestation of early problem-solving ability, a key component of fully developed cognitive ability.

Another important contributor to the notion that the first three years of life was critical to the development of intelligence was Burton White, director of the Harvard Preschool Project and the Brookline Early Education Project in the 1960s and 1970s. His work emphasized the importance of parenting behaviors during the first three years of life for producing high levels of cognitive functioning that would influence learning throughout a person's life.[43] Interestingly, he did not think that high-quality parenting behaviors could be replicated by full-time child centers. He felt parents were in the best position to create the optimal environment to maximize early learning opportunities.

Finally, a more recent example of observational research on the timing of cognitive development is that of Hart and Risley. They observed the daily parent-child interaction and behaviors of forty-two children in families from each major socioeconomic (SES) category—upper, middle, lower, and welfare recipients.[44] They found extreme differences in both the quantity and quality of parent-child interaction that led to significant differences in vocabulary growth curves and subsequent intelligence tests. Hart and Risley also found that, although vocabulary could always be increased through intervention, a vocabulary *growth curve* is established quite early and usually becomes fixed.

The authors noted a number of similarities between the families studied: all children learned to talk at about the same age, all were stimulated with very similar games, and all were prompted to say words when they began to talk. More importantly, there were substantial variations in language richness, quality, and quantity. For example, when the children were between ages two and three, parent utterances per hour ranged from 34 (lowest SES) to 783 (highest SES). When multiplied by the total hours awake during a year, the cumulative difference in exposure to language, according to the authors, is staggering. After devising various measures of the quality and quantity parent-child interactions, Hartley and Risley found that parent-child interactions accounted for over 60 percent of the variation in vocabulary growth, vocabulary use, and IQ scores at age three. Finally, in a follow-up study when the children were in third grade, they found that the parent-child interaction measures before age three explained 61 percent of the variation in IQ at ages nine and ten. The authors concluded that these parenting variables are "powerful characteristics of everyday parenting that cause important outcomes in children."

In one respect Hart and Risley agree with Bruer: they do not take the position that the first three years of life are the only important years. However, they are years in which infants are uniquely vulnerable and dependent upon adults for everything from physical needs to learning and stimulation. In addition, since experience is cumulative, changing the quality and diversity of language accumulated during the first three years of development might be very difficult once the child gets to school.

In summary, the review of timing issues in the development of intelligence leads to three major conclusions. First, there is evidence that the development of intelligence extends beyond the first three years of life, which is consistent with the status of brain research as reviewed by Bruer. Second, there is equally convincing evidence that intelligence is not plastic throughout life, and in fact there is very little change in normed IQ or achievement scores after age eight or nine (i.e., the relative ranking of children with respect to cognitive ability). Finally, the stability or plasticity of IQ appears to be a continuum that varies over time, such that the younger the age, the more plasticity and less stability of IQ. While these conclusions differ from the Zero to Three theory, they are consistent with the view that early influences are more important than later influences. In effect, the probability of being able to maximize a child's IQ diminishes with time, and that probability becomes fairly small after a child has finished the first grade or two of elementary school.

These conclusions about the timing of intellectual development have serious implications for other agents of change, particularly the capability of special school programs to influence IQ. If the probability of changing a child's cognitive ability diminishes with age, then interventions to improve a child's ability during the formal school years are likely to have small or no effects on academic achievement. A detailed discussion of this topic is found in chapter 5.

Why IQ is Important

Perhaps as recently as twenty years ago it would not have been necessary to have a discussion of why a child's cognitive development, as measured by IQ and achievement test scores, should be important to those who are concerned about a person's educational and occupational success. In recent years, however, the concept of intelligence and the practices of aptitude and even achievement testing have come under increasing attacks from a variety of sources.

Some of the attacks on testing are related to civil rights issues, and particularly the thorny problem of affirmative action and the use of aptitude tests in college admissions. A good example is a proposal by the president of the University of California to abandon the use of SAT aptitude scores in college admissions.[45] This proposal followed the passage of a state constitutional amendment that barred use of race in admissions decisions, along with a number of federal court decisions holding that the use of race can create illegal "reverse discrimination" against equally qualified white applicants. Given the racial and ethnic differences in aptitude test scores on the SAT, African American and Hispanic students may have lower admission priorities than white students unless their race or ethnicity is given special consideration. One of the grounds used by the UC president is that the SAT test no longer has predictive value for success in college, and therefore its use as an entrance requirement leads to improper racial discrimination. Similar attacks have been made on other types of tests used for admission to graduate or professional schools, such as the Graduate Record Exam, the Law School Aptitude Exam, and the Medical school exams.

I discussed some aspects of this problem earlier, particularly the problems of definition and some of the more fundamental attacks on the concept of intelligence itself. The issue addressed here is criticism of IQ and aptitude testing on the grounds that they are not good predictors of a person's educational and occupational success. While I will not get into the issue of whether particular tests predict college performance, which is a test validity issue, I do want to address the broader questions of whether IQ and achievement test scores matter for educational attainment and certain occupational statuses.

There are few studies that allow a comparison of the earliest measures of IQ (usually about age three or four) with adult educational and occupational outcomes for the same group of persons, which require a longitudinal study extending over a period of thirty years or more. There is, however, a great deal of national longitudinal research that compares various age groups at two points in time, often ten to fifteen years apart. Accordingly, this discussion of the predictive value of IQ will be broken into three chronological stages: predicting early school achievement from preschool IQ, predicting later school achievement from early school achievement, and predicting educational attainment and occupational outcomes from the academic aptitudes of teenagers.

Predicting Early Achievement from Preschool IQ

One of the technical problems in predicting early school achievement from preschool intelligence is that it is very difficult (and perhaps impossible) to measure IQ until a child has a modicum of language and reasoning skills, so that a range of meaningful questions can be used in the test. The problem is inherent in all developmental processes, including the biological process of growth. It is akin to the problem of predicting a person's adult height from birth length, where the variance is very small (compared to the adult variance) and hence its measurement is less reliable. Intelligence as defined today cannot be reliably measured until a child is at least three years old, and even then some types of reasoning skills (especially quantitative skills) may not be sufficiently developed for reliable testing until the age of four or five. The verbal IQ test used in the CNLSY can be administered to three-year-olds, but in fact it was not administered to the full sample of children until they reached the age of four.

In the CNLSY, verbal IQ measured at age four or five has correlations of .44, .46, and .54, with achievement at ages 7, 8, and 9, respectively. The correlations between verbal IQ (at four or five) and achievement remain about the same for achievement measured at ages 10 to 14, suggesting that the content of verbal IQ at preschool ages may be too narrow to give high predictions for early school achievement. Support for this interpretation is provided in Figure 2.6, which showed IQ to IQ correlations of nearly .7 for ages 5 to 9 and ages 5 to 11. Nonetheless, even a correlation of .45 still makes pre-school verbal IQ the strongest predictor of early school achievement scores, as compared to all other risk factors in the CLNSY study including mother's IQ.

Predicting Later Achievement from Early Achievement

Regarding the prediction of later school achievement from earlier achievement, much of the earlier discussion on the stability and change of individual IQ and achievement levels is relevant here. It was demonstrated that both IQ and academic achievement become quite stable at fairly young ages. IQ stabilizes before achievement test scores, so that by the ages of six or seven IQ is quite stable, and IQ to IQ correlations with older ages average over .7. Achievement scores stabilize at about age eight or nine, and correlations with older ages average .8 and higher.

In other words, once a child has reached grade three or four in elementary school, there is very little change in the relative position of achievement levels as the children progress through the later grades. Again, I emphasize that this does not mean no learning is occurring; the content of these achievement tests demonstrates increasing mastery of new knowledge and skills throughout junior and senior high years. But the ranking of students' achievement scores, relative to one another, remains quite stable after the third or fourth grade.

Predicting Educational and Occupational Attainment from Youth Aptitudes

One of the problems in using the much-discussed SAT for predicting educational and occupational attainment is that the test is usually taken only by those high school students who are considering college. Thus, even a national sample of students with SAT scores is a highly self-selected group that excludes many students with low academic achievement levels, and its correlation with educational outcomes could be seriously underestimated.

An alternative is the Armed Services Qualifying Test (AFQT), a test that is used as a screening device for enlistment into military service.[46] While there are differences between the SAT and AFQT tests, they both generally measure a person's verbal, logical, and quantitative skills. Although both are called aptitude tests, in fact they include many questions that depend on knowledge acquired in school (crystallized abilities), and therefore they are considered by many psychologists to be very similar to achievement tests.

The AFQT was administered to a large, representative sample of youth as part of the National Longitudinal Study of Youth in 1979 (from which the CNLSY data also originated). The original national sample of youth was followed up every four years starting in 1986 and continuing through 1996. The prediction analyses presented here are based on a subsample of approximately 4500 youth who took the AFQT test when they were between the ages of fifteen and eighteen in 1979, and who were resurveyed in 1996 (age thirty-two to thirty-six) to determine their educational attainment and their family income levels at that time.[47] This sample provides a prediction analysis that spans a period of about seventeen years, from the teens to the young adult years.

The correlation between teenage AFQT scores and total years of education completed by the early thirties is .63, which means that 40 percent of the variation in years of education can be explained by this single academic aptitude test. While the correlation leaves ample room for the influence of other characteristics, such as motivation, financial resources, and other family background factors, the AFQT score is the single strongest predictor of educational attainment in the NLSY study.

The aggregate relationship shown in Figure 2.8 illustrates the remarkably strong relationship between youth aptitude and ultimate educational attainment. For youth at the lowest end of the aptitude continuum—below the twentieth percentile—85 percent did not attend college and only 3 percent graduated from college; almost 30 percent dropped out of high school.[48] For the highest category of aptitude—above the eightieth percentile—90 percent attended college and 75 percent graduated from college; none dropped out of high school. Generally, for each increase of twenty percentile points in youth IQ, the probability of attending college is increased by nearly 20 percent.

What about occupational and career outcomes? There are various occupational attributes that might be measured, such as employment status, type of job and industry, and annual income. Clearly, one of the most valued career outcomes is annual income, since it can impact on a number of other life satisfaction measures.

The correlation between youth aptitude and family income is .4, and while this is a substantial relationship, it is considerably lower than correlation between aptitude and educational attainment. One of the reasons is that some

Figure 2.8
Youth IQ in 1979 and Education Completed by 1996

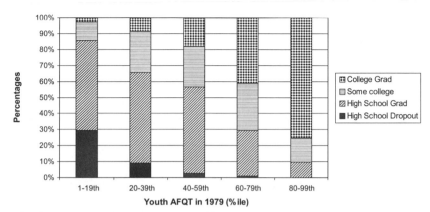

professional occupations, such as teaching and the academic professions, may require high IQ levels but have modest salaries compared to many business careers. People in the upper management levels of large businesses may have much higher salaries but lower IQs than those in academic jobs. Also, success in business careers may require social and personal skills not required in academic professions. In general, however, the higher the aptitude, the higher the family income.

Figure 2.9 shows the aggregate relationship between youth aptitude and family income, and again the aggregate relationship is quite impressive. Those in the highest aptitude group earn nearly $70,000 annuallycompared to just over $30,000 for those in the lowest aptitude group, and an increase of twenty percentile points in youth aptitude predicts an increase of about $10,000 in annual income. Aside from education, another reason for this relationship is that higher-IQ people are more likely to be married than lower-IQ people, creating the possibility of two-earner households. For example, about 70 percent of those with an AFQT score above the eightieth percentile were married, compared to only about 40 percent of those below the twentieth percentile.

The importance of IQ is clearly demonstrated by this national study. Higher IQs promote learning in school, which is manifested in higher achievement test scores. Early achievement scores have a very strong influence on achievement in the higher grades, and teenage achievement levels strongly predict a person's ultimate educational attainment. In turn, both aptitude and educational attainment affect income, not only because people with more education can obtain higher-paying jobs, but also because higher-achieving teens have a greater likelihood of marriage. Thus, a causal chain is established: from a child's IQ, to school achievement, to years of education completed, and finally to type of job and income.

Figure 2.9
Youth IQ in 1979 and Family Income in 1996

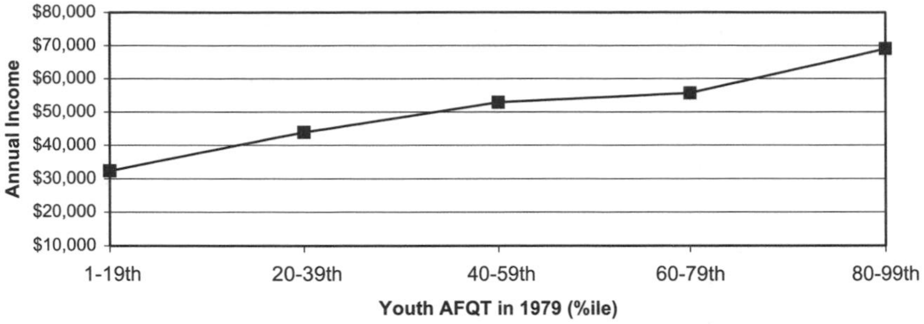

This is not to say that IQ and academic achievement are the only factors that affect educational and occupational success. The correlations are high, and the predictions are significant, but they are not so high as to preclude the importance of other human attributes such as motivation, creativity, and interpersonal skills in attaining career success and life satisfaction. The main point here is to establish, firmly, that intellectual ability as measured by IQ and achievement tests is a significant predictor of academic and occupational success. This fact clearly justifies a concern about maximizing a child's IQ, providing it is feasible to do so.

I should mention one other way in which intelligence is important. Certain professions, particularly math, science, and many other academic fields require people who possess high levels of academic intelligence. Just as individuals who are gifted in art, music, or athletic ability make the major contributions to these fields, people gifted with very high IQs generally make the most important contributions in math, science, and other academic fields. Individuals who possess these special talents and who apply them in their jobs and careers make major contributions to the larger society.

Notes

1.   C. Spearman, *Abilities of Man*, New York: MacMillan, 1927.
2.   A. Jenson, *Bias in Mental Testing*, New York: Free Press, 1980.
3.   L. L. Thurstone, *Primary Mental Abilities*, Chicago: University Press, 1938.
4.   J. B. Carroll, *Human Cognitive Abilities*, Cambridge, England: University Press, 1993.
5.   R. G. Cattell, *Abilities: Their Structure, Growth, and Action*, Boston: Houghton Mifflin, 1971.
6.   H. Gardner, *Frames of Mind*, New York: Basic Books, 1983.
7.   D. Goleman, *Emotional Intelligence*, New York, Bandtum, 1995.
8.   R.J. Sternberg, *Beyond IQ*, New York: Cambridge University Press, 1985.
9.   A standard deviation is a measure of dispersion; in a normal distribution, which is approximated by most IQ and aptitude tests, plus or minus one standard deviation encompasses about two-thirds of the population.

10. Like most individual attributes than can be represented on a numerical continuum (e.g., height and weight), properly designed cognitive test scores approximate a bell-shaped "normal" distribution which has these sd characteristics.

11. This same point has been made by Stephen Ceci. See Stephen Ceci et al., "The Shrinking Gap between High- and Low-Scoring Groups," in U. Neisser, ed., *The Rising Curve*, Washington, DC: APA, 1998.

12. C. Fischer, et al, *Inequality by Design*, Princeton, NJ: University Press, 1996.

13. S. J. Gould, *The Mismeasure of Man*, New York: W.W. Norton, 1996.

14. W. T. Dickens and J. R. Flynn, "Heritability Estimates Versus Large Environmental Effects: The IQ Paradox Resolved," *Psychological Review*, 108: 346-369, 2001.

15. S. J. Wadsworth, et al., "Covariation among measures of cognitive ability and academic achievement in the Colorado Adoption Project: sibling analysis," *Personal Individual Differences*, Vol. 18, No. 1, 1995.

16. Dorret I. Boomsma and G. Caroline M. van Baal, "Genetic influences on childhood IQ in 5- and 7- year-old Dutch twins," *Developmental Neuropsychology*, Vol. 14, No. 1, 1998.

17. S. Scarr, "Behavior-Genetic and Socialization Theories of Intelligence," in R. J. Sternberg and E. Grigorenko, eds., *Intelligence, Heredity, and Environment*, Cambridge University Press, 1997.

18. M. Daniels, B. Devlin, and K. Roeder, "Of Genes and IQ," in B. Devlin, S. Fienberg, D.P. Resnik, and K. Roeder, eds., *Intelligence, Genes, and Success*, 1997.

19. U. Neisser, et al., "Intelligence: Knowns and Unknowns," *American Psychologist*, 51: 77-101.

20. M. W. Feldman, S. P. Otto, and F. B. Christianson, "Genes, Culture, and Inequality," in K. Arrow, S. Bowles, and S. Durlaf, eds., *Meritocracy and Economic Inequality*, Princeton, NJ: University Press, 2000.

21. R. Martorell, "Nutrition and the World Wide Rise in IQ Scores," in Neisser, *The Rising Curve*, op cit.

22. A standardized score can also be used in this case, provided the same test level is used both times and the same norms are used.

23. Of course, most rigorous designs would also include a control group to rule out the possibility that the school as a whole was experiencing losses relative to national norms, in which case the intervention group would be seen as preventing losses that would otherwise have occurred.

24. J. Flynn, "IQ Gains over Time: Toward Finding the Causes," in Neisser, *The Rising Curve,* op cit.

25. J. R. Campbell, C. M. Hombo, J. Mazzeo, *NAEP 1999 Trends in Academic Progress*, Washington, DC: U.S. Department of Education, 2000.

26. U. Neisser, *The Rising Curve*, op cit.

27. D. Armor, "Why is Black Educational Achievement Rising?" *The Public Interest*, Summer, 1992; C. Jencks and M. Phillips, eds., *The Black-White Test Score Gap*, Washington, DC: Brookings Institute, 2000.

28. D. Grissmer, A. Flanagan, and S. Williamson, "Why Did the Black-White Score Gap Narrow in the 1970s and 1980s," in Jencks and Phillips, *The Black-White Test Score Gap*, op cit.

29. More precisely, to obtain the "true" correlation between two sets of test scores, the actual correlation should be divided by $\sqrt{\rho_1 \rho_2}$, where ρ_1 is the reliability of the first test and ρ_2 is the reliability of the second test. If both tests have reliability close to .9, then the divisor would be approximately .9.

30. Reported in Niesser, et al., eds., "IQ: Knowns and Unknowns," op cit., p. 81.

31. T. E. Moffitt, A. Caspi, A. R. Harkness, and P. A. Silva, "The Natural History of

Change in Intellectual Performance," *Journal of Child Psychology and Psychiatry*, 34: 455-506, 1993, Table 1.

32. L. G. Humphreys, "Intelligence: Three Kinds of Instability and their Consequences for Policy," in R. L. Linn, ed., *Intelligence*, Urbana: University of Illinois Press, 1989.

33. Only a randomly drawn 5 percent subsample is plotted (about 2000 cases) for clarity.

34. This under- and over-prediction is due in part to the statistical phenomenon of regression toward the mean.

35. H. Clinton, *It Takes a Village*, New York: Touchstone Books, 1996.

36. R. Shore, *Rethinking the Brain: New Insights into Early Development*, New York: Families and Work Institute, 1997; Carnegie Task Force on Meeting the Needs of Children, *Starting Points: Meeting the Needs of Our Youngest Children*, New York: Carnegie Corporation of New York, 1994.

37. John T. Bruer, *The Myth of the First Three Years: A New Understanding of Early Brain Development and Lifelong Learning*, New York: The Free Press, 1999.

38. W. T. Greenough, "We Can't Just Focus on Ages Zero to Three," *APA Monitor* 28:19, 1997.

39. There are studies of components of IQ, such as word usage or physical reaction times to various stimuli, which can be assessed at ages earlier than three, but it is not established that these are full measures of IQ, particularly reasoning ability, which is hard to measure in most children until after age three.

40. Lynn A. Karoly, et al, *Investing in Our Children: What We Know and Don't Know About the Costs and Benefits of Early Childhood Interventions*, Washington, DC: RAND Publishing, 1998.

41. Ibid.

42. Jean Piaget, "The Origins of Intelligence in Children," Margaret Cook, translator, in H.E. Gruber and J. J. Voneche, eds., *The Essential Piaget*, Northvale, N.J., Jason Aronson Inc., 1995.

43. Burton L. White, *The First Three Years of Life*, Englewood Cliffs, N.J., Prentice Hall, 1985.

44. Betty Hart and Todd R. Risley, *Meaningful Differences in the Everyday Experience of Young American Children*, Baltimore, MD: Paul H. Brookes Publishing Co., 1995.

45. Richard C. Atkinson, The 2001 Robert H. Atwell Distinguished Lecture, delivered at the 83rd Annual Meeting of the American Council on Education, Washington, D.C., February 18, 2001.

46. Generally, colleges look for candidates with high test scores, while the military screens out applicants with low test scores.

47. The study actually started in 1979 and surveyed 12,000 youth between the ages of fourteen and twenty-two; the sample was restricted here to get youth before they had entered the job market.

48. The AFQT scores are shown as percentiles.

3

The Risk Factors for Intelligence

The ten major risk factors that influence a child's intelligence were listed and described briefly in chapter 1. This chapter discusses the risk factors in greater detail, explaining what each factor means and showing their potential impact on both IQ and achievement. There are two preliminary matters concerning how the discussion of risk factors is organized as well as the nature and sources of research evidence used to support my proposition about risk factors.

With respect to organization, the ten risk factors are classified according to their chronology and the associated feasibility of changing the risk factors by parents, prospective parents, or other child caregivers. The most important chronological distinction is whether the factor occurs before or after the birth or conception of a child. This distinction is critical for parents. Clearly, those risk factors that operate prior to birth must be controlled or optimized by parents or prospective parents before a child is conceived. Moreover, parents-to-be are the only people who can exercise control over these factors, although other people might be in a position to give advice. In contrast, those risk factors that operate after a child is born (e.g., cognitive stimulation) can be modified or optimized during a child's early development years, and it is also possible for persons other than parents to play a significant role (e.g., childcare center staff).

Evidence for the Risk Factors

The primary sources of evidence for the risk factors are two comprehensive national studies. The most important of these is the Children of National Longitudinal Study of Youth (CNLSY or Youth Study). In 1979, as part of another study, a national representative sample of approximately 5000 women ages fifteen to twenty-one was selected and interviewed. Starting in 1986, the women were re-contacted every two years in order to assess the development of their children. By 1994 the Youth Study had assessed approximately 9000 children born to this sample of women.

The Youth Study represents the most comprehensive and longest-running national assessment of young children from birth to adolescence. Over a fifteen year period parents were interviewed about their education, employment, earnings, marital status, behaviors and attitudes about parenting, and a host of other important family characteristics. Trained interviewers observed children and parents in the home in order to document the type and quality of the home environment, parenting behaviors, and parent-child interactions. Children received a variety of cognitive ability tests, including the Peabody Picture Vocabulary Test (PPVT), which measures verbal IQ, and the Peabody Individual Achievement Tests (PIAT) in mathematics and reading. Finally, a very important feature of the Youth Study is that the original sample took the Armed Forces Qualification Test (AFQT), which provides a measure of the mother's IQ when she was a teenager or young woman.

The other major national study used in this book is the National Assessment of Educational Progress (NAEP). This is the most comprehensive national assessment of academic achievement in existence. Starting around 1970, large national samples of children ages nine, thirteen, and seventeen (grades four, eight, and twelve) have been tested in reading, math, and science every two or four years. The NAEP study also collects extensive data on students' family background as well as information about their school, classroom, and teachers.

Greatest reliance will be placed on the Youth Study because it measures more potential risk factors than any other national study. In order to establish and assess the importance of each risk factor, this chapter examines the correlation between a given risk factor and two different measures of a child's intelligence: the Peabody verbal IQ test and the PIAT test in mathematics. The verbal IQ test was given to all children aged three years or over in 1986 and 1992 (ages range up to fifteen). The verbal IQ scores used in this chapter are those available when children are between the ages of three and five. In order to have a measure of IQ before most children have started their formal schooling, the analysis of IQ scores is restricted to children younger than six. The verbal IQ score has been standardized to have a mean of 100 and a standard deviation of 15.

The math achievement test was given to all children aged five years or older in each assessment between 1986 and 1994. The math achievement scores are based on children ages five to fifteen, with an average age of nine years (two-thirds were between seven and twelve). The math achievement score has also been standardized to have a mean of 100 and a standard deviation of 15. Since many children learn math at school rather than at home, math achievement scores mostly reflect content that children have learned in schools. The important question in this chapter, however, is whether the risk factors that affect a child's IQ before they start school also affect math achievement after a child has been in school for several years. Since both the IQ and achievement tests are normed, the correlation between a risk factor and a test score measures the extent to which a given risk factor influences the ranking of children's relative to each other or to the national norm. It does not assess the absolute level of skill or knowledge that the children might possess.

The Role of Parent IQ

Many studies have shown that there is a fairly strong correlation between a child's IQ and the IQ of either parent. The fact of the correlation is not so much at issue as the interpretation of the correlation. Behavioral scientists who believe that IQ is largely inherited quite naturally believe that this correlation reflects primarily a genetic effect and, indeed, the authors of *The Bell Curve* endorse this interpretation. As indicated by the sweeping criticisms of *The Bell Curve*, however, this interpretation is still controversial in a large segment of the social science community. At least five scholarly books have now been published in reaction to this book, comprising dozens of separate reviews and commentary, most of which criticize the conclusions of *The Bell Curve*.[1] Most of the criticism focuses on the book's thesis that heredity plays a much larger role in determining intelligence than environmental factors.

Despite the controversy over *The Bell Curve*, many behavior scientists do accept the proposition that heredity plays at least some role in shaping a person's intelligence. Although evidence for this conclusion comes from a variety of research studies, the strongest evidence comes from studies of identical twins, two of which were mentioned in chapter 2. Identical twin studies are important because identical twins have identical genetic structures, and they show that the IQs of identical twins are very similar, whether the twins are raised together or raised apart. Statistically speaking, the IQs of identical twins have very high correlations, where a correlation ranges from −1.0 for a perfect negative relationship, 0 for no relationship, and +1.0 for a perfect positive relationship. In one comprehensive study, the correlation of IQs between identical twins raised in the same family is .86, and when identical twins are raised in different families (due to adoptions, etc.) the average correlation drops to about .75.[2] In other words, even when identical twins are raised in different families with presumably different environments, knowing the IQ of one twin leads to a very good prediction of the other twin's IQ.

Family studies have shown that the IQ correlations between parents and their biological children are also fairly high, although not nearly as high as the correlation between identical twins. Since a child inherits only one-half of his or her genes from each parent, the correlation of a parent-child IQ should be smaller than that for identical twins. For example, the correlation of IQs between biological siblings raised together, who share one-half of their genes, averages about .5, and correlations between the IQ of either biological parent and their child's IQ range from .3 to .5. But the size of sibling or parent-child correlations is subject to other interpretations, because siblings are usually raised by the same parents. High sibling and parent-child correlations could reflect the effects of similar home environments as well as genetic influences.

A high parent-child IQ correlation can be interpreted as an environmental effect if it is understood that parents largely control and determine a child's home environment. A high IQ parent might create an environment that promotes higher IQs for their children, while a low IQ parent may fail to do so. For example, higher IQ parents generally have higher educational attainments and higher incomes, as shown in chapter 1. Therefore, they may place greater emphasis on teaching various skills to their children, and they may have more resources for doing so (e.g., educational toys, books, time). Perhaps most important, a parent with a higher IQ may have a richer intellectual interaction with their child, offering more complex words, ideas, games, etc. which provide greater stimulation for the child's intellectual development. Thus the parent-child IQ correlation might reflect this richer home environment as well as the effects of heredity.

For the purpose of this book, it is not important to decide how much of the relationship between a parent's IQ and the child's IQ is due to heredity or environment. The most important fact is that a young mother or mother-to-be cannot change her IQ in the same way she can change the other risk factors. By the time a person reaches the late teens, IQ scores and academic ability are fairly well established and will not change much over the child-bearing years. Thus, whether the correlation between a parent's IQ and a child's IQ indicates mostly environmental or mostly genetic effects, attempting to change this particular risk factor would not be a particularly promising way to maximize a child's IQ.

Having said this, it is nevertheless important to evaluate the role of parent's IQ when considering the effects of the remaining risk factors. First, we assume that a given environmental risk factor may be caused in part by a parent's IQ level. Second, in order to understand how the environmental factor affects a child's IQ, we have to separate out the effect due to the parent's IQ and the effect due to the environmental factor. For example, Figure 1.8 in chapter 1 showed that youth IQ exerts a very strong influence on subsequent educational attainment. In deciding how much parent education affects a child's IQ above and beyond parent IQ, we need to know how much of the education effect is due to the parent's IQ and how much is due to parent education *independent* of parent IQ. In order to do this, we need to remove the contribution of the parent's IQ to the relationship between a parent's education and a child's IQ. This is done using the statistical technique of multiple regression.[3]

The same process can also work in reverse. In order to test how much of the relationship between parent and child IQ might be due to environmental risk factors, we first consider the unadjusted relationship between parent and child IQ and then see how this relationship changes when the other environmental factors are removed by regression analysis.

Figure 3.1
Effect of Mother's IQ on Child's IQ,
Before and After Removing Environmental Factors

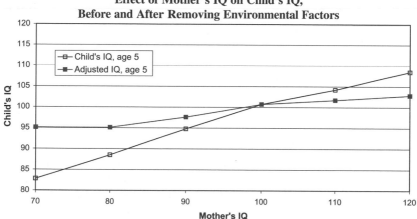

For example, figure 3.1 shows the relationship between mother and child's IQ from the Youth Study data before and after removing the effects of all remaining environmental risk factors.[4] The environmental factors are those listed in chapter 1. The unadjusted relationship between mother and child IQ is very strong, and the overall correlation is a little over .5. Children whose mothers have the highest IQs (about 120) score 26 points higher, on average, than children whose mothers have the lowest IQs (about 70). For each increase of ten points in a mother's IQ, the child's IQ is raised five points.

However, when the effects of other environmental risk factors are removed from the relationship (the chapter 1 list), the effect of mother's IQ is reduced considerably. After removing these environmental effects, children whose mothers have IQs around 120 score about ten points higher, on average, than those whose mothers have IQs around 70. After removing environmental effects, each ten-point increase in a mother's IQ is associated with an increase of only two points in the child's IQ. In other words, mother's IQ still has a strong effect on a child's IQ, even when we remove the most important environmental risk factors. But the relationship between a mother's IQ and her child's IQ is less than half as strong when other environmental effects are removed. This indicates that, even if the effect of mother's IQ is assumed to be genetic (which is not assumed here), all the other environmental factors combined have greater effects on a child's IQ than this presumed genetic factor.

This finding has been reported in other research. Perhaps the most comprehensive analysis of the effect of a mother's IQ on her child's IQ was undertaken by Meridith et al., using the Youth Study data as of 1992.[5] Analyzing the verbal IQs of five-year olds, they found an effect of .4 for mother's IQ after controlling for race (a one-point increase in mother's IQ is associated with a .4 point increase in the child's IQ). When a large number of family environment variables were added as controls, however, including the parenting behaviors of cognitive stimulation and emotional support, the effect of mother's IQ dropped by more than half, to around .17. They conclude that while the effect of mother's IQ may reflect genetic influences, family environment factors also exert substantial influence on a child's IQ.

In *The Bell Curve*, Herrnstein and Murray relied on the Youth Study to show not only the strong correlation between mother and child's IQ, but also strong correlations between mother's IQ and many environmental factors, such as education, family income, and parenting behaviors. Because these latter variables are more weakly related to a child's IQ, they argued that these environmental factors themselves are simply reflections of parent's IQ, implying they have little or no independent effects of their own. If a child's IQ is largely influenced by the parent's IQ, and if the family environment itself is largely determined by parent's IQ, then there is very little room left for improving IQ by changing environmental factors.

This chapter comes to a very different conclusion using the same data. While no single environmental factor has as strong an effect on a child's IQ as the mother's IQ, it will be argued here that when all of the potential environmental effects are combined, as in Figure 3.1, there is considerable room to improve a child's IQ by altering environmental conditions.

The Sequence of Risk Factors

Apart from parents' IQ, the other nine risk factors can be changed and optimized after a person has reached the teen years, but the timing of changes is critical. In this respect, it is important to distinguish between those risk factors that must be optimized before a child is born (or conceived) and those that can be optimized after a child is born. Those that can be altered after birth, such as nutrition and the parenting behaviors of cognitive stimulation and emotional support, have perhaps the greatest potential for impact because there is some chance that they can be modified, to good effect, during a child's early development. The parenting behaviors are especially important here because they can also be influenced or optimized, at least to some extent, by persons other than the parents, such as grandparents, other relatives, or the professional staff of an early childcare center.

Those factors that cannot be changed easily (or at all) immediately after a child's birth include the factors of parent education, family income, family structure, number of children, and mother's age at birth. Practically speaking, these factors usually must be altered by the decisions of a potential parent before a child's conception. For example, a prospective parent must decide not to drop out of high school or college, not to have a baby as an unmarried teenager, not to have a baby until adequate financial resources are available, or not to have a baby after two or three are already born. Technically, parents can alter their education, income, and marital status after a child is born; for example, a new mother can stay in school or can marry the father. But if the change in status is going to have an impact on the child's early intellectual development, the change must come very soon after a child's birth.

Before addressing each of the environmental risk factors, two caveats are in order concerning interpretation of the risk factors. First, because all risk factors are interrelated, it is very difficult to quantify the specific *independent* effect of each risk factor. For now, a condition or behavior is a risk factor if it is correlated with a child's IQ score after controlling for the mother's IQ. This ensures that each risk factor has some influence on a child' s IQ independent of the mother's IQ. Later in this chapter I will discuss multivariate analyses where the effect of each factor is estimated controlling for all other factors. Some risk factors seem more important than others because they retain a significant correlation with a child's IQ even after all other risk factors have been removed. It should be noted that, given the strong relationship between IQ and education, removing the effect of mother's IQ to some extent also removes the effect of socioeconomic levels.

Second, correlation and regression analyses alone can establish a relationship, but they do not prove causation. An inference of causation depends on the totality of research concerning each risk factor. For this reason, correlational results from the large national studies are supplemented by references to a large body of research literature on each risk factor.

Risk Factors after Birth or Conception

The environmental conditions that can influence a child's academic ability after birth (or conception) are especially important to parents and childcare workers, because they can be altered after the fact. Their significance is amplified for families at the lower end of the socioeconomic spectrum whose children are already at risk for lower academic achievement. Given that lower education, lower income, and single parenthood have potential adverse effects on a child's IQ, optimizing parenting behaviors may offer the best pathway for maximizing a child's IQ. But even for families better positioned on the socioeconomic continuum, parenting behaviors must also be optimized in order to maximize the academic ability of any child.

The four post-conception factors identified here fall into two groups. The first group includes the parenting factors of cognitive stimulation and emotional support, and by definition they clearly operate after a child is born. These parenting behaviors are usually seen as most important during the early years of a child's life, although they might continue to exert influence throughout a child's intellectual development. It will become clear that these two risk factors are the most important environmental influences on a child's IQ and academic achievement.

The other post-conception group includes the interconnected factors of nutrition and birth weight, which are also implicated in the health and physical well being of a child. The timing of these factors differs from the parenting behaviors, since they can involve environmental conditions and parental behaviors between conception and birth. In the case of nutrition, the period of potential effect can also extend to the years of infancy and early childhood.

Cognitive Stimulation

The term "cognitive stimulation" is a rather academic term for what most parents would simply call "instructing" their children. For most parents (and grandparents, for that matter), nothing is more natural than teaching their infant children, which usually starts with language: giving names to family members and common objects around the home (mama, baby, etc.), reading stories, and many other types of verbal and nonverbal interaction with the baby. During infancy most parents also introduce a great variety of toys designed to stimulate, entertain, and educate. When the child is a little older, parents begin teaching the alphabet, numbers, more complicated words, shapes, and so forth, and introducing increasingly complex toys such as puzzles and building blocks.

At older ages—but before school age—parents can introduce a great variety of teaching activities: more serious reading material in more advanced topics such as science and history, more complex toys such as computer games, and instructional outings to museums, zoos, concerts, and so forth. All of these teaching activities and educational experiences can happen before a child starts formal schooling, and it usually continues throughout the elementary grades and beyond, or at least until a parent feels that the topics have become too advanced or complex for their own teaching skills.

There is now substantial research to show that these natural parenting activities, which behavioral scientists often call "cognitive stimulation" to distinguish it from other types of parenting activities, are not merely helpful but in fact crucial to a child's mental progress. That is, the more time that parents spend on these sorts of teaching activities during infancy, the higher the children's IQ by the time they reach school age and the higher their academic achievement after they have started school.

The best evidence for the importance of cognitive stimulation for a child's academic ability again comes from the Youth Study. During the visits to each family in the study, interviewers administer an instrument called the HOME Inventory.[6] This inventory consists of questions and interviewer observations across a wide variety of parenting behaviors, parent-child interactions, and conditions in the home. There are fifteen specific activities or conditions that go into a parent's cognitive stimulation score for children aged three to nine, although they differ somewhat by age group; there are nine elements for children under three. The elements of the inventory for ages three to five are as follows:

- Mother reads stories to child at least three times per week

- Ten or more children's books in the home

- One or more magazines in the home

- Child has a record or tape player

- Family member helps child to learn alphabet

- Family member helps child to learn numbers

- Family member helps child to learn colors

- Family member helps child to learn shapes and sizes

- Outings (shopping, parks, etc.) at least twice a month

- Has gone to a museum at least once

- Play areas judged safe

- Home is reasonably clean

- Home is minimally cluttered

- Home is not dark or monotonous

- Building has no structural or health hazards

Each child in a family can receive a raw score from 0 to 15 points, depending on how many of these activities are taking place for that child. During the 1992 assessment the average score for children ages three to nine was about 10 points, and most children fell in the range of 5 to 13 points. It should be noted that the specific activities are not as important as the range of activities and conditions in the list, since each activity contributes only 1 point to the score. Other similar activities (playing games, having educational toys, etc.) can be substituted without changing the relative ranking of a child's score. These raw scores are standardized to resemble an IQ score with a mean of about 100. To understand the relation between the standardized and raw scores, each additional parent activity or home condition would translate into an increase in the standardized score of about 7 points.[7]

Figure 3.2a confirms the strong relationship between parents' cognitive stimulation scores and a child's IQ at age five or math achievement at age nine. The IQ gap between the highest and lowest-scoring groups is 22 points, and the math achievement gap is 17 points. In fact, cognitive stimulation has a

Figure 3.2a
Cognitive Stimulation and Child's IQ and Achievement

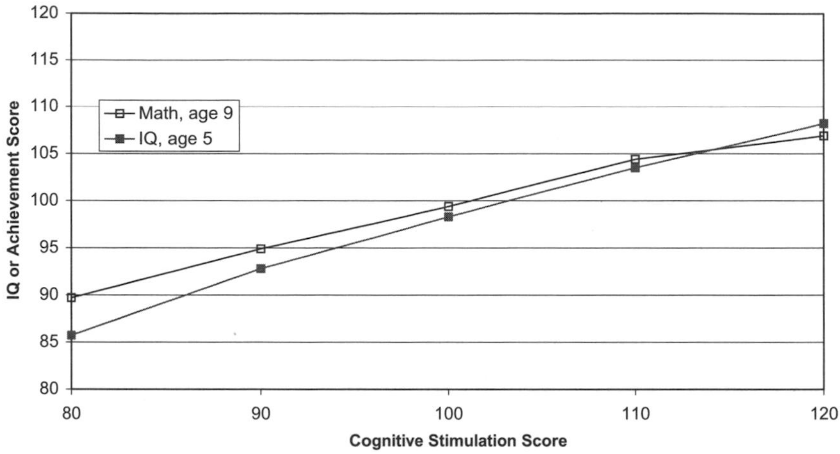

stronger association with a child's academic ability than any other environmental risk factor, and it is only slightly weaker than the relationship between child IQ and mother's IQ. This is especially good news, because cognitive stimulation is one of the few risk factors that can be altered and enhanced after a child is born, and it can also be offered by persons other than a child's parents.

Not surprisingly, cognitive stimulation is also strongly related to a mother's IQ, which raises the possibility that it may be a mother's IQ that causes the strong relationship rather than cognitive stimulation. As shown in Figure 3.2b, however, removing the influence of mother's IQ reduces the relationship but still leaves a very significant impact of cognitive stimulation on a child's academic ability. Mother's IQ removes about half of the relationship; the gap between the highest and lowest scoring groups is now 12 points for IQ and 8 points for math achievement. Although not shown in a figure, this strong relationship persists even if we remove the effects of all other environmental factors including number of children, income, family status, mother's age, and so forth (see later section on multivariate analysis).

Another way to describe this relationship is that, after removing the effect of the mother's IQ, an increase of 10 points on the cognitive stimulation score raises a child's IQ score by approximately 3 points and the math achievement score by about 2 points. Given the relationship between the number of activities and the standardized score, an increase of about three activities (out of the fifteen) translates into an increase of 6 IQ points or 4 math achievement points after removing the effect of mother's IQ. These are very strong effects, indeed, and they could mean the difference between a child's IQ being several points below the national average to several points above it.

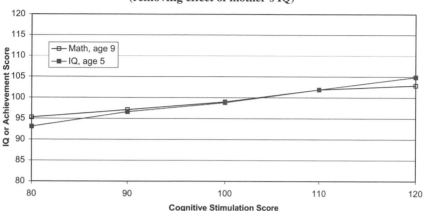

Figure 3.2b
Cognitive Stimulation and Child's IQ and Achievement
(removing effect of mother's IQ)

Other research supports these findings. A study of a sample of 121 healthy, full-term, non-minority infants used HOME scores and socioeconomic measures to predict the IQ scores of participants at three to eight years of age.[8] The study concluded that the home environment was the most important variable for predicting intelligence scores at all ages, although the influence declines from year five onward. Other studies have used the Youth Study data and other national data to come to similar conclusions about the importance of HOME scores on a child's IQ. The most important of these to date is by Philips and others. They found large effects of HOME scores on verbal IQ after controlling for many other family variables, including mother's IQ, in both the Youth Study data and an independent national study called the Infant Health and Development Study.[9] They conclude that "The HOME is an important predictor of children's test performance, even after controlling other measures of children's family environment."

There has been much debate among behavioral and biological scientists about the exact mechanism behind the relationship between cognitive stimulation during infancy and a child's later academic ability. It might seem odd to some that there is a debate, because it seems self-evident that the more time and effort spent on teaching children or exposing them to various kinds of experiences, the more they will learn. But the debate is actually over the timing of this process, and whether this type of teaching is effective at all ages or just during the years of early childhood.

Those scientists who believe that cognitive stimulation has an effect on IQ only during infancy have argued that there is a direct link between cognitive stimulation and brain development, specifically the formation of synapses among brain cells (neurons), which is especially intense during the early years of childhood.[10] Other scientists, while agreeing that the rate of synapse formation appears highest during very early childhood, disagree that a specific causal link has been proven between cognitive stimulation, synapse formation, and human intelligence.[11] The relationship between brain development and IQ change was discussed in greater detail in chapter 2.

It is beyond the scope of this chapter to evaluate the mechanisms that explain how cognitive stimulation affects a child's IQ. It is not necessary for present purposes, which is to establish whether early cognitive stimulation is a risk factor for a child's academic ability. Since a strong correlation exists between cognitive stimulation and a child's subsequent academic ability, and since it remains strong after the effect of mother's IQ and other risk factors are removed, it is reasonable to conclude that cognitive stimulation is an important risk factor for a child's intelligence.

Emotional Support

Like cognitive stimulation, the risk factor of "emotional support" also has a common-sense meaning among non-experts, which might be called simply a "loving" or "nurturing" family. For decades (if not centuries for some cultures) good parents have believed that a child learns best when the home environment is warm and supportive, and when parents express their love, care, and respect for their children. There are many ways in which a nurturing environment is manifested, and there may be some legitimate disagreement between parents and experts about some issues, particularly the role of physical punishment in discipline. But most parents and experts alike agree that for healthy development a young child needs a great deal of love and affection and, when a little older, needs to be recognized as an individual and treated with appropriate respect.

There is not a well-established theory that explains the precise link between an emotionally supportive home and intellectual development. Many books on child development emphasize that love and affection are important for building a "trusting" relationship between a parent and child, which is necessary for healthy mental and emotional development.[12] Whether such a theory is proven or not, the values of most Western civilizations, and many developing societies as well, emphasize loving and caring relationships among family members (as well as among friends, neighbors, etc.). Most people believe that affection and respect are necessary for good mental health of children, and its absence in childhood produces adults who are unfulfilled, insecure, and maladjusted. Most people also believe that rules, discipline, and authority are necessary for healthy child development in a family, although a balance must be struck: too little and children become spoiled, demanding, and self-centered; too much and children become weak, passive, and self-doubting.

Like cognitive stimulation, there is substantial evidence that emotional support is strongly related to the development of a child's academic ability. In the Youth Study, the HOME Inventory assesses a number of parenting activities and behaviors that are combined to form an emotional support score. It includes several questions answered by the mother about various parenting practices, but about half of the behaviors are based on the interviewer's observations of interactions between the mother and each child during the home visit. The specific parenting activities that go into the emotional support score differ somewhat by age group: there are twelve elements in the score for three to five year olds. The twelve parenting behaviors that make up the three to five score are as follows:

- Child is introduced to interviewer by name

- Mother talked to child at least twice during visit

- Mother answered child's questions verbally

- Mother hugged or kissed child during visit

- Child was not physically restrained during visit

- Child was not slapped or spanked during visit

- Mother's voice showed positive feelings about child

- Child has at least some choice in foods for breakfast/lunch

- Television is on no more than four hours per day

- Non-physical punishment if child hits parent

- Child spanked no more than once per week

- Child has meal with mother and father/father figure once a day or more

Note that the score includes mostly indications of positive interaction between mother and child as well as several items dealing with discipline. To get a perfect score on this measure of support, a mother would have to show mostly positive interactions with her child and could not spank her child more than once a week. Each child in a family gets a raw score for emotional support by adding up the number of activities or behaviors on this list; the maximum score is 12 and the average is about 8 or 9. This discussion uses standardized scores that have a national average of 100. An increase in the raw score of one activity would translate into an increase of about 8 points in the standardized score.

Figure 3.3a shows that the relationship between an emotionally supporting environment and a child's academic ability is nearly as strong as that for cog-

Figure 3.3a
Emotional Support and Child's IQ and Achievement

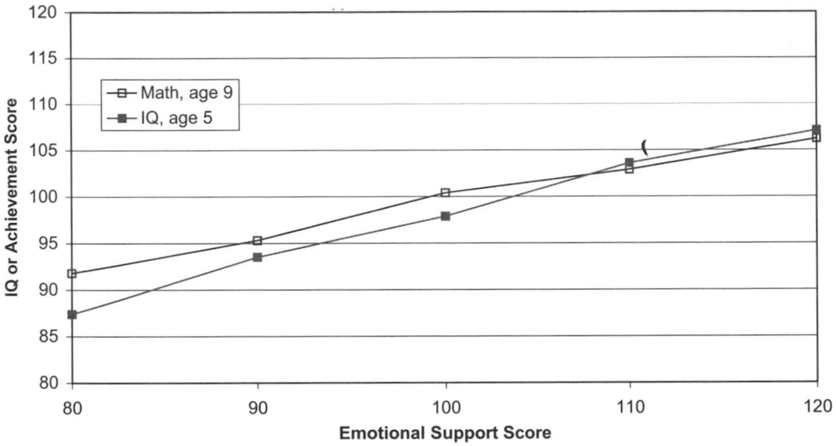

nitive stimulation. The IQ gap between groups with the lowest and highest emotional support scores is 20 points, and the math achievement gap is 14 points. Without regard for mother's IQ, an increase of 10 points in parent's emotional support is associated with a 5-point increase in a child's IQ and about 3.5 points in math achievement.

Again, the relationship remains strong when the effect of mother's IQ is removed, as seen in Figure 3.3b. Adjusting for mother's IQ, the IQ gap is reduced to 12 and the math achievement gap is reduced to 8 for highest and lowest support scores. For each 10-point increase in the emotional support scale, or approximately one more supporting behavior, we expect an increase of about 3 points in a child's IQ and an increase of about 2 points in the math score.

Although mother's IQ explains about half of the relationship between emotional support and child's IQ, the influence of emotional support is second only to cognitive stimulation among all of the environmental factors. If a group of children has raw scores of 7 on the emotional support scale, and the mothers could add three positive or subtract three negative behaviors from the list above, then those children could experience a 6-point rise in their IQ scores, on average.

Other research has used different measures of maternal attitudes and behaviors to arrive at the same conclusion. For example, a study of 234 Scandinavian children investigated the link between maternal attitudes and children's cognitive abilities controlling for mother's IQ and socioeconomic status.[13] Maternal attitudes were assessed using a version of the Child Rearing Practices Report. Although maternal IQ was found to be the best predictor of intelligence, it was determined that a nurturing maternal attitude and less severe discipline was related to cognitive ability.

Figure 3.3b
Emotional Support and Child's IQ and Achievement
(removing effect of mother's IQ)

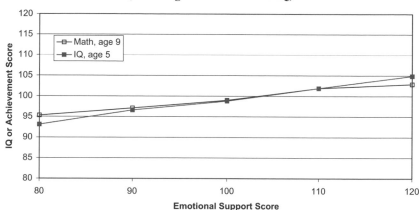

That intelligence and academic ability also flourish in families with strong emotional support may come as a surprise to some, particularly those who believe that better learning takes place in highly structured environments with a lot of rules and strict discipline. The most likely explanation is that most children learn better when they are not anxious about whether they might fail, and when they feel secure in their relationship with their parents—that they will still be loved regardless of whether they pronounce a word correctly, count properly, and so forth. Mothers who offer strong emotional support form a healthy emotional bond with their children where this type of security is fostered.

As might be expected, cognitive stimulation and emotional support scores are themselves related, meaning that mothers who bestow high stimulation scores also tend to produce high support scores. Is it possible that cognitive stimulation causes the apparent relationship with emotional support or vice-versa? The answer is no, although the relationship between emotional support and academic ability diminishes when both mother's IQ and cognitive stimulation are taken into account. For children with very high or very low cognitive stimulation scores, there is no significant gain in math achievement for children from the lowest and highest categories of emotional support: math achievement remains at about 103 for the former group and 95 for the latter (with mother's IQ removed). For children in the middle ranges of cognitive stimulation scores, however, there is a gain of about 4 points for children in the lowest to highest categories of support.

If the comparison is reversed, cognitive stimulation improves math achievement regardless of whether a child has low, middle, or high levels of emotional support: the gain is 6 or 7 points across all levels of support. It is fair to conclude, then, that cognitive stimulation is somewhat more beneficial to academic achievement than emotional support, and emotional support seems to play the biggest role for children in the middle ranges of cognitive stimulation. Another way to put this is that parents who are really good or really poor teachers seem to get good or bad results, respectively, regardless of how much emotional support they provide to their children. Those parents who are average teachers, or somewhat below or above average, get better results from their teaching as their emotional support grows for their children.

Birth Weight

The issue of a child's birth weight is usually raised as a threshold issue. That is, the question is not the general relationship between birth weight and intelligence, but whether low birth weight in particular has an adverse impact on a child's IQ. An expectant mother in good health can expect to give birth to a baby weighing, approximately, from five to ten pounds.[14] In the medical research, low birth weight is traditionally defined as about 5.3 pounds or less (2500 grams), and sometimes a distinction is made for very low birth weights under about 3.2 pounds (1500 grams). Very low birth weights often occur in premature or multiple births. A considerable body of research indicates that low birth weight children are at higher risk for a number of health problems, including impaired cognitive ability.

The reasons for the negative effects of low birth weight on cognitive functioning involve a variety of developmental factors that may also be tied to the causes of low birth weight. Some of these causes may be biological in nature, including inadequate nutrition, restricted blood supply (as in the case of teenage mothers), hypertension, and the biological effects of substances such as nicotine, alcohol, and illegal drugs.[15] Other factors may be social in nature and can include such factors as stress (abuse, illness, incarceration) and economic disadvantage.

How important are the effects of low birth weight on a child's IQ? The full relationship between birth weight and a child's IQ and math achievement is shown in Figure 3.4a using Youth Study data. The relationship for actual math scores suggests a low-weight threshold between 5.2 and 5.3 pounds, but a threshold is less clear for actual IQ scores. After the threshold, math scores continue to rise until birth weights reach about eight pounds, and then the relationship flattens. IQ scores seem to rise until about seven pounds and then they flatten out. Therefore, the relationship between weight and intelligence may be more than a threshold issue. The IQ and achievement differences between children with low and high birth weights are not as large as those seen for parenting behaviors. The ability gaps between children with low versus normal birth weights is about 10 points for math scores and only about 5 points for IQ scores.

Figure 3.4a
Birth Weight and Child's IQ and Achievement

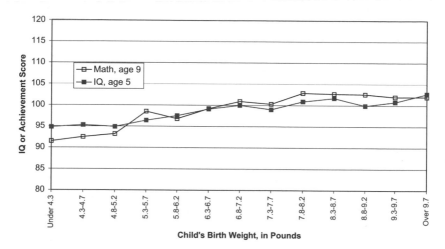

When the effect for mother's IQ is removed (Fig. 3.4b), the relationships definitely weaken, suggesting that much of the original relationship between birth weight and IQ may be due to mothers' intelligence and related socioeconomic levels. That is, lower IQ (and hence less educated) mothers may have lifestyles that contribute to nutritional or other physiological problems during pregnancy, which in turn contribute to reduced birth weights. The relationship is weakest for IQ, where there is only a small difference between low and normal weight children: an average IQ of 98 versus an average IQ of 100, respectively. The trend for math scores suggests a stronger influence of birth weight independent of mothers' IQ. In fact, there is still a distinct threshold at about 5.3 pounds, and low birth rate children have adjusted math scores of 95 compared to 101 points for children above 7.7 pounds.

The effect of low and very low birth weights on intellectual ability is well documented. A study conducted at Johns Hopkins Medical Institution matched 150 very low birth weight babies with 124 normal birth weight controls with similar sociodemographic background.[16] The average IQ of the low weight group was 13 to 18 points lower than the controls at ages eight and sixteen.

A similar study followed thirty-nine very low birth weight children matched with normal weight controls on grade, gender, race, maternal education, birth order, and SES.[17] Another study compared 367 very low birth weight babies to 553 low birth weight and 555 normal birth weight babies matched on maternal race, maternal age, and city of residence.[18] The results indicate that approximately one-fourth of the very low weight children had either a questionable or abnormal performance on a developmental test.

Figure 3.4b
Birth Weight and Child's IQ and Achievement
(removing effect of mother's IQ)

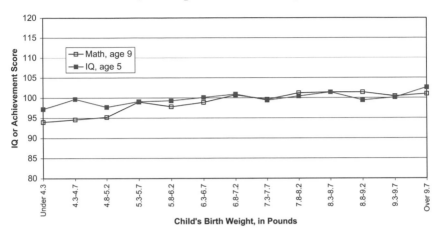

One of the largest and longest-running studies on low birth weight was published in the *Journal of the American Medical Association*. The study followed 14,000 full term infants born in Great Britain in 1970 of which 1064 were low birth weight (small for gestational age or SGA). Data was collected at ages five, ten, sixteen, and twenty-six.[19] Significant cognitive deficits for the SGA children were observed at both ages five and sixteen, and at age ten SGA children had significantly lower math scores. The long term results were that the SGA adults were significantly less likely to have professional or managerial occupations and more likely to work as unskilled, semi-skilled, or manual laborers than the normal birth weight adults even after controlling for social class.

Nutrition

Like low birth weight, the nutrition risk factor can involve physiological and biological processes that occur during pregnancy, but nutritional influences can also occur throughout a child's growth years. The major concern here involves nutritional deficiencies that can have adverse effects on cognitive development if they fall below certain levels. While children do not necessarily gain higher intelligence by adding more of these critical nutrients to a diet, some psychologists believe that the overall gain in IQ scores observed over the last fifty years is partly due to improved general nutrition.[20]

Although malnutrition can adversely affect a host of physical and mental characteristics of children, the specific nutritional deficiencies with the greatest involvement in a child's cognitive development concern iodine, iron, and fatty acids.[21] Mothers who are deficient in iodine before and during pregnancy are at risk of bearing children with brain damage, mental retardation, and a variety of other disabilities. At the present time iodine deficiency is primarily a problem in the developing world; diets with normal amounts of salt are generally sufficient to provide the necessary amount of iodine to prevent brain damage or retardation.

While anemia is primarily a problem in developing countries, iron deficiency has also been documented in the United States. It is believed to affect at least 5-10 percent of women in the U.S. between the ages of twenty to forty-four, with slightly higher rates for pregnant women.[22] Significantly, iron deficiency is higher among black than white mothers, suggesting that poverty and other socioeconomic factors may play a role in causing iron deficiency. The potential impact of iron deficiency on a child's IQ may involve the causal mechanism of oxygen circulation in the blood and brain, which is particularly critical in the periods of rapid brain growth during the fetal and postnatal periods. There are still some questions about the efficacy of iron supplementation, suggesting that iron deficiency may be caused by other less understood physiological or dietary mechanisms.[23]

The third major factor in nutritional deficiencies is fatty acids, and in particular the types of fatty acids found in mother's milk but not in certain types of infant formula used by non-nursing mothers. The suggested causal mechanism here is the fact that a substantial portion of the brain's "gray matter" is composed of complex fatty acids, and that a diet deficient in these fatty acids during rapid brain development (late pregnancy and early infancy) might impair mental and cognitive development.

There is no consensus yet on the precise types of fatty acids that infant formula should contain to prevent adverse effects on a child's mental development, but there is substantial evidence that breast-fed babies have better cognitive outcomes than babies who are not breast-fed. A review of twenty separate studies on this issue has determined that after adjusting for the appropriate factors, breast-feeding is still associated with significantly higher cognitive scores than formula feeding.[24] It is not yet settled whether this result is caused by nutrition or by other behaviors of mothers who breast-feed, but there is little question that breast-feeding does represent a risk factor for a child's IQ and achievement.

The Youth Study contains information on whether a child was breast-fed or not, and the relationship between being breast-fed and subsequent IQ and achievement is shown in Table 3.1. Without regard to mother's IQ, there is a 7-point difference in IQ and a 6-point difference in math achievement between children who are breast-fed and those who are not. When the effect of mother's IQ is removed, the difference drops to two points. Although this is not a large difference, the 2-point difference remains after all other environmental effects are also removed, including mother and father's education, income, family status, family size, and parenting behaviors (and it is statistically significant).

Table 3.1
Breast-Feeding and Child's IQ and Achievement (CNLSY)

	IQ age 5	Math age 9
Actual scores		
Not breast-fed	96	98
Breast-fed	103	104
Mother's IQ removed		
Not breast-fed	99	99
Breast-fed	101	101

Based on the Youth Study data, then, it appears that when all other environmental factors are equal, breast-feeding confers an IQ and achievement advantage of about 2 points. Since the most important socioeconomic and environmental factors have been removed from this result, and given the consistency with other research, it is reasonable to conclude that this benefit is derived from the unique nutritional characteristics of mother's milk.

Summary of Post-conception Risk Factors

All of the post-conception risk factors have strong correlations with both IQ and math achievement, but the correlations are reduced when the effect of mother's IQ is removed. This is especially true for birth weight and breast-feeding, where the adverse effect of low birth weight is minus 2 IQ points and the benefits of breast-feeding is about plus 2 IQ points after removing the effect of mother's IQ. The potential influence of parenting behaviors (cognitive stimulation and emotional support) is much stronger, perhaps because the range of possible scores is much greater. For example, after removing the influence of mother's IQ, a 20-point increase in cognitive stimulation is associated with a 6-point increase in a child's IQ and a 20-point increase in emotional support is also associated with a 6-point increase in a child's IQ. More will be said about the strength of these various influences at the end of this chapter, and the technical details of how these effects are calculated are provided in Appendix A.

Environmental Risk Factors before Birth

The environmental risk factors that arise before a child is conceived present a different utility for maximizing IQ than the post-conception factors. First, it is generally difficult to change these factors after a child is born, at least during early years of a child's development when they may have the greatest impact. Second, the only persons who can modify most of these pre-conception factors are the parents themselves, especially the mother. Unlike nutrition and parenting behaviors, which can be provided by non-parents, the pre-conception factors involve decisions made only by parents. These risk factors include the well-known socioeconomic cluster of education, income, poverty, and family structure. In addition, this group of factors includes the number of children in a family and the age of the mother at conception. In the case of income, it can be supplemented through welfare programs.

Virtually every major study of children's IQ and academic achievement, from the earliest to the most recent, have observed strong correlations between a child's academic ability and the parents' socioeconomic status. The higher the socioeconomic status of the parents, meaning higher education, income, and having both parents at home, the higher a child's IQ and academic performance in school. While this correlation is universally acknowledged, there is less agreement about whether it represents a true cause-and-effect relationship, or whether the socioeconomic status itself is determined by a parent's IQ. In other words, do these socioeconomic characteristics have a direct influence on a child's IQ and achievement, or does higher parental IQ cause both higher education, income, etc., and higher ability in the child, thereby explaining the correlation? One way to evaluate this possibility in the Youth Study data is to examine the relationship for each of these risk factors after removing the effect of mother's IQ. If parental IQ explains the socioeconomic effects, then we should see little or no relationship remaining after removing the effect of parents' IQ.

Parent's Education

Virtually every study of the relationship between a child's IQ or academic achievement and a parent's education has found a strong relationship between these two characteristics. In many cases, a parent's education has a stronger relationship with IQ or achievement than any other socioeconomic indicator such as income or family status.

The largest and most comprehensive study of academic achievement in the nation is the National Assessment of Educational Progress, which has been carried out every two years since 1970. The 1998 National Assessment of reading documents the strong relationship between reading proficiency and parent's education for fourth graders, eighth graders, and high school seniors. For a high school senior, being "proficient" in reading was defined as being "able to extend the ideas of the text by making inferences, drawing conclusions, and making connections to…personal experiences and other readings."[25] A rating of "basic" was defined as having "an overall understanding and make some interpretations of the text." Nationally, just over three-fourths of all high school seniors were at the basic reading level and about 40 percent were at the proficient level in 1998.

For high school seniors with a parent who was a college graduate, more than 80 percent had attained a "basic" level or better in reading, while over 50 percent reached the "proficient" level. But for seniors whose parents were high school dropouts, just over 50 percent reached the basic or better level and only 20 percent reached the proficient level. For seniors whose parents had some college, 80 percent were basic and about 40 percent were proficient, which dropped to about 70 and 30 percent, respectively, for seniors whose parents were high school graduates.[26] In other words, the higher the education of a parent, the higher the reading skill of seniors. The same strong relationships were documented for other grade levels, and in earlier assessments they have also been documented for other content areas like math and science.

While the association between parent education and a child's IQ and achievement is well established, there has been a major problem in interpreting exactly what this relationship means. Since IQ influences the amount of education a person attains, as shown in chapter 1, and since a parent's IQ also influences the child's IQ, the question becomes whether parent education affects a child's IQ above and beyond the parent IQ. Few national studies, including NAEP, have measures of a parent's IQ. One exception, of course, is the Youth Study. Unfortunately, only the mother's IQ was assessed, so the effect of the father's IQ on a child's IQ cannot be addressed. However, the Youth Study data allows one to sort out the effect of mother's education from mother's IQ.

Figure 3.5a shows a very strong relationship between mother's education and child's IQ and achievement before adjusting for mother's IQ. At age five, children whose mothers are high school dropouts have an average IQ of 93, while children whose mothers finished college have an average IQ of 108, a spread of 15 points. The IQ of children whose mothers finished high school or had some years of college were in between at about 100 and 102, respectively. The relationship between mother's education and math achievement at age nine is very similar, with a spread of 16 points between mothers with the lowest and highest levels of education.

The relationship between mother's education and child's IQ and achievement weakens considerably after removing the effect of mother's IQ, as shown in Figure 3.5b, although there is still a small positive relationship. Adjusted for mother's IQ, the children whose mothers have the lowest education levels have average IQs of 100 versus 102 for children whose mothers have the highest levels of education. For math achievement the spread is somewhat larger at 4 points (99 versus 103). This indicates that nearly all of the relationship between mother's education and child's IQ at age five is due to the mother's IQ, but there is still a modest effect of mother's education on math achievement after removing mother's IQ.

What explains the stronger relationship between a parent's education and a child's math achievement, after removing the effect of mother's IQ? Several explanations are possible. One is that parents with more education (especially college graduates) are more motivated and better equipped to help their children learn math while they are infants and during the early school years. Such

Figure 3.5a
Mother's Education and Child's IQ and Achievement

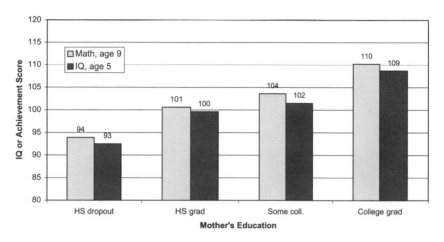

Figure 3.5b
Mother's Education and Child's IQ and Achievement
(removing effect of mother's IQ)

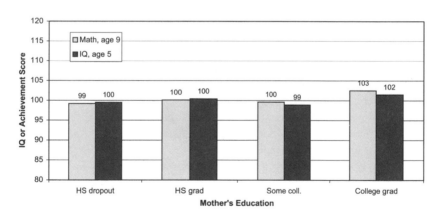

parents may place more emphasis on teaching their children numbers, counting, and simple arithmetic during the early years. Later, when children are in
school and learning more complicated arithmetic, college graduates may be
better equipped to help their children in math concepts and to assist with math
homework. They may also place more stress on the importance of learning
math, and thereby give more rewards or encouragement to their child for doing
well in math.

Figure 3.5c
Effect of Mother's IQ and Education on Cognitive Stimulation

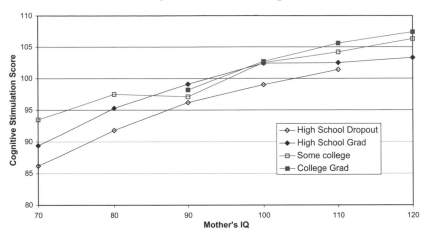

Some support for this interpretation is revealed in Figure 3.5c, which shows the relationship between mother's IQ, mother's education, and the child's cognitive stimulation (instruction) score. For each education level, there is a substantial relationship between mother's IQ and the stimulation score; this indicates, as expected, more intelligent mothers spend more time instructing their children regardless of their education level. But for each IQ level, higher education is generally associated with higher instruction, particularly at the lower and upper ends of the IQ continuum. This is especially true for mothers who are high school dropouts: the children of these mothers have the lowest cognitive stimulation scores regardless of IQ level. For mothers with IQs below 90, those who are high school dropouts score 6 to 8 points lower in cognitive stimulation than those with some college and 3 points lower than high school graduates. The benefits of education are weaker and less consistent in the average IQ ranges, but high school dropouts always have the lowest instruction scores. For mothers with IQs over 100, those with college degrees have cognitive stimulation scores 3 to 4 points higher than high school graduates.[27]

There is another reason for the stronger effect of parent education on math achievement, one that is less related to parenting behavior per se and more related to possible school effects. Parents with more education may seek out better schools for their children, or better preschools, so that the effect seen in Figure 3.5b might be due to better schools rather than home instruction and other parenting skills. Even under this scenario, however, the school effect can still be credited to the parent's education, if that is why the better schools are chosen. The specific effects and benefits of school programs will be discussed in greater detail in chapter 5.

Whatever the reasons, the greater the education of a mother, the greater the math achievement of her child, even when the effect of the mother's IQ is removed. Accordingly, parent education is an environmental risk factor, and more so for math achievement than IQ.

Family Income

The influence of family income and poverty on a child's IQ and academic achievement is even better documented than the influence of a parent's education. The reason for this is that most public school systems track student poverty as part of the federal free lunch program, whereby students from families below the poverty line are eligible for free lunches. Since most public school systems also give standardized achievement tests, it is relatively easy to document the achievement levels of students whose families are in poverty.

For example, Table 3.2 shows average math achievement scores (in percentiles) for students in the free lunch program in five cities where I have conducted comprehensive academic achievement studies. On the basis of percentiles, the national average is 50 by definition; that is, the average child in the nation scores at the fiftieth percentile. In Charlotte, North Carolina and Wilmington, Delaware, students in poverty score only at the thirty-eighth percentile in math, which is 12 percentile points below national averages. Math scores are even lower in the other three cities—thirty-second percentile for Kansas City, twenty-eighth percentile for Tampa, and twenty-fifth percentile for St. Paul. The scores vary in part because of other socioeconomic differences and also because of different achievement tests used in the five cities. No matter what city is chosen, it is very likely that its students below the poverty line will have below-average achievement levels.

Table 3.2
Math Achievement for Students in Poverty

Average Percentiles (national average = 50)

Charlotte, NC	(grade 5, 1998)	38
Kansas City, MO	(grade 5, 1995)	32
St. Paul, MN	(grade 6, 1995)	25
Tampa, FL	(grade 5, 1995)	28
Wilmington, DE	(grade 6, 1992)	38

There are also national studies of the relationship between poverty and school achievement. One of the largest (mentioned in chapter 2) is a study called Prospects, which is a national evaluation of the federal compensatory education program called Title 1. Title 1 gives special funds to schools for remedial reading and math instruction for at-risk students; namely, students in poverty who have low achievement test scores. In October 1992, the Prospects study tested a national sample of 9000 first graders who were just beginning their formal schooling. Those first graders who were below the poverty level scored at only the thirty-first percentile on a standardized reading test. That is, poor students were almost 20 points below the national average of 50 points.

This is an especially important finding, since it shows that the achievement deficit for poor children across the nation exists at the beginning of their school career, before school programs have had much chance to impact learning. Similar results have been found in a more recent national study of 20,000 children just beginning kindergarten.[28] Some critics of public schools blame school programs for the low achievement of poor children, but the Prospects and kindergarten studies make it clear that poor children have low achievement at the beginning of their schooling.

Another major study of the impact of poverty on a child's IQ found that the most adverse effects are found for children who live in continuous rather than transient poverty. Using data from the Youth Study and from a national study of low birth weight children, this study found that "duration of poverty has very negative effects on children's IQ, verbal ability, and achievement scores. Children who lived in persistently poor families scored 6-9 points lower on the various assessments than children who were never poor."[29]

As with parent's education, interpreting the relationship between family income and children's IQ can be problematic. Is the low achievement due to poverty itself or does it arise from lower levels of parent education and other social characteristics, which are influenced by parent's IQ? Since persons with less education generally have lower paying jobs, and since parents with less education generally have lower IQs, it is possible that the relationship between poverty and a child's academic ability is also traceable to parent's IQ. This possibility can be tested with the Youth Study data.

Figure 3.6a shows the relationship between family income and a child's IQ and math achievement before adjusting for mother's IQ. Like parents' education, the relationship between family income and IQ or math achievement is very strong. There is a 13-point difference in both IQ and math scores between families in the highest and lowest income brackets (over $50,000 vs. under $20,000 annual income, 1994 dollars). It is also noteworthy that the IQ and math scores of children from families with moderate income ($35,000-50,000) are quite similar to those of children from families with high incomes (over $50,000). This suggests a threshold effect for income. That is, a family needs

Figure 3.6a
Family Income and Child's IQ and Achievement

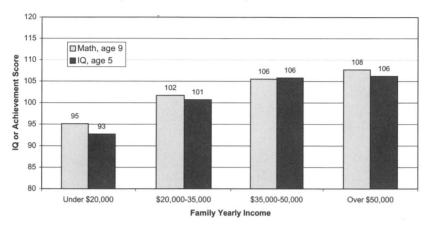

adequate income to provide a good environment for cognitive development, but beyond a certain income level a child's intelligence may not benefit from increasingly higher income levels.

The relationship between family income and a child's intelligence diminishes when the effect of mother's IQ is removed, as seen in Figure 3.6b, but a moderate effect remains. Children from families in the lowest income categories have math scores 3 points lower than children from middle- and higher-income families (over $35,000). For IQ scores, the spread is even larger; children from families in the lowest income bracket have IQ scores 5 points lower than children from middle-income families. The adverse effects of poverty, and in particular being below the poverty line for extended periods of time, are even stronger than the effects of low income shown in Figure 3.6b. Children from families who were below the poverty line continuously between 1990 and 1994 had average IQs of only 93, after removing mother's IQ, and they had average math scores of only 96. Family income and poverty remain strong predictors of a child's IQ and achievement even when the effect of mother's IQ is eliminated from the relationship.

Why do income and poverty play an important role in a child's IQ and achievement, above and beyond parent IQ and education? Perhaps the most important explanation is that families with adequate income have more resources to enrich a child's home environment in any number of ways. First, they can afford to buy more books and more educational toys that aid in the instructional process at home. Second, parents with more financial resources (but not necessarily wealthy) can afford to spend the time and money it takes for important educational and recreational outings such as zoos, museums, aquariums, and similar types of activities. Third, more affluent families have

Figure 3.6b
Family Income and Child's IQ and Achievement
(removing effect of mother's IQ)

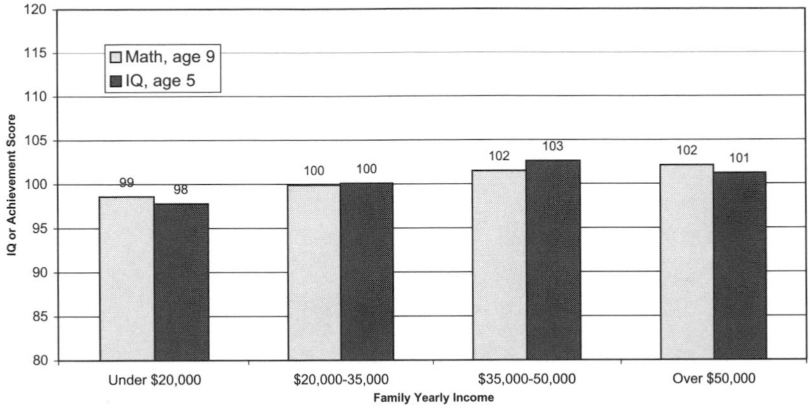

larger homes, often in safer neighborhoods, where children can have their own study and play areas and where they can play and interact with other children both indoors and outdoors.

Finally, and perhaps most important, one of the reason that some families have adequate income is that there are two parents in the home, sometimes with both parents working. In the Youth Study, nearly 60 percent of never-married single mothers are below the poverty line, while less than 7 percent of two-parent families are below the poverty line. Thus part of the income effect is actually the effect of having a two-parent family. The advantages of a two-parent family in promoting a child's IQ are discussed next.

Family Status

Like education and income, there is growing evidence that children raised in intact families experience greater success in any number of life endeavors including educational attainment, vocational satisfaction, and social adjustment. By intact family, I mean a family with both biological parents married and living in the children's household. The benefits of being in an intact family appear to extend to a child's IQ and school achievement as well. Some researchers question whether these benefits come directly from the intact family itself or, rather, from other advantages offered by intact families such as higher income or more parenting attention.

In discussing this risk factor, I will distinguish several types of families with children. The two most important are families headed by a single parent (either a mother or a father) and families with two parents at home. In some cases I will distinguish single mothers who never married versus those whose husbands are absent (e.g., by divorce), and in other cases I will identify families where neither parent is at home, such as a foster family. Finer distinctions can be made among family types, such as biological versus stepparents, but most studies do not gather such detailed information.

Some of the best evidence about the benefit of two-parent families on academic achievement comes from the National Assessment studies. The National Assessment studies allow distinction among four types of families: two parents at home, the mother only at home, the father only at home, and neither parent in the home. For this discussion the test scores have been standardized so that the national average is 100. In the 1992 national assessment of mathematics for eighth graders, those with both parents at home scored 103. Children with only a mother or only a father at home score 97 and 96, respectively, and children with neither parent in the home score lowest at 92. Similar patterns are observed in different subject matters such as reading and science and in different years of assessment. According to the National Assessment, then, children from single-parent homes have a substantial achievement disadvantage compared those with two-parent families.

Other national studies have also concluded that children from single parent families have a higher risk of academic problems compared to children from two-parent families. For example, a study using the High School and Beyond survey found that children from single-parent families are more likely to have low achievement scores, lower expectations for college, lower grades, and higher dropout rates than children from two-parent families after controlling for other family socioeconomic factors.[30]

The potential effect of family status is also apparent in the Youth Study. The Youth Study documents marital history as well as whether both parents are in the home, so it is possible to distinguish three types of families: single mothers who never married, single mothers who were married but the father is absent, and both parents present. Remarkably, even though the Youth Study and the National Assessment are completely independent studies, the relationships between family status and achievement are nearly identical.

The relationships between family status and IQ and math achievement are shown in Figure 3.7a. Family status has a powerful relationship with both IQ and math scores, and the potential effects are largest for mothers who never married. Children with both parents at home score 103 points on math compared to 99 for children whose fathers are absent and only 92 for children whose mothers never married. This is an achievement gap of 11 points between two-parent families and never-wed mothers. The gap for IQ scores is even larger: IQs average 103 for children in two-parent families versus 88 for never-wed mothers, an IQ gap of 15 points. This difference is especially troubling because children whose mothers never married comprise 8 percent of this national sample, and another 32 percent have fathers absent. This leaves only about 60 percent of children with both parents at home, the family status associated with the highest IQ and math achievement scores.

Figure 3.7a
Family Income and Child's IQ and Achievement

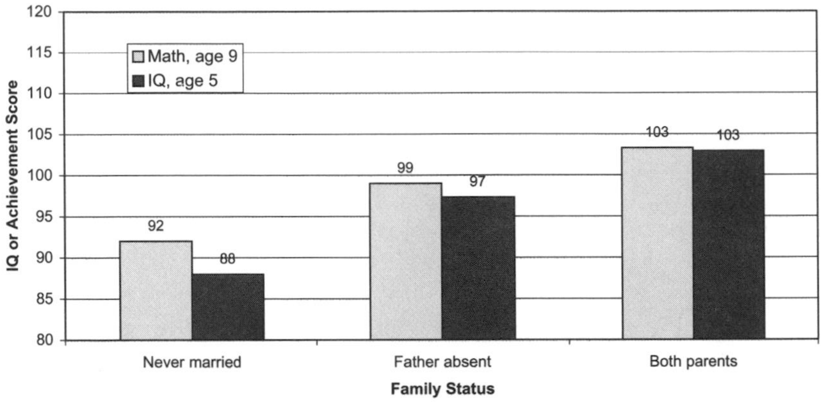

The potential adverse effects of unwed mothers and broken marriages are especially serious given the high rate of births to unwed teenagers and the high divorce rates that evolved during the 1970s and 1980s. In 1965, only one in five births to teenagers were outside marriage; by 1985 it had risen dramatically to nearly three out of five—a three-fold increase in only twenty years.[31] Similarly, divorce rates rose during the same period, and the percentage of children being raised in single-parent families increased correspondingly.

Some studies have concluded that the impact of family status on a child's IQ or achievement is actually an effect of parent education and income rather than an effect of family status itself.[32] Since single mothers have less education and income than two-parent families on average, these studies say the real reason for lower child achievement is not marital status, but rather the mother's deficient education and income. Other studies, such as *The Bell Curve*, argue that the real reason is the lower IQs of single mothers, and therefore the mother's IQ explains the lower IQs of their children.

The role of mother's IQ in the family status factor is revealed in Figure 3.7b, which shows the relationship between test scores and family status in the Youth Study data after removing the effect of mother's IQ. The relationship between family status and IQ or achievement is diminished after controlling for mother's IQ, but a relationship remains nonetheless. The IQ gap is now 5 points between children whose mothers never wed and those who have two parents, and the math achievement gap is 3 points. Therefore, while mother's IQ may be one of the reasons for the relationship between family status and a child's ability, it does not explain all of it.

Figure 3.7b
Family Status and Child's IQ and Achievement
(removing effect of mother's IQ)

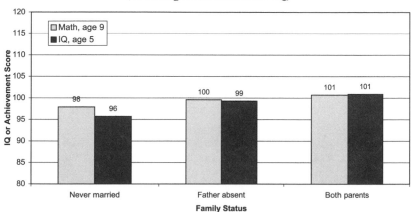

What about the role of education and income? If we collapse all of the Youth Study families into two income groups (over $35,000 vs. under $35,000) and two education groups (some college or more vs. high school or less), a relationship between family status and a child's intelligence still remains, even with mother's IQ removed. Importantly, the relationship between family status and a child's intelligence is strongest in the lowest socioeconomic group—those with lower income and with lower education. In this lowest SES group, children with never-wed mothers have adjusted IQ scores of 96, those with father absent score 99, and those with both parents at home score 100. In the group with lower income but higher education, children with never-wed mothers have adjusted IQ scores of 94, those with father absent score 99, and those with both parents at home score 100.[33] Interestingly, the most adverse effects occur for never-wed mothers; the IQ difference between children with divorced single mothers and children with two parents is only one point (controlling for education, income, and mother's IQ). This suggests that even an absent father may contribute enough to the home environment to enable a child to have adequate cognitive development.

This last finding points to the reasons why family status matters in the intellectual development of a child. It is perhaps as simple as the old adage, "two heads are better than one." To the extent that a child's mental growth depends on frequent, positive, and informative interactions with parents, then two parents at home or even an absent but active father may do this better than a never-wed mother who has no one to help raise her children. Of course, simply having two active parents does not guarantee that more or more positive parent-child interactions will occur. A very attentive single parent can spend more time with a child than two less attentive parents, and two parents who are unhappy and arguing a lot may create a more negative environment than a single parent.

This notion can be tested in the Youth Study by looking at the influence of family status on cognitive stimulation and emotional support scores after removing the effects of education, income, and mother's IQ. For families with low education and low income, children with never-wed mothers have instructional scores of 95 compared to 99 for children with two parents at home (mother's IQ removed). For families with low income and high education, the differences are a bit smaller—instructional scores are 99 and 101, respectively. The impact of family status is even greater for emotional support. For low education-low income families, children with never-wed mothers have support scores of 92, those with absent fathers score 98, and those with two parents score 102. For families with low income and high education, the differences among family statuses are similar—92, 98, and 103, respectively. It is quite clear in the Youth Study that the effect of family status on a child's intelligence operates through the parent's instructional and nurturing behaviors, and these impacts are independent of parent education, family income, and mother's IQ.

Mother's Age at Child's Birth

The concern about a woman's age when she becomes a mother is not only over age itself but also over the circumstances confronting young mothers, especially in the case of young teenagers. A woman who becomes a mother at age sixteen or seventeen is more likely to drop out of high school or not attend college, to be unmarried, and to have less income than older mothers. Given the importance of these socioeconomic factors for academic ability, it is not surprising that children of teenage mothers have lower IQ and achievement test scores.

Other than education and income, there are additional reasons why very young mothers might raise children with lower cognitive ability. Teenage mothers have a higher risk of low birth weight children, and low birth weight is itself a risk factor for a child's IQ and achievement. Young mothers are also not fully mature, physically, and some studies have suggested that very young mothers might, during pregnancy, compete with their child for nutrients, another risk factor for IQ (and also a reason for low birth weight). Finally, and most importantly, teenage mothers may be less skilled in the types of parenting behaviors that are most conducive for intellectual development, namely the critical risk factors of cognitive stimulation and emotional support.

These concerns are very much justified on the basis of many national studies, including the Youth Study. Using data from the Youth Study and the National Survey of Children, one major study concluded that "Children of the youngest teen mothers are less likely to have received well-baby care in the first year of life, have less cognitively stimulating and less nurturing home environments, and obtain lower cognitive achievement scores than peers whose mothers were 20 to 21 at their births."[34]

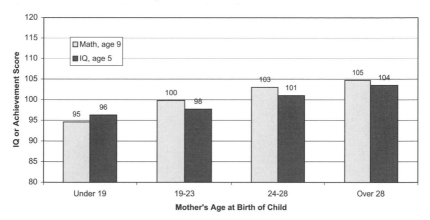

Figure 3.8a
Mother's Age and Child's IQ and Achievement

In the 1994 Youth Study, for example, half of the women who had their first child when they were eighteen or under did not finish high school, while only one in ten had some post-high school education. Three out of four were single mothers, about a third of whom had never married, and nearly 60 percent had annual family incomes less than $20,000. In contrast, for those mothers who had their first child in their late twenties, 70 percent attended college, 75 percent were married with husband present, and more than half have incomes over $35,000. The differences on these established risk factors alone dictate a relationship between mother's age and a child's intelligence.

For the 1994 Youth Study, the relationship between mother's age and a child's IQ and achievement is shown in Figure 3.8a. Children whose mother's were younger than nineteen when they were born have average IQ scores of 96 and math scores of 95; those whose mothers were in their late twenties have average scores of 101 and 103, respectively. Of course, mothers who are attending college are more likely to defer childbearing until they finish their schooling, so part of the effect in Figure 3.8a is undoubtedly explained by a mother's educational level and IQ rather than her age. Another confounding factor is the number of children born to a mother, a risk factor discussed in the next section. Mothers with large numbers of children must necessarily be older by the time of their third or fourth child.

Figure 3.8b attempts to untangle some these confounding factors by showing the relationship between mother's age and IQ or achievement for first-born children after removing the effect of mother's IQ. Removing the mother's IQ does substantially reduce the effect of mother's age on her child's IQ, although the children of teenage mothers still have IQs 3 points less than children whose mothers were in their late twenties when they were born. For math scores, removing mother's IQ still leaves a strong influence of mother's age.

Figure 3.8b
Mother's Age and Child's IQ and Achievement
(removing effect of mother's IQ)

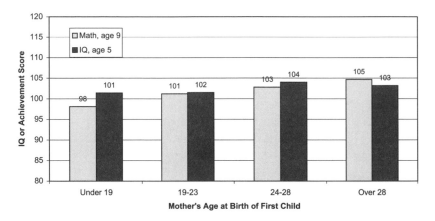

After the effect of mother's IQ is removed, children of teenage mothers have math scores of 98 while children whose mothers were over twenty-three score about 6 points higher at 104. As discussed for the education factor, the stronger influence of the mother's age on math scores may reflect more experience and greater interest older mothers may have in helping their child learn mathematics.

The reduction in the relationship for IQ does *not* mean that mother's age is not a serious risk factor for a child's IQ. If having a baby as a teenager prevents a mother from completing her education, reduces her chances of having a husband and father present to help raise the child, and lowers her income potential, then teenage childbearing is still a risk factor for a child's academic ability. The difference is that part of the effect of mother's age operates indirectly on IQ by lowering socioeconomic status, while the rest of it operates as a direct age effect.

The relationship between a mother's age and her child's intelligence is amply supported in the research literature. Another study using Youth Study data concluded that, if children experience adverse environmental conditions such as poverty, an absent father, many siblings, or a mother who is a high school dropout, it is difficult to overcome the disadvantage of being born to a teenage mother.[35]

Number of Children and Birth Order

Most studies of children's IQ and achievement find that the larger the number of children born to a mother, the lower the IQ or achievement of all of her children. The most common explanation for this phenomenon is the "dilution

Figure 3.9a
Family Size and Child's IQ and Achievement

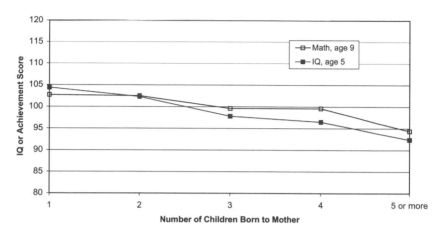

of resources" theory.[36] According to this theory, the more children born to a family, the fewer resources and the less time parents have to devote to each child. Because more resources and attention are required for higher ability, the larger the number of children, the lower the resources and time for each child, and therefore the lower their academic ability.[37]

The research has not been clear as to whether it is the number of children or the birth order that is the most important reason for lower IQs and achievement. Of course, it is very hard to disentangle the two aspects because they are so intertwined. If the resource dilution theory is correct, then a larger family would dilute resources for all children, but it would dilute resources differently depending on when a child was born. First-born children could have a year or two of undivided attention, during which they would be the sole recipients of their parents' attention, interaction, and nurturing. The second-child born would have less attention than the first-born but more than the third-born, and so on. Thus, the resource dilution theory would predict effects of both family size and birth order, with the greatest advantage going to an only child and the greatest disadvantage going to the last-born child in a large family.

There is another theory, called the "confluence model," that acknowledges resource dilution but also suggests positive effects for younger children due to tutoring effects of older siblings.[38] The results from the Youth Study (below) do not support this model. Also, an article in the *American Psychologist* disputes both the resource dilution and the confluence theories, concluding that the effect of family size on a child's IQ is explained almost entirely by a mother's IQ.[39] Not only is this conclusion inconsistent with the Youth Study results discussed below, but the study had a number of methodological flaws.[40]

Figure 3.9b
Family Size and Child's IQ and Achievement
(removing effect of mother's IQ)

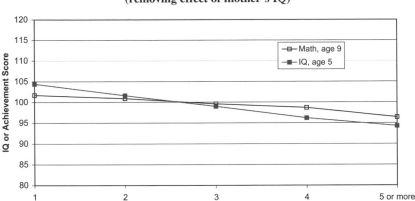

Number of Children Born to Mother

Figure 2.9a shows a strong relationship between the number of children in a family and children's IQ or achievement. Children from one-child families score 104 and 103, respectively, on the IQ and math tests. The test scores decline fairly steadily as the number of children rises, so that children from four-child families have IQ and math scores of 97 and 100, respectively. The lowest scores occur for children in families with five or more children, where the average IQ and math achievement scores are 92 and 95, respectively. These trends yield IQ and math score gaps of 12 and 8 points between the smallest and largest families.

These are large differences and they call for some explanation. Like the socioeconomic factors, some of this relationship might be due to a mother's IQ, on the assumption that higher IQ (and therefore more educated) women may be more likely to engage in family planning and restrictions on family size. While the correlation between mother's IQ and family size is negative, it is not very strong at -.09. The correlation between mother's education and family size is about the same magnitude. Accordingly, neither of these risk factors is a likely explanation of the substantial relationship between number of children and a child's IQ.

As shown in Figure 3.9b, removing mother's IQ does not eliminate the strong impact of family size on a child's intelligence. After adjusting for mother's IQ, the children's IQ gap is still 10 points between families with one versus five or more children, and the math achievement gap is 6 points. In other words, the reduction in a child's academic ability as the number of his or her siblings increases cannot be explained by the fact that mothers with lower IQs tend to have somewhat larger families. Moreover, effect of family size is not explained by mother's or father's education, either. The adjusted IQ gap between children from single-child vs. five-child families is even larger where neither parent has gone beyond high school (12 points). The IQ gap is reduced for families where one or both parents have attended at least some college (8 points). The fact that the effect of family size is larger for less educated parents tends to support the resource dilution theory. More educated parents usually have higher incomes and may be able to make resource tradeoffs to reduce the impact of having larger numbers of children, while less educated and lower income parents may not have these options.

To what extent do these differences arise from the possible effects of birth order? Looking only at the number of children in a family provides just a partial test of the resource dilution theory, because it averages IQ scores across the number of children in each family. If a second-born child receives less attention than a first-born, then the drop in IQ from one- to two-child families may be due to the lower scores of the second child, the drop from two- to three-child families may be due to lower scores from the third child, and so forth.

The joint impact of family size and birth order is revealed in Figure 3.10, with the effect of mother's IQ removed. It appears that both family size and birth order contribute to lower IQ scores, thereby offering even more support to the resource dilution theory. Children who are the only child in a family have the highest adjusted IQ scores at 104. In two-child families, the first-born scores slightly lower than the only child (103), while the second-born scores much lower (100). The pattern is repeated for three-child families, with the first-born scoring lower than the first-born in two-child families, the second-born scoring lower than the second-born in two-child families, and so forth. The pattern breaks down somewhat for after four or more children, perhaps because of smaller numbers of cases for large families. Nonetheless, third-born and later children from families with four or more children have IQ scores of 95 or lower on average.

Being later-born has a somewhat larger effect on IQ than having more siblings. The scores of first-born children decline about one point for each additional family child until families reach four or more children; second-born scores do about the same. But the gap between adjacent siblings in same size families averages about 3 points until family sizes reach four or more. This makes some sense under the resource dilution theory, because first-borns enjoy some period of undivided parental attention regardless of family size, and even second-born children in larger families can receive less divided attention until their next siblings arrive.

The strong relationship between birth order and academic ability raises serious questions about the theory that IQ is genetically determined. Children born to the same parents have the same genetic inheritance. Assuming that the specific genetic inheritance for a given child has some non-predictable aspects (e.g., brown-eyed parents can give birth to blue eyed children), the absence of environmental effects should produce roughly equal numbers of first-born chil-

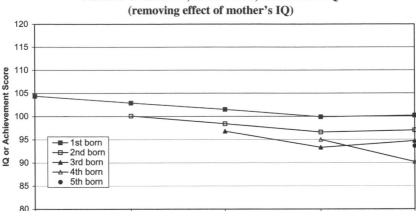

Figure 3.10
Number of Children, Birth Order, and Child's IQ
(removing effect of mother's IQ)

dren with higher IQs and second-born children with higher IQs. This should lead to relatively equal IQ scores for first- and second-born children when averaged across a large sample of children. Since there is a consistent IQ advantage for the first-born child, as shown in Figure 3.10, the genetic inheritance explanation breaks down, and an environmental explanation becomes more tenable. The resource dilution theory is a good candidate for an environmental explanation.

Let me pause at this point for readers who are third- or fourth-born children and who do not feel cognitively impaired. Like all risk factors discussed here, the potential effects of family size and birth order are averaged across all families, and they do not predict the IQ scores of any single child. Many very bright and talented people have been the youngest children in large families. The Youth Study, in fact, has about ninety children who are the last-born children in four-child families, and seven of these children have IQs over 110. On the other hand, thirteen have IQs below 70.

Moreover, it turns out that the relationship between academic ability and number of children is a bit more complicated than indicated in Figure 3.9b. The effect of number of children appears to depend in part on the level of a mother's education, so that the impact of family size is greater for women with less education and is largely absent for mothers who are college graduates. This pattern is shown for math achievement in Table 3.3 (a similar pattern occurs for IQ but is not shown). Family size has the greatest adverse impact for mothers who are high school dropouts, with a 9-point difference in math scores between a one-child family and a four-child family (or more). The second largest impact, 5 points, occurs for high school graduates. For mothers with some college or who are college graduates, the relationship between family size and math scores weakens and virtually disappears.

Table 3.3
Child's Math Achievement by Mother's Education and
Number of Children (CNLSY)

No. of Children	High School Dropout	High School Graduate	Some College	College Graduate
One	99	104	103	106
Two	97	101	105	111
Three	94	100	102	108
Four or more	90	99	102	112

Under the resource dilution theory, these results make some sense. On the one hand, mothers with the least education are more likely to be unwed and have the lowest incomes, and as a result their parenting resources are already severely limited. The dilution of these meager resources therefore has more drastic effects. College educated mothers, on the other hand, are more likely to be married with husband (and father) present and higher incomes, and therefore they are in a better position to make resource tradeoffs that compensate for the greater parenting attention demanded by a larger family.

The resource dilution theory can be tested in part by examining the relationship between number of children and cognitive stimulation scores. If scarcity of resources is the reason why family size has the strongest impact on children with less educated mothers—and little effect for college educated mothers—a similar pattern should emerge for cognitive stimulation. The cognitive stimulation score is a direct measure of parenting resources, since it is a tally of actual activities and conditions in a home. If the number of children can dilute parenting resources, then this dilution should be reflected in the cognitive stimulation score.

Table 3.4 shows the cognitive stimulation scores for various combinations of mother's education and family size. The pattern of declines is very close to the pattern for math achievement shown in Table 3.3. Children whose mothers are high school dropouts receive lower stimulation scores generally, but the impact of having larger families is dramatic for this group. Their stimulation scores drop several points for each additional child, and the total decline is 12 points between the smallest and largest families. For mothers who have finished high school or who have some college, stimulation scores also drop as family size increases, but the drop is smaller for these groups, on the order of 4 to 6 points. But for mothers who are college graduates, there appears to be no "dilution" effect at all as family size grows. Children of college graduate mothers with four or more children have virtually the same cognitive stimulation scores as those from one-child families. The resource dilution theory seems valid, then, but only for mothers who are not college graduates.

Table 3.4
Cognitive Stimulation Scores by Mother's Education and
Number of Children (CNLSY)

No. of Children	High School Dropout	High School Graduate	Some College	College Graduate
One	101	102	104	105
Two	98	101	105	106
Three	92	100	102	108
Four or more	89	98	98	106

The fact that there is no relationship between family size and cognitive stimulation scores for children whose mothers are college graduates suggests that parenting resources are not fixed, depending only on the number of parents. It is true that three-fourths of college graduate mothers are married with husband present, and that is one reason for their higher stimulation scores overall; two-thirds of the high school dropouts are single mothers. But if parenting resources are fixed, even in two-parent families the stimulation scores should still fall as the number of children grows and the parenting workload increases. Rather, these results imply that parenting resources are flexible, and that college graduate parents may be working harder and putting more effort into parenting as their family size increases.

There is an encouraging lesson here for all parents, regardless of education levels. Highly educated parents may be more motivated to put greater effort into teaching their children, because they want their children to be better prepared for school. There is no reason, however, why less educated parents cannot do the same, and indeed many do. For example, consider the group in Table 3.3 consisting of mothers with high school diplomas and four or more children. Looking only at those who are single mothers (formerly married), their average stimulation score is 96, but more than 10 percent of these mothers have cognitive stimulation scores 110 or higher, and their children are rewarded by having average math scores 10 points higher than the rest of the group.[41]

Summing Up Pre-conception Risk Factors

When considered separately, the risks associated with most of the pre-conception risk factors are reduced substantially once mother's IQ is taken into account. This is especially true for mother's education and family status, and to a lesser extent for family income and mother's age. The reason is because mother's IQ strongly influences all of these factors, which means that more intelligent mothers tend to stay in school longer, defer childbearing until they are older, marry and raise children in intact families, and attain higher income levels. When the effect of mother's IQ is removed, the relationship between each of these factors and a child's intelligence is weakened. The major exception is the number of children in a family, which is only weakly related to a mother's IQ.

Saying that the relationships for these factors are weakened does not mean they disappear. Each of the factors still has a small effect, which raises the possibility that when they are considered together, their combined effects may be larger. Moreover, looking at combined effects makes sense because all of these factors are interrelated. Most women who want to finish high school or attend college will delay marriage and childbirth until they are older, and those who do attend college are more likely to marry when they want to start a family. Because they have more education and a husband, they also have higher incomes. Thus, all of these factors mutually reinforce each other, creating a profile that may advance or hinder their child's intelligence.

Table 3.5 shows the impact of two contrasting family profiles on a child's intelligence. The first profile assumes children with two married parents, the mother has some college and was over eighteen at the child's birth, and their family income in 1994 was over $35,000. The second profile assumes children with a single, never-wed mother who did not attend college and was under nineteen at the child's birth, and whose family income was under $35,000. IQ and math scores are shown for the children in each group before and after removing the effect of mother's IQ.

Before adjusting for mother's IQ, these differing profiles produce a 10-point gap for children's math scores and an 11-point gap for IQ scores. After adjusting for mother's IQ, the combined effect of these risk factors still produces 5-point gaps in both math and IQ scores. Thus, when all the socioeconomic factors are considered together, they have a sizeable impact on their child's academic ability even after removing the effect of mother's IQ.

By removing the effect of mother's IQ when looking at the impact of socioeconomic factors, I want to stress again that parent IQ is not viewed here as solely a genetic effect. Part of the effect may be genetic, but not all of it. Indeed, more intelligent parents may find any number of ways to boost their child's intellectual development other than by bestowing their genes. The most important reason for removing this factor is that, unlike the socioeconomic factors, by the time mothers reach their late teens and are contemplating children, their IQ is relatively fixed and not subject to change. The other preconception risk factors, such as education, family status, income, and family size are subject to decisions made by teenagers and young adults. The results here demonstrate that their choices can have a significant impact on their future children's intelligence levels.

Table 3.5
Combined Effects of Mother's Education, Income, Family Status,
and Mother's Age at Birth (CNLSY)

Children with both parents married and present, mother having some college or more, family income over $35,000 and mother over 18 when child born:

	Actual Scores	Mother's IQ Removed
Math, age 9	109	102
IQ, age 5	108	101

Children with single mother who never married, with high school education or less, family income less than $35,000, and who was 18 or younger when child born:

Math, age 9	89	97
IQ, age 5	87	96

Summary of the Risk Factors for Intelligence

Summarizing the effects of the ten risk factors for a child's intelligence is complicated by the fact that they are all highly interrelated. Each of the risk factors has a significant correlation with a child's IQ at age five and math achievement, but most of them also have significant correlations with one another. Mother's IQ is significantly correlated with many of the risk factors, especially the risk factors of mother's education, family income, family status, mother's age at birth, and breast-feeding. When mother's IQ is removed the correlation between each of these risk factors and the child's intelligence is weakened. Mother's IQ is also significantly related to cognitive stimulation and emotional support but large effects remain for these risk factors after mother's IQ is removed. Mother's IQ is only weakly related to number of children and birth weight.

But there are also strong interconnections among the environmental factors as well. Women who stay in school longer tend to delay marriage and childbirth, are more likely to marry, and will have higher family incomes—by virtue of their own education as well as having a husband. Education, income, family status, and family size are also strongly related to cognitive stimulation and emotional support, sometimes in complex ways, and some of those relationships have already been mentioned. Family status is especially critical in this regard, because two-parent families are much more likely than single-parent families to have higher income and higher parenting scores.

What can be said about the rankings of these risk factors regarding potential influence on intelligence and regarding the capability of parents or prospective parents to change them? The only way to sort out the reliable effects of such a large number of interacting risk factors is to use a fairly complex statistical technique called path analysis. The discussion that follows is based on, and summarizes, multivariate regression and path analyses using Youth Study data that are presented in detail in Appendix A. The potential influence of each of the risk factors discussed here is statistically significant and is estimated after controlling for all other environmental factors.

Considering risk factors singly, mother's IQ has the strongest impact on a child's IQ and math achievement. It is not known precisely what portion of this relationship may be genetic and what portion is due to creating a better home environment, but the allotment makes little difference from the standpoint of a potential parent. IQ is already largely determined by the time a person reaches late adolescence, and it is not subject to substantial modification for most prospective parents.

Most of the other risk factors can be changed by parents or prospective parents before or shortly after they start a family. This is particularly true for marital status, family size, age of mother, and parenting behaviors including nutrition. Education is probably the hardest environmental factor to change, not only because it depends so much on IQ, but also because of decisions made during high school that might determine whether a person will be admitted to college. Individual income is also hard to change—at least by large amounts—since it depends so much on education. Family income can be increased, however, by changing marital and family status: at any given level of education, two-parent families generally have higher income than a single mother, and even a formerly-married single mother can have more income than a never-married mother by virtue of child support. Family income can also be supplemented by welfare programs.

The risk factor of low birth weight has important effects on a child's academic ability, but whether a mother has control over it depends on its cause. If it is a consequence of poor nutrition, then it can be prevented with adequate nutrition; if it is a consequence of other health factors, perhaps unknown, then obviously it may not be preventable. Fortunately, it is a relatively uncommon condition; in the Youth Study, only about thirty-six out of 1000 children were low birth weight.

Given these considerations, then, the most important risk factors in terms of impact on intelligence and their potential for change are family status, number of children, income, age of mother, and the parenting behaviors of breast-feeding, cognitive stimulation, and emotional support. Some of these risk factors affect academic ability by operating through other risk factors; this is especially true for family status and to some extent family size. That is, the benefit of a two-parent family is manifested through higher income and better parenting scores, rather than operating directly on academic ability; the benefit of a smaller number of children also operates partly through better parenting scores. The parenting behaviors of cognitive stimulation and emotional support appear to impact directly on academic ability without other intervening conditions.

Given the dependence of parent education on IQ, and since father's IQ was not measured in the Youth Study, for this summary the potential effects of all risk factors were adjusted for mother's IQ and the education of the parent with the higher education (generally the father's education in two-parent families and the mother's education for never-wed women). That is, any potential effects of mother's IQ or a father's education, if higher than the mother's, are removed from the effect of each risk factor on a child's IQ and math achievement.

Starting with family status, the potential benefit of two-parent families compared to single mothers is apparent by their income differences. Removing the effects of mother's IQ and parent education, two-parent families have about double the income of never-wed single mothers—about $43,000 compared to $24,000. They also have about $15,000 more than single mothers with husband absent whose incomes average $29,000. Formerly-married single mothers have moderately higher income than never-wed single mothers ($5,000). The two-parent family thus has greater financial resources that can benefit the learning environment of their children.

Perhaps the easiest way to see the combined effects of the most important risk factors is to demonstrate the average IQ and math achievement scores for several groups of families with differing profiles on these factors. This is shown for various combinations of family status, family size, and the parenting behaviors of cognitive stimulation and emotional support. The effect of mother's IQ is removed from all comparisons.

Table 3.6 shows the effects of family status and number of children by themselves. The number of children generally has larger effects than family status, about 4 points for IQ and 2 points for math. Nonetheless, the highest scores are seen in families with both parents present and one or two children, whose children score 6 points higher in IQ and 3 points higher in math than children in families with never-wed mothers and the same number of children.

The next set of profiles, shown in Table 3.7, adds variations for cognitive stimulation, which is the single most important risk factor for a child's ability after mother's IQ. The effect of parental instruction is fairly constant across all combinations of family status and number of children, so the two examples given are representative of other types of families. Holding constant family status and number of children, cognitive stimulation has even stronger effects than family status and family size. For children with never wed-mothers and one or two siblings, having above or below average cognitive stimulation scores creates an 8-point difference in IQ and a 6-point difference in math. For children with both parents at home and the same number of children, having above or below average stimulation scores makes a 4-point difference in test

Table 3.6
Effects of Family Status and Size (Mother's IQ Removed; CNLSY)

Family status and size	IQ age 5	Math age 9
Never-wed mother, 3 or more children	97	98
Never-wed mother, 1 or 2 children	99	100
Married mother, father absent, 3 or more children	100	100
Married mother, father absent, 1 or 2 children	104	102
Both parents present, 3 or more children	100	101
Both parents present, 1 or 2 children	105	103

Table 3.7
Effects of Family Status, Size, and Parenting (Mother's IQ Removed; CNLSY)

Family status, size, and parenting	IQ age 5	Math age 9
Never-wed mothers, 1 or 2 children:		
Below average cognitive stimulation	96	96
Above average cognitive stimulation	104	102
Both parents present, 1 or 2 children:		
Below average cognitive stimulation	101	100
Above average cognitive stimulation	105	104

scores. It is especially encouraging that the effects of cognitive stimulation appear greater for children with never-wed mothers than for children with intact families, since this group is most at risk for lower intelligence. The suggestion is that some women who find themselves in this unfavorable marital situation can nonetheless create an above average stimulating environment for their children, especially if they keep their family small, and it pays off in higher academic achievement for these children.

Similar results are observed for the emotional support scores. Holding all other risk factors constant, for each additional behavior or condition on the emotional support list, a child's IQ is increased about 1.5 points and math achievement is increased about 1 point. Generally, when all other risk factors are taken into account, the cognitive stimulation factor maintains a slightly stronger relationship with a child's intelligence than the emotional support factor.

Another way to summarize the risk factors' influence on a child's IQ and achievement is to show the potential effect of each risk factor controlling for all other factors simultaneously through multiple regression and path analysis. Table 3.8 shows the "direct" effects for each of the risk factors and also the "indirect" effects for selected factors. This analysis uses father's education as a

Table 3.8
Estimated Effects of Risk Factors on Child's IQ and Math Achievement

	Amount of Change	Estimated IQ	Effect on: Math achievement
DIRECT EFFECTS			
POTENTIAL GENETIC			
Mother's IQ	+10 points	3.3	2.9
Father's Education (for IQ)	+ 2 years	0.6	1.1
TOTAL		3.9	4.0
ENVIRONMENTAL			
Cognitive Stimulation	+10 points	1.8	1.3
Emotional Support	+10 points	1.3	0.9
No. of Children	- 1 child	1.8	0.5
Breast-fed	yes vs. no	1.7	b
Birth Weight	+ 1 lb.	0.4	0.7
Family Structure[a]	2 vs. mom never married	1.8	b
Family Income	+ $10,000	0.3	0.2
Mother's Age at First Birth	+ 5 years	b	1.2
TOTAL DIRECT		9.0	4.8
SELECTED INDIRECT EFFECTS (via cognitive stimulation and emotional support)			
Mother's IQ	+10 points	0.5	0.5
Father's Education (for IQ)	+ 2 years	0.3	0.2
Family Structure[a]	2 vs. mom never married	1.7	1.6
No. of Children	-1 child	0.5	0.4
Family Income	+ $10,000	0.3	0.3

[a] Two parents=2; one parent married=1; mother never married=0
[b] Not significant

surrogate for father's IQ, since father's IQ is not assessed in the Youth Study.[42] Since parent education may have a small effect on a child's IQ apart from the parent IQ effect, this is a conservative assumption. The details of this analysis can be found in Appendix A.[43]

As seen in Table 3.8, the potential genetic effect of mother's IQ is considerably stronger than the effect of any other single risk factor. A 10-point increase in mother's IQ predicts a 3.3-point increase in her children's IQs. Using father's education as a surrogate for father's IQ, a two-year increase in father's education (which is about equivalent to a 10-point IQ difference) has an additional effect of .6 points, for a combined estimated effect of nearly 4 points on a child's IQ. The results are about the same for math scores.

The combined estimated effects of similar increases in environmental risk factors, however, are even stronger, at 9 and nearly 5 points for IQ and math achievement. The strongest and most consistent direct environmental influences occur for the parenting behaviors of cognitive stimulation and emotional support, and the number of children. Breast-feeding and family structure have sizable impacts on IQ but not math achievement; birth weight and mother's age at first birth have sizable effects on math achievement but smaller effects on IQ. Income has a smaller impact on both outcomes.

Several indirect effects are also shown for risk factors operating through cognitive stimulation and emotional support. Both mother's IQ and father's education have significant indirect effects operating through the two parenting behaviors, as does number of children. But family structure has the largest indirect effect on IQ, 1.7 points, through the parenting behaviors. That is, since family structure has sizable effects on cognitive stimulation and emotional support, and these in turn have strong effects on a child's IQ, the effect of two-parent families in raising parenting scores leads to an additional gain of 1.7 points in a child's IQ. Thus the total effect on IQ of a two-parent family versus a never married single mother, including indirect effects through parenting behaviors, is more than 3 points. More information on indirect effects is provided in Appendix A.

It appears, then, that the most promising and most consistent environmental effects for improving a child's IQ and academic achievement are the following:

(1)   parenting behaviors that create a cognitively stimulating and emotionally supportive home environment,

(2)   limiting the number of children to one or two, especially for single mothers whose education and financial resources are low,

(3)   having both parents in the home to increase parenting resources and income, and

(4)   practicing breast-feeding for nutritional (and possibly nurturing) benefits.

Based on the data from the Youth Study, it appears that if all of these key risk factors could be at optimal levels, a child's IQ might be raised on the order of 10 points or so, perhaps somewhat less for math achievement. While an IQ change of this magnitude would not convert a semiskilled factory worker into an electronic engineer, it does translate into about two additional years of education. Two more years of education produces non-trivial gains in lifetime income. Also, a change of 10 IQ points is about two-thirds of a standard deviation, which is very large compared to the strongest schooling effects that will be discussed in chapter 5.

It should be emphasized that these potential gains are statistical probabilities that apply to groups of children rather than individual children. Based on the Youth Study, if these environmental factors were changed for a large group of children, we should expect to see average IQ increases in the group as a whole. This means that optimizing risk factors increases the probability that a child's intelligence will be maximized; it does not guarantee a result for a particular child.

Notes

1.   Steven Fraser, ed., *The Bell Curve Wars: Race, Intelligence, and the Future of America*, New York: Basic Books, 1995; C. L. Schultze, W. T. Dickens, T. J. Kane, *Does "The Bell Curve" Ring True?* Washington, D.C.: The Brookings Institution, 1995; J. L. Kincheloe, S. R. Steinberg, and A. D. Gresson, III, eds., *Measured Lies: The Bell Curve Examined*, New York: St. Martin's Press, 1996; C. S. Fischer, et al., *Inequality by Design: Cracking the Bell Curve Myth*, Princeton: University Press, 1996; Bernie Devlin, et al., eds., *Intelligence, Genes, and Success*, New York: Copernicus/Springer-Verlag, 1997.
2.   Sandra Scarr, "Behavior-Genetic and Socialization theories of intelligence: Truce and reconciliation," in R. J. Sternberg and E. Grigorenko, eds., *Intelligence, Heredity, and Environment*, London: Cambridge University Press, 1997.
3.   This is accomplished by means of a statistical procedure called "multiple regression." It is analogous to procedures used in medical studies for calculating age-adjusted disease rates, since the risk of many diseases are known to increase with age.
4.   Since the child's IQ scores have been scaled so that the population averages are 100 and the standard deviation is 15, a score of 85 is at about the seventeenth percentile while a score of 115 is at about the eighty-third percentile.
5.   M. Phillips, J. Brooks-Gunn, G. J. Duncan, P. Klebanov, and J. Crane, "Family background, parenting practices, and the black-white test score gap," in C. Jencks and M. Phillips, *The Black-White Test Score Gap*, Washington, DC: Brookings Institution Press, 1998.
6.   The HOME inventory was developed by B. M. Caldwell and R. H. Bradley; see B. M. Caldwell and R. H. Bradley, *Home Observation for Measurement of the Environment*, Little Rock: University of Arkansas, Center for Applied Studies in Education, 1984. Internet: www.ualr.edu/~crtldept
7.   The minimum standard score is 20 and the maximum score is 135, corresponding to raw scores of 0 and 15.
8.   Victoria J. Molfese, et al., "Prediction of the intelligence test scores of 3- to 8-year-old children by home environment, socioeconomic status, and biomedical risks," *Merrill-Palmer Quarterly,* Vol. 43, No. 2, April 1997.
9.   M. Phillips, et al., op. cit.
10. For a general statement of this view, see Alison Gopnik, Andrew N. Meltzoff, and Patricia K. Kuhl, Ph.D., *The Scientist in the Crib*, New York: William Morrow & Co., 1999, chapter 6.
11. John T. Bruer, *The Myth of the First Three Years*, New York: The Free Press, 1999.
12. Burton L. White, *The First Three Years of Life*, New York: Prentiss Hall, 1990.
13. Helle W. Andersson, et al , "Maternal child-rearing attitudes, IQ and SES as related to cognitive abilities of 5-year-old children," *Psychological Reports,* Vol. 79, 1996.
14. Jeffery Roth, et al., "The risk of teen mothers having low weight babies: implications of recent medical research for school health personnel," *Journal of School Health*, Vol. 68, No. 7, September 1998.
15. Hugo Lagercrantz, "Better born too soon than too small," *The Lancet,* Vol. 350, No. 9084, October 11, 1997.

16. Mary Ann Moon, "ELBW infants show cognitive deficits at ages 8, 16," *Family Practice News,* Vol. 29, No. 13.

17. Barbara D. Schraeder, "Academic achievement and educational resource use of very low birth weight (VLBW) survivors," *Pediatric Nursing,* Vol. 23, No. 1, January-February 1997.

18. Diana E. Schendel, et al., "Relation between very low birth weight and developmental delay among preschool children without disabilities," *American Journal of Epidemiology,* Vol. 148, No. 9, 1997.

19. Richard S. Strauss, "Adult functional outcome of those born small for gestational age: twenty-six-year follow-up of the 1970 British birth cohort," *Journal of the American Medical Association,* Vol. 283, No. 5, February 2, 2000.

20. Marian Sigman and Shannon E. Whaley, "The Role of Nutrition in the Development of Intelligence," in Ulric Neisser, ed., *The Rising Curve: Long Term Gains in IQ and Related Measures,* Washington, DC: The American Psychological Association, 1998.

21. Norman Kretchmer, John L. Beard and Susan Carlson, "The role of nutrition in the development of normal cognition," *American Journal of Clinical Nutrition,* Vol. 63, No. 6, 1996.

22. US Preventive Services Task Force, "Routine iron supplementation during pregnancy: review article," *Journal of the American Medical Association,* Vol. 270, No. 23, December 15, 1993.

23. *Journal of the American Medical Association,* "Routine Iron Supplementation during Pregnancy: Review Article," 270 (23): 2848-2854, December 15,1993.

24. James W. Anderson, et al., "Breast-feeding and cognitive development: a meta-analysis," *American Journal of Clinical Nutrition,* Vol. 70, No. 4, 1999.

25. P.L. Donahue, et al., *NAEP 1998 Reading: Report Card for the Nation and the States,* Washington, DC: National Center for Education Statistics, 1999, p. 19.

26. Ibid, Table 3.3, p. 73.

27. In all of these comparisons, the cognitive stimulation scores apply to the children and not just the mothers (e.g., fathers also contribute to the scores), but it is easier to word the comparisons assuming the scores belong to the mothers. The bulk of the score, however, can be attributed to the mother who is usually the primary caregiver.

28. Jerry West, Kristin Denton, and Elvira Germino-Hausken, *America's Kindergartners,* Washington, DC: National Center for Educational Statistics, 2000.

29. Judith R. Smith, Jeanne Brooks-Gunn, and Pamela K. Klebanov, "Consequences of Living in Poverty for Young Children's Cognitive and Verbal Ability and Early School Achievement," in Greg. J. Duncan and Jeanne Brooks-Gunn, eds., *Consequences of Growing Up Poor,* New York: Russell Sage Foundation, 1997.

30. Sara McLanahan and Gary Sandefur, *Growing Up with a Single Parent,* Cambridge, MA: Harvard University Press, 1994.

31. Susan Williams McElroy and Kristen Anderson Moore, "Trends over Time in Teenage Pregnancy and Childbearing," in Rebecca A. Maynard, ed., *Kids Having Kids,* Washington, DC: Urban Institute Press, 1997.

32. See David Grissmer, et al., *Student Achievement and the Changing American Family,* Santa Monica, CA: The Rand Corporation, 1994.

33. In the other two SES groups there are insufficient numbers of never-wed mothers for reliable comparisons.

34. Kristin Anderson Moore, Donna Ruane Morrison, and Angelo Dungee Greene, "Effects on the Children Born to Adolescent Mothers," in Rebecca A. Maynard, ed., *Kids Having Kids,* Washington, DC: The Urban Institute Press, 1997.

35. Eric F. Dubow and Tom Luster, "Adjustment of children born to teenage mothers: the contribution of risk and protective factors," *Journal of Marriage and Family,* Vol. 52, May 1990.

36.   For the most complete statement of this theory, see Judith Blake, *Family Size and Achievement*, Berkeley, CA: University Press, 1989.

37.   The adverse effect of family size on academic achievement was recently confirmed in Douglas B. Downey, "Family Size, Parental Resources, and Children's Education," *American Sociological Review*, 60: 746-761, 1995.

38.   R. B. Zajonc and P. R. Mullally, "Birth Order: reconciling conflicting results," *American Psychologist*, 52: 685-699.

39.   Joseph Lee Rodgers, et al., "Resolving the debate over birth order, family size and intelligence," *American Psychologist*, Vol. 55, No. 6, June 2000.

40.   For a critique, see David J. Armor, "Family size and intelligence," Comment in the *American Psychologist*, June-July, 2001.

41.   Burton White, in *The First Three Years of Life*, op. cit., argues that parents of any education level can provide an appropriate level of cognitive stimulation.

42.   When regressions are run for child's IQ using mother's IQ, mother's education, and father's education, mother's education has no significant effect while father's education does. It seems reasonable, then, that father's education can be used as a conservative surrogate for father's IQ. If father's education is unknown, mother's education is used to avoid loss of cases.

43.   A few of the measures in this analysis differ from the measures described earlier in this chapter. In order to maximize available cases, all IQ and math scores are used regardless of age (average ages are about seven for IQ and nine for math). In addition, because the age of a mother at a child's birth is confounded with the number of children she has (a mother must be older with each subsequent child), this analysis uses age of mother at first birth.

4

Race, Family, and Intelligence

The strong links between family characteristics and a child's intelligence raises the important question of the relationship between race and intelligence. This topic has generated a great deal of controversy, much of it over the causes of test score differences between white and African American children—the so called IQ or achievement "gap." It is a highly charged and emotional issue, which is understandable given the history of racism in America and the early uses of IQ testing to support racist theories of black inferiority.[1]

In spite of the controversy over causes, countless educational and social science studies have established beyond doubt that racial differences in IQ and achievement do exist in the United States. A study by the late sociologist James Coleman et al., *Equality of Educational Opportunity*, commissioned by Civil Rights Act of 1964, was one of the first to generate national controversy over the causes of the black-white gap.[2] The Coleman study found sizeable academic achievement gaps between black and white students at all grade levels—first, third, sixth, ninth, and twelfth grades. In the elementary grades the achievement gaps were just over one grade level. This means, for example, that the average black student in the sixth grade scored at about the same level as the average white fifth grader. These achievement gaps were documented for a variety of cognitive skills, including verbal, nonverbal, and mathematics ability.

Since the Coleman study, many other studies have supported and extended the original Coleman findings. Black-white achievement gaps have been documented in national studies of the Armed Forces Qualifying Test (AFQT), many national longitudinal studies including High School and Beyond, and the National Assessment of Educational Progress (NAEP). A major study that attempts to explain the race gap is *The Black-White Test Score Gap* edited by Christopher Jencks and Meredith Phillips.[3]

It is also well known that African American and Hispanic families lag behind white families with respect to a host of socioeconomic characteristics, including poverty, income, education, single parent families, and the like. African American mothers as a group also tend to give birth at younger ages, to have more children, and to have more low birth weight children than white

mothers. Since all of these characteristics are risk factors for IQ and achievement, it is not surprising that black and Hispanic children, as groups, have
lower IQ and achievement test scores than white children.

Not all social scientists agree, however, that family socioeconomic characteristics are the primary cause of black-white IQ differences. In *The Bell Curve*,
for example, Richard Herrnstein and Charles Murray take the position that
considerable portions of the race differences in IQ or achievement are due to
genetic differences between the races. They also argue that IQ causes lower
socioeconomic status (SES) rather than the other way around. That is, they
argue that genetic differences are major reasons why blacks have lower IQs
than whites, and these lower IQs in turn cause black families to have less
education, lower income, higher poverty rates, and fewer intact families. In
other words, the causal interpretation of the correlation between parent SES
and child IQ is that low parental IQs cause both the lower parental SES levels
and the lower IQs of their children.

Other social scientists argue that a genetic link between race and IQ has not
been established with sufficient rigor, and they also argue that at least some of
the causality runs the other way: black children have lower IQs because their
parents tend to have lower SES levels. They point out that the most rigorous
evidence for a genetic basis of IQ comes from identical twin studies, but obviously there is no way to study racial differences using data from identical
twins. The correlation of IQs between identical twins may establish a causal
link between genes and IQ within racial groups, but it cannot do so between
racial groups.

Finally, other social scientists and many educators believe that at least
some, if not most, of the academic achievement differences between minority
and white children are due to differences in the quality of schools that they
attend rather than the low SES of the families. The school deficiency argument
made by this group has several components:

(1)   Most black and Hispanic students attend public schools that are segregated,
       both racially and economically;

(2)   their teachers are less qualified with respect to education and training;

(3)   their facilities, resources, and academic programs are inferior, and

(4)   they are held to lower standards as compared to the schools attended by white
       children.

While these observers may agree that socioeconomic factors play a role in
creating a gap even before schooling starts, they believe firmly that properly
staffed and well-programmed schools should be able to overcome the achievement gap as the child progresses through the K-12 school years.

Thus, three distinct theories attempt to explain the racial gap in intelligence. One theory emphasizes the heritability of IQ and explains racial differences in IQ scores by genetic differences between the races. The second theory emphasizes differences in family environments and explains IQ differences by virtue of racial differences in socioeconomic status and family characteristics. The third theory sees IQ and achievement differences as arising from differences in policies, programs, and resources in the schools children attend. Of course, there is no reason why the IQ gap cannot be explained by contributions from all three theories.

While genes may or may not play a role in determining IQ and achievement gaps, this book places higher priority on learning about the influence of all risk factors on the IQ gap, and then deciding which ones provide the maximum opportunity to close the gaps. Whatever the correlation between parent and child IQ signifies regarding genetic effects, the parent IQs are largely determined by the time they decide to have a child and are not very malleable at that point. There are other family risk factors more amenable to change, including two-parent families, family size, and parenting behaviors, as discussed in chapter 3. Finally, to the extent that school programs and policies contribute to the IQ and achievement gaps, school reform would represent one of the most feasible scenarios for closing the gaps, given the strong commitment that most educators have to equity of outcomes for all students. Clearly, these different explanations have very different implications for policies that might help reduce the racial gaps in IQ and achievement scores.

The role of family and school effects on racial differences in IQ and achievement will be explored in this chapter. First, the magnitude of the IQ and achievement gap will be described, along with historical trends showing a reduction in the gap. Second, the chapter will assess racial and ethnic differences in the ten risk factors identified in chapter 3, relying on evidence from both the U.S. Census and the Youth Assessment. Third, the extent to which school factors might explain the IQ gap are assessed and discussed using both national and case study information. Finally, all of these components will be evaluated to determine which of the domains offer the most feasible and effective ways to reduce IQ and achievement gaps.

Racial Differences in IQ and Achievement

Before discussing the causes of racial differences in IQ, it will be helpful to first consider the size, nature, and trends of racial gaps in IQ and achievement. There are numerous studies and many sources of data that document racial differences in IQ and achievement, but the most comprehensive national data comes from the National Assessment of Educational Progress (NAEP). A second important source of information is the national Youth Study, whose results

Figure 4.1
National Reading Trends by Race, age 9

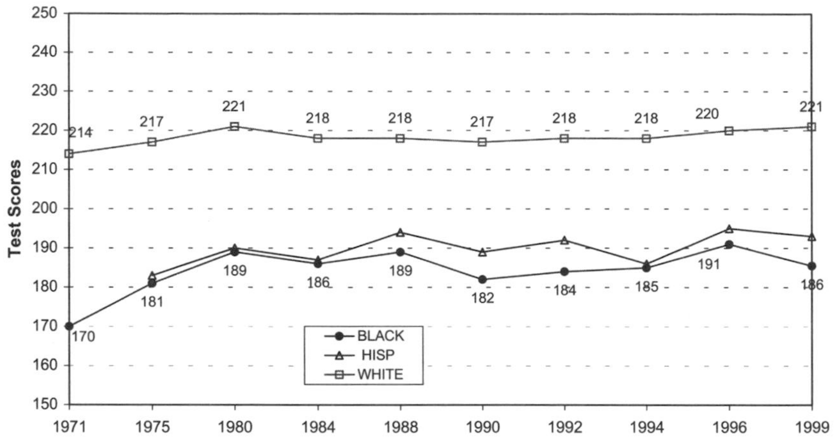

are especially valuable because the Youth Study has the most complete data for documenting racial differences in family characteristics and parenting behaviors.

Trends in the NAEP Studies

The best information about academic achievement gaps and trends comes from NAEP, which has the longest term achievement results for nine-, thirteen-, and seventeen-year-olds in both public and private schools. Large, representative samples of students have been tested periodically since 1970 in such topics as reading, mathematics, science, history, and writing. Unlike many other testing programs, NAEP maintains the same test content for its long-term trend studies, so that changes in test scores over time reflect real changes in student skills rather than changes in test content.

Since the very beginning of these tests, large achievement gaps have been documented between black and Hispanic youth on the one hand and white youth on the other. In the early 1970s, the gaps had a magnitude of about one standard deviation, which is about the same as the gaps observed in the Coleman study.[4] As mentioned in chapter 2, over the next twenty years the achievement gaps diminished appreciably, due primarily to the rising scores of black and Hispanic students while white scores remained flat. The minority student scores leveled off in 1988 or 1990, and between 1990 and 1999 the achievement gap has fluctuated around three-fourths of a school year.

Figure 4.1 shows the national trends in reading achievement for nine-year-olds in the National Assessment between 1971 to 1999. White reading scores

Figure 4.2
National Reading Trends by Race, age 13

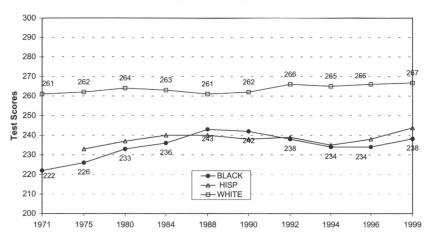

rose slightly during the 1970s, from 214 to 221, but they were relatively flat between 1980 and 1999. In contrast, black reading scores rose dramatically by nearly 19 points during the 1970s, from 170 to 189, which represents about one-half of a standard deviation. After 1980 black scores fluctuated quite a bit, from a low of 182 (in 1990) to a high of 191 (in 1996), and in 1999 their average scores were 186. This represents a total rise in black reading achievement of 16 points. The black-white reading gap for nine-year olds started out at 44 points, and by 1988 the gap had been reduced to 29 points. Between 1990 and 1999 the gap widened again, and by 1999 the gap stood at 35 points for only a 9-point reduction over the entire period. The trend for Hispanic nine-year-olds is similar, except that the gap is a little smaller. In 1975, the first year Hispanic data is available, the Hispanic-white gap was 34 points, and it shrunk to 24 points by 1988. After that, the Hispanic-white gap fluctuated in the mid-20s, ending the period at 25 points.

The reading trends for thirteen-year-olds, shown in Figure 4.2, are similar to those for nine-year-olds, although the reduction of the reading gap by 1990 was greater. White student test scores remained fairly steady between 1971 and 1988, while black scores rose significantly, cutting the black-white gap in half (from 39 to 18 points). After 1990 white scores began rising somewhat and black scores started declining, and thus the reading gap for this age group began widening again, reaching 32 points in 1996. It narrowed slightly to 29 points in 1999, so that over the entire time period we can say the black-white reading gap for thirteen-year-olds was reduced by about 10 points, resembling the 9-point reduction for nine-year-olds. The patterns for Hispanic students are similar to that for black students.

Figure 4.3a
National Math Trends by Race, age 9

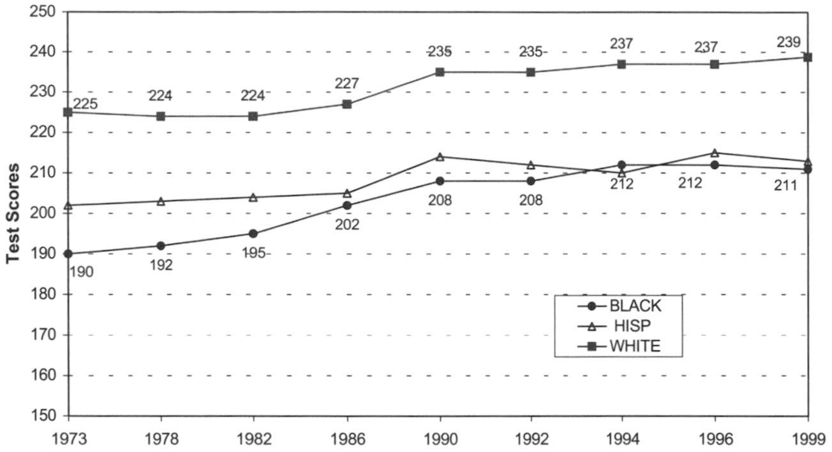

Figures 4.3a and b plot the national trends in math achievement, which reveal some different patterns compared to the reading trends. The math skills for nine-year-olds increased significantly for all three groups between 1973 and 1990, but black students gained at a somewhat higher rate. The effect was to reduce the black-white math gap from 35 to 27 points over that seventeen-year period. Between 1990 and 1999 both blacks and whites continued to gain ground but at a slower rate, so the math gap has remained fairly constant in recent years and was 28 points in 1999; the total reduction is therefore just 7 points. Over the entire period black students gained a total of 21 points compared to 14 points for whites. Hispanic students did not experience the same large gains as black students, and in fact their gains resembled white students more than black students. As a result, the Hispanic-white gap for nine-year-olds remained relatively constant over the entire period, starting at 23 points in 1973 and ending at 26 points in 1999.

For thirteen-year-olds, white math achievement rose fairly steadily over the whole period, gaining about 9 points. Black and Hispanic math achievement, in contrast, rose rapidly until about 1986 and then stabilized. The net result is that the black-white gap shrunk dramatically in the first half of the period, from 46 to 25 points, but because of the steady white gains the gap expanded to about 35 points by 1999. The Hispanic-white gap started at about 35 points and ended the period at 24 points.

It is clear, then, that both black and Hispanic students have gained in reading and math skills as compared to white students, but most of these improvements took place between 1970 and 1990. There have been few improvements since then and, in fact, there has been some widening of the gaps during

Figure 4.3b
National Math Trends by Race, age 13

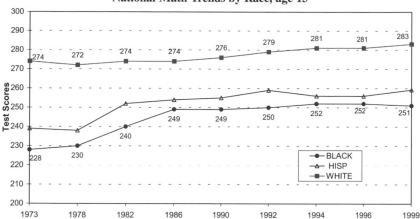

the 1990s. It is not clear why minority students would gain over such a long period of time and then suddenly stop improving. There are several complications when trying to interpret these trends. The NAEP reading and math scores represent different content; they have differing standard deviations; and until 1990 the math tests and reading tests were administered in different years.

Figures 4.4a and b help clarify the trends by showing the black-white reading and math gaps on the same time scale and by converting the achievement gaps into standard deviations, which can be interpreted as approximately one school year for younger children.[5] In 1971, black nine-year-olds were more than one full school year behind whites in reading, but the gaps in both reading and math diminished uniformly until 1988 when they reached their lowest level of about seven-tenths of a school year. After 1988, the gaps first increase and then decrease for both tests, fluctuating between .7 and .8 school years with a final upturn in 1999. For nine-year-olds, then, the reading gap closes by only .15 standard deviations and the math gap closes by less than .1 school year. The fluctuations are even larger for thirteen-year-olds. The reading gap starts out at 1.1 years, falls to just over .5 years in 1988, and then rises to over .8 again in 1996 before falling back to .7 in 1999. The math gap starts out at just under 1.1 years, falls only to .8 years by 1986, and then rises again to 1.0 years in 1999. While the reading gap for thirteen-year-olds seems to have closed appreciably, the math gap has closed only slightly.

Why would black achievement first improve and then retreat? Such patterns cannot be explained by genetic factors, because the changes and fluctuations have occurred over relatively short time spans. Indeed, as pointed out in chapter 2, the NAEP achievement trends offer some of the best evidence that children's intelligence levels can change in response to some types of environmental influences. The key question is whether the environmental factors that

Figure 4.4a
National Trends in the Black-White Achievement Gap (Age 9)

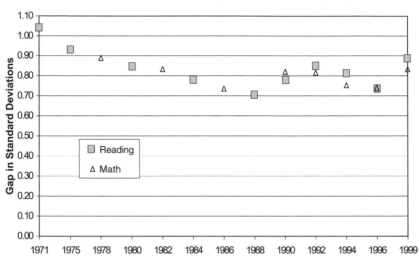

explain the improvement in black achievement during the 1970s and 1980s and then a drop during the 1990s can be identified. Before trying to answer this question, it is important to investigate IQ and achievement gaps in the Youth Study, because that study offers the richest source of information to help identify the causes of these gaps.

Race and Ethnic Gaps in the Youth Study

The Youth Study also reveals gaps in the IQ and achievement levels among black, Hispanic, and white children. This data is especially important because, unlike NAEP, the gap in IQ is assessed at age five before children start school, thereby removing school programs as explanations of the gap.

Figure 4.5 shows the IQ and achievement gaps in the Youth Study. The black-white gap for verbal IQ at age five is 18 points and the Hispanic-white gap is 14 points. Although few of these children are in school, these differences are the equivalent of 1.2 standard deviations for black children and just shy of one standard deviation for Hispanic children.[6] For math achievement at age nine, when most children are in the fourth grade, the black-white gap is 12 points and the Hispanic-white gap is 9 points. When these math differences are transformed into standard deviations (.8 and .6, respectively), they correspond quite closely to the math achievement gaps shown in Figures 4.3b and 4.4b for the NAEP studies.

Whatever the causes of the achievement gaps between white and minority students, the evidence is strong that the differences are real. They show up in virtually every type of study that uses standardized achievement tests, regard-

Figure 4.4b
National Trends in the Black-White Achievement Gap (Age 13)

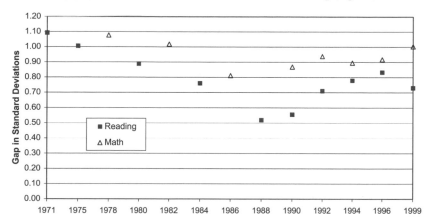

less of test content, age, and year of the test. It is highly unlikely that such consistent differences would be observed if in fact there were no differences in the basic cognitive skills of white as compared to black and Hispanic students. While the reduction in the achievement gaps between white and minority students is a very encouraging result, the minority-white achievement gaps are still very large. Both black and Hispanic test scores indicate that they are nearly a school year behind white students in reading and math skills.

The facts that the black-white achievement gap has closed by a modest amount, and that the gap is smaller for math achievement than for IQ, suggests that at least some of the racial differences in academic achievement can be explained by changes in children's environments. Furthermore, since the reductions arise mainly from improved black achievement rather than declines in white achievement, changes in black environments, either family risk factors or schools program, provide the most likely explanations.

In order to reduce these gaps further, it will be necessary to raise the IQ and achievement scores of minority students relative to the achievement of white students. That is, minority students will have to experience greater gains in standardized test scores than white students. It is therefore important to understand the causes of the achievement gaps as well as the reasons why the achievement gaps first diminished, then stopped, and in some cases actually expanded.

At the outset, it should be stated that school policies and programs are not the most likely explanations of the achievement gap nor of changes in the gap, simply because the IQ gap at age five is more than one standard deviation. This means that a serious cognitive gap exists before schools can have any significant effect on verbal skills. This fact alone leads us to look first at family risk factors as the most likely causes of IQ and achievement gaps.

Figure 4.5
IQ and Math Achievement by Race (CNLSY)

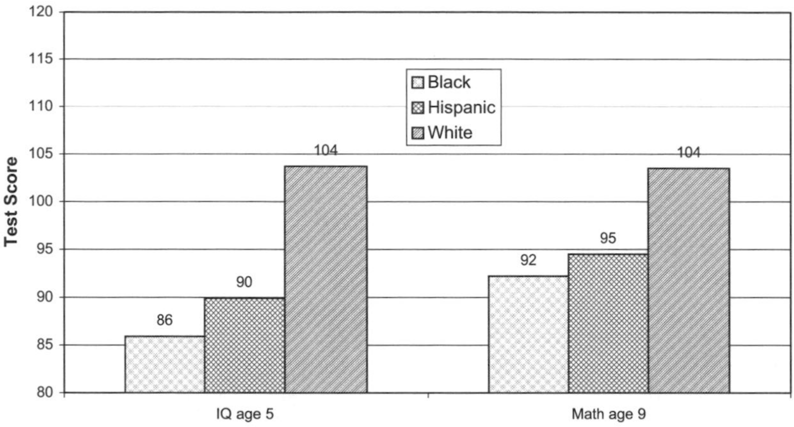

Racial Differences in Risk Factors

Racial differences in a number of family risk factors, especially the socio-economic characteristics of poverty, education, and family structure and size, are well documented in many different sources of data, most notably that collected by the U.S. Bureau of the Census. Racial differences in other family risk factors, especially parenting behaviors such as cognitive stimulation and emotional support, have received less attention in the research literature, no doubt because this type of data is not commonly collected. The same might be said about other risk factors such as birth weight and nutrition. As shown in chapter 3, some of these other risk factors have greater influence on IQ than socioeconomic status, and therefore might also help explain gaps in IQ and academic achievement.

This section will examine the extent of racial differences in the ten risk factors for IQ and achievement. Some of the most reliable evidence on socio-economic status comes from the U.S. Bureau of the Census, which conducts annual surveys to determine the economic and social condition of the U.S. population.[7] For decades these census reports have provided detailed information about differences between white and minority families on many socio-economic indicators such as income and poverty, educational attainment, job and employment status, and family status. For the other risk factors, some of the best data available to date is drawn from the Youth Study.

Socioeconomic Differences

The advantage of U.S. Census data over other types of information is that Census data can assess changes in socioeconomic status over time. For certain socioeconomic characteristics, the condition of black families has improved substantially in comparison to white families; this is especially true for educational attainment. For other SES indicators, however, the trends show either slight improvements or even increasing disparities between the races. This complex and mixed picture of improvement and decline in SES factors could very well explain the initial increase and subsequent stagnation of achievement for black and Hispanic students.

The risk factor with the greatest improvement of African Americans relative to whites is educational attainment. Figure 4.6 shows the trend in high school graduation rates for young adults, which shows the most impressive gains of all the education indicators. In 1957 high school graduation rates were much lower than they are today, but they were especially low for black youth. Only 31 percent of young black adults completed four years of high school in 1957 compared to 62 percent for young white adults, a graduation rate for whites almost double that for blacks. Over the next twenty years high school graduation rates for whites increased steadily to just under 90 percent by the late 1970s, and then the white rate leveled off. Graduation rates increased more rapidly for blacks, reaching nearly 80 percent by 1980. The high school graduation gap continued to close during the 1980s, and by the mid-1990s there was virtually no difference in the high school graduation gap between black and white youth.

Hispanic youth show a very different trend. Their high school graduation rate has been stuck at about 60 percent since 1976, with virtually no improvement even during the 1990s. This lack of progress may be due to increasing Hispanic immigration, which over time causes the youth cohorts to reflect more individuals with fewer years spent in American schools.

Figure 4.6
U.S. High School Graduation Rates for Ages 25-29
(CPS)

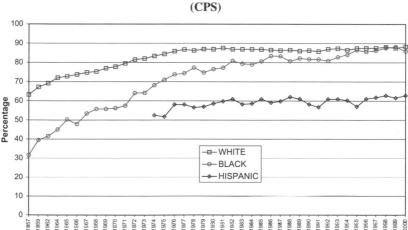

Figure 4.7
Percent of Parents with Some College (Age 13 NAEP)

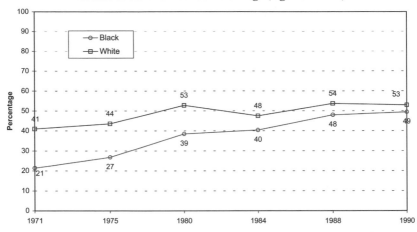

A similar trend of black improvement is observed for the percentage of parents in the NAEP studies who completed at least some college. Figure 4.7 shows the educational attainment of parents of thirteen-year-old students who were tested in the NAEP studies from 1971 to 1990, as reported by the students. In 1971 there was a 20-point gap in the percentage of parents who had completed some college (41 percent for white parents compared to 21 percent for black parents). Between 1971 and 1980, the college attendance of white parents increased from 41 to 54 percent, and then the college rate for white parents shows very little change after that. In contrast, college attendance by black parents gained steadily over this period, from 21 percent to 49 percent over the entire period. By 1990 there was only a 4-point difference in college attendance rates between white and black students.

While the trends in high school graduation rates and college attendance show definite reductions in the black-white education gap, the trends in the percentage of young adults who graduate from college reveal a less positive picture. Figure 4.8 shows the percentage of college graduates for black and white young adults between 1957 and 2000. African American young adults have increased their rates of college graduation over the whole period, but the college graduation rates for whites has risen slightly faster than the black rate, particularly during the early part of the period.

Between 1957 and 1977, the white college graduation rate rose from 12 to 25 percent, and then flattened until about 1995. The black rate also increased between 1957 and 1977, but only from 4 to 13 percent. Accordingly, the college graduation gap actually increased during this period from about 7 to 12 percentage points. The black rate remained relatively flat from 1977 to 1990. Starting in 1995, the college graduation rate began rising again for whites, and

Figure 4.8
Percent College Graduates, Ages 25-29 (CPS)

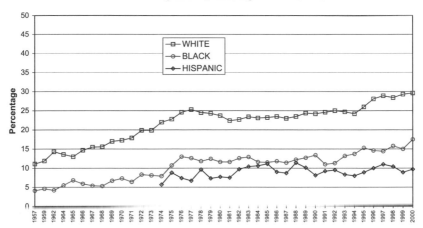

the black rate also rose from 1990 to 2000. As of the start of the twenty-first century, the black-white gap was about 12 points, about where it was in the late 1970s. Thus the black-white gap in college graduation rates remain as large or larger than it was just after the Korean War.

Why do two educational trends show a narrowing of the gap, while another shows a widening? The answer might be found in the achievement trends discussed earlier, showing that after a period of black gains the achievement gap stabilized during the 1990s. Most of the early gains may have been among lower-scoring students, many of whose parents were high school dropouts. As black parents increased their high school completion rates, proportionately fewer black students scored at the lowest achievement levels. Indeed, a recent analysis of NAEP trends indicates that most of the gains in black achievement during the 1970s and 80s were at the lower end of the test score continuum rather than at the upper end.[8] If black students have not improved as much at the higher end of the achievement continuum, this may mean that many black students may still lack sufficient academic skills to complete a four-year college program. This should not, of course, diminish the importance of black improvements that have eliminated the gap in high school graduation rates and that have narrowed the gap in some years of college completed, such as two-year community college programs.

Switching to family economic levels, Figure 4.9 shows the trends in median income for black and white families between 1967 and 2000 (2000 constant dollars). Both groups experienced rises in family income during this period, although the increase for white families was somewhat greater than for black families. White family income rose steadily over the entire period, with brief downturns for each of the major recessions of the period—mid-1970s,

Figure 4.9
U.S. Median Family Income (2000 dollars; CPS)

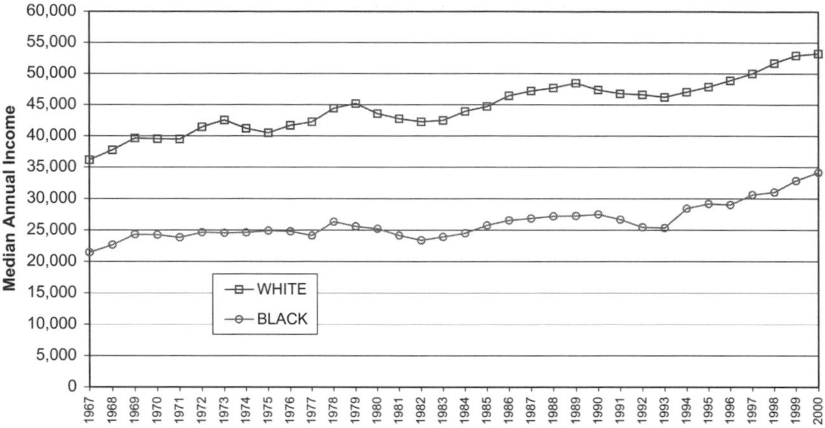

early 1980s, and early 1990s. Black family income rose during the late 1960s, but then remained relatively flat except for brief downturns during the recessions. Black income also rose relatively rapidly from 1993 to 2000, but since white income was also rising during the same time, the income gap was not reduced. Basically, the black-white family income gap increased slightly over the past three decades, but it has remained relatively constant at about $20,000 since 1980. Of course, since both groups have experienced increasing incomes, the ratio of black to white earnings increased from 55 percent in 1980 to 63 percent in 200. In relative terms, blacks have improved their income position with respect to whites.

The trends for poverty present a similar picture, with a fairly constant poverty gap of 25 points between 1970 and 1995 (whites 10 percent poverty, blacks 35 percent poverty). Coming out of the 1991-93 recession, black families experienced a rapid downturn in poverty rates to about 30 percent by 1998, so the poverty gap had diminished to about 20 points in 2000.

While the education trends and to a lesser extent income show progress in reducing economic and social inequality among the races, other Census trends and other sources of information show that there is a long way to go before full socioeconomic parity can be declared. Of particular concern are the trends in family structure, of which the most important indicator is the percentage of families headed by single parents.

Of all the socioeconomic indicators, the trends in family structure may have the most important implications for the achievement gap. Not only does family structure—meaning the percentage of families headed by single parents—reveal the largest gap between black and white families, unlike education and income it shows a deteriorating condition for black families. Moreover, black families have the highest rate of mothers who never married. The significance of this trend has been debated and discussed by many social commentators, including Senator Daniel Patrick Moynihan in a famous article written when he was serving in the Department of Labor during the Johnson administration.[9] Moynihan was concerned about the decline of two-parent black families during the 1960s, but the decline actually got much worse after his paper appeared. The most heated debate was whether welfare policies, which got a big boost during the Johnson administration, played a significant role in breaking up the black family.[10]

While the causes of increasing single-parent families are still being debated, the fact of the increases is not. Figure 4.10 shows that the rate of single-parent black families increased for three decades. During the 1970s (and the 1960s, not shown) the rate of single-parent families increased more rapidly for black than white families, reaching 50 percent for blacks in 1978 as compared to only 15 percent for white families, or a gap of 35 percentage points. From the late 1970s on, the rate of single parents among white families also began to increase, so that the black-white gap remained about the same for the next twenty years. The single-parent rate also rose among Hispanics during the 1980s, but it was never as high as the black rate. Among blacks, the rate of single parents reached a high of 65 percent in 1994, compared to 25 percent for white families, or a gap of 40 percent.

Interestingly, the rate of single-parent families began decreasing for blacks in 1995, and the same for Hispanics and whites several years later. By 2000 the rate had fallen to 61 percent for blacks and 26 percent for whites, the first reduction in the single-parent gap since 1970. The possibility that this decline might be explained by welfare reform is discussed in chapter 5.

Figure 4.10
Percentage of Single-Parent Families in U.S. (CPS)

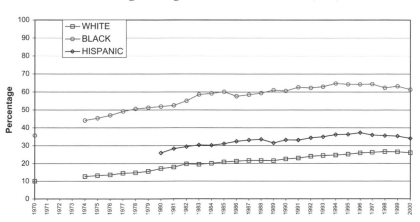

Given the continuing and sizeable gaps in income, college education, and family structure, all of which are risk factors for a child's IQ and achievement, it is not surprising that there are still achievement gaps between black and white children. But these are not the only risk factors for IQ and achievement. What about the possibility of racial differences in other important risk factors such as family size, and the parenting behaviors of cognitive stimulation and emotional support?

Other Risk Factors

Like differences in socioeconomic status, national studies have also found racial differences in most of the other risk factors identified in chapter 3. These differences can be examined most thoroughly using data from the 1994 Youth Study. Figure 4.11 shows the results for four environmental risk factors involving birth weight, number of children, age of mother at child's birth, and nutrition. For every factor, black and Hispanic children are in a less favorable condition than white children, and in three out of the four factors black children are more disadvantaged than Hispanic children. Starting with birth weight, 11 percent of black children were considered of low birth weight (weight less than 5.3 pounds) compared to only 5 percent for white parents; Hispanic children were in between, at 7 percent low birth weight.

Considering family size, about 60 percent of both black and Hispanic children are in families with more than two children, compared to 46 percent of white children. In terms of average number of children, white mothers in the Youth Study have an average of 2.5 children per family, compared to nearly three for black and Hispanic families. While this is not a striking difference, it must be emphasized that a large majority of black families are single-parent families, while a large majority of white families have both parents at home. So the typical black family has three children per parent while the typical white family has a little more than one child per parent. This means there are substantially greater parenting resources on a per capita basis for white families as compared to black families. Hispanic families fall somewhere in between these two extremes (they have a somewhat lower rate of single-parent families than black families).

Black mothers start their families at a younger age than white mothers and are much more likely to have a baby as a young teenager. Figure 4.11 shows that about 22 percent of black children were born when their mothers were eighteen or younger, compared to 11 percent for white children; Hispanic children are in between. If we look only at first-born children, about 35 percent of black mothers have their first child when they are eighteen or younger compared to 14 percent for white mothers. Moreover, 24 percent of black mothers have their first child at age seventeen or younger compared to only 8 percent of white mothers—a difference of three to one. This may be the reason

Figure 4.11
Racial Differences in Selected Risk Factors (CNLSY)

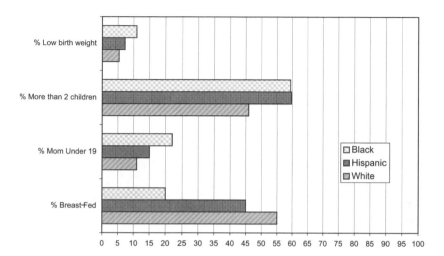

why black mothers are twice as likely to have a low birth weight child than a white mother. Hispanic mothers, again, fall in between these two extremes with respect to their age when they have children.

Finally, with regards to possible nutritional differences, the Youth Study finds that white children are most likely to have been breast-fed and black children are least likely. About 55 percent of white children have been breast-fed compared to 45 percent of Hispanic children and 20 percent of black children. To the extent that mother's milk confers a nutritional advantage for cognitive growth compared to alternatives, white and Hispanic children may have a head start from the moment of birth.

While the risk factors shown in Figure 4.11 are important for children's cognitive development, they are not as influential as the parenting characteristics of cognitive stimulation and emotional support. The racial and ethnic differences in these two parenting behaviors are shown in Figure 4.12. The minority-white gaps are very large for these two critical risk factors. White children average 103 points in both cognitive stimulation and emotional support scores, while black children score only 93 and 91 points, respectively. Hispanic children score about the same as black children in cognitive stimulation (94) but are closer to white children in emotional support. Since a difference of 10 points in either of these parenting behaviors is associated with a 5-point difference in a child's IQ or math scores, the racial and ethnic differences in parenting behaviors might be among the major causes of the IQ and achievement gaps.

The differences in parenting behaviors should not be surprising, considering some of the other socioeconomic differences already discussed. The racial

Figure 4.12
Cognitive Stimulation and Emotional Support (CNLSY)

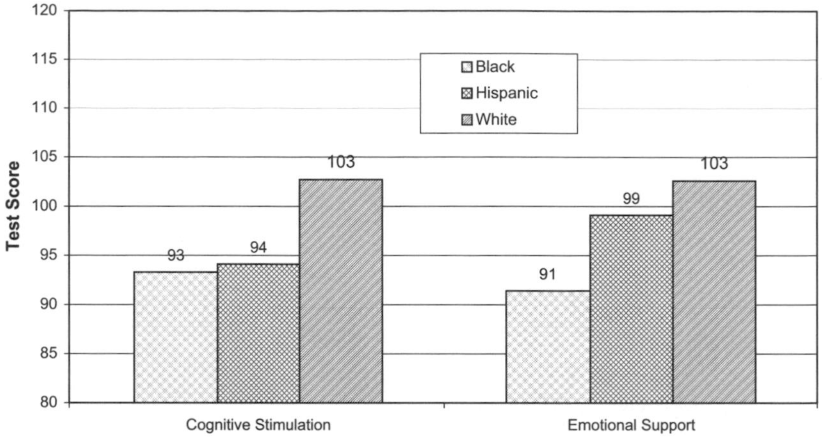

differences in family income, family structure, and family size, all of which are interrelated, could go a long way in explaining parenting behaviors. Compared to white families, black families are much more likely to be headed by a single and never-married mother and to have more children (see Figure 4.10). The absence of a spouse or former husband lowers family income and raises the parent-child ratio, which means fewer parents sharing in child-rearing responsibilities. Compared to two-parent families, this leads to less intensive instructional activities and lower support scores.

This finding does not imply that single, never-married mothers are not doing the very best job that they can to raise their children. But they are at a substantial disadvantage when compared to a two-parent family. A single parent with several children simply has fewer parenting resources per child in terms of both time and money: less time for instruction, less time for interaction and attention, less money for educational outings, and less money for reading materials, toys, and other educational materials.

The above description is a reasonable scenario for explaining the lower test scores of black and Hispanic children as compared to white children. Before this socioeconomic and environmental scenario can be adopted as the best explanation for the racial achievement gap, however, two other factors need to be considered: parent IQ and non-family environmental factors, especially school policies and resources. The reason why parent IQ is important, of course, is that it has high correlations with a child's IQ. This does not necessarily mean genetic effects: the IQ of a parent may also influence the quality of parenting behaviors, such as helping a parent teach or communicate more effectively, or by increasing the amount of information a parent can transmit to a child. Thus a parent's IQ can combine both genetic and environmental effects.

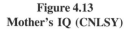

Figure 4.13
Mother's IQ (CNLSY)

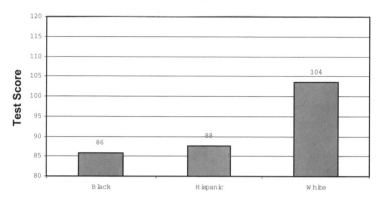

Figure 4.13 confirms that there is a substantial difference in mother's IQ among white, black, and Hispanic children. The black-white gap for mother's IQ is 18 points, and the gap for Hispanic and white mothers is only slightly less at 16 points. These racial differences are of the same magnitude as the racial differences documented in other populations, such as the achievement differences shown in the National Assessment. Since there is a significant correlation between the IQ of parents and their children, the racial differences shown in Figure 4.13 are undoubtedly responsible in part for the racial IQ gaps among the children in the Youth Study.

The magnitude of parent IQ differences also raises the important question of whether and to what degree the IQ difference might explain the socioeconomic gaps discussed earlier. Since parents with higher IQs are more likely to finish college and to enter higher-paying skilled careers, the question becomes how much of the correlation between parent's SES and children's IQ might be traceable to parent IQ. Before addressing this complex issue, another potential cause of the achievement gap must be addressed first: the impact of school environments, particularly the quality of resources and programs available to white and minority students.

Racial Differences in Schooling

In one respect, the question of school effects has already been answered. The various studies and data sources reviewed in the previous section demonstrate that large race and ethnic gaps exist before or at the beginning of children's regular schooling. For example, the verbal IQ scores measured in the 1994 Youth Study reveal large race and ethnic gaps in IQ before children enter the first grade (Figure 4-5). A similar finding for first graders was reported by Coleman et al. in the classic study on The Equality of Educational Opportunity. Whatever causes pre-school IQ and achievement differences, they cannot be blamed on school programs and policies. Coleman first made this observation in 1966 and it remains true today, thirty years later.

But even if the early achievement gaps are due to differences in home environments, many educators and social scientists believe that appropriate school programs and resources can close the gaps. In particular, it is often argued that low-achieving minority students do not receive sufficient programs and resources to overcome their disadvantaged socioeconomic background. If disadvantaged children could receive the proper level of support and a high quality education, many critics argue that minority achievement could be raised and the achievement gaps eliminated or at least reduced substantially. This viewpoint was expressed explicitly in a lawsuit against New York State brought on behalf of students and teachers in the New York City schools.[11] Similar arguments have been made in "educational adequacy" lawsuits brought in a number of states.[12]

It is useful, therefore, to consider the extent to which school policies and resources might be responsible for the national achievement gap documented above. This has been a very difficult and contentious issue among education researchers, with many debates over exactly how to study the problem. There is a great deal of educational data that can be used to conduct a study, but little agreement regarding the methodology.

National Assessments of School Resources

The National Assessment not only has the most complete information on the achievement gap, beginning in 1996 it also began to gather extensive information on the school resources available to the students who were being tested. The school resource information includes many of the quantitative indicators used to evaluate the quality of education, and these indicators are frequently the focus of school improvement or reform efforts. These quality indicators include expenditures on instructional materials; classroom size; teacher quality in terms of training, experience, and certification; and finally, the intensity and content of instructional programs. This information can be used to compare school resources available to white and minority students throughout the nation.

The major expenditure calculation available in NAEP data is per pupil expenditures on instructional materials, which includes textbooks, computers, lab equipment, and other educational supplies. Figure 4.14 displays this information by race or ethnicity of students who are age thirteen and who are attending middle or junior high schools, most being in the eighth grade. The average instructional dollars in schools attended by black students averages $602 per student, compared to $569 for schools attended by white students. The schools attended by Hispanic students also spend slightly more than white students at $579 per student. Similar results are observed for students who were ages nine and seventeen in 1996.

Figure 4.14
Instructional Expenditures by Race of Student
(1996 NAEP Age 13)

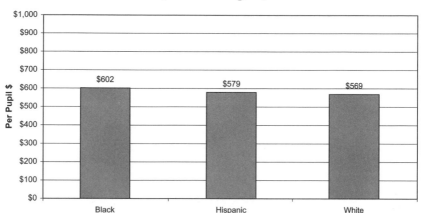

It would appear, then, that to the extent that there are school differences in expenditures for instructional materials, they tend to favor black and Hispanic students rather than white students, although the differences are not large. This result may surprise some observers, particular given the oft-heard criticism that large urban school systems have inadequate resources. It must be remembered, however, that there are many state and federal compensatory programs, such as Title 1, that offer additional funds for schools with large proportions of students who are both low achieving and below the poverty line. It appears that these programs have, in fact, led to a situation where black students, and to a lesser extent Hispanic students, actually receive more funds for educational materials than white students.

Despite the fact than many urban school leaders insist on the need for more funding, expenditures may not be a very good measure of school quality because they do not indicate how the expenditures are being spent. For example, additional funds can be used simply to buy more computers without regard to how they are used in the instructional process. The 1996 National Assessment included detailed information on teacher quality and other classroom characteristics, including teachers' education level (percent of teachers with an MA degree), experience, certification information, college majors and minors, and class size.

Figure 4.15 summarizes these teacher and classroom characteristics for eighth-grade math students and teachers in the 1996 math assessment. Black and Hispanic students fare as well as or better than white students on three of the five indicators. Black students are more likely than white students to have a math teacher with a Masters or higher degree; the rates for Hispanic and white students are about the same. All three groups have math teachers with

Figure 4.15
Teacher Resources by Race of Student
(1996 NAEP Age 13; Math Teachers Only)

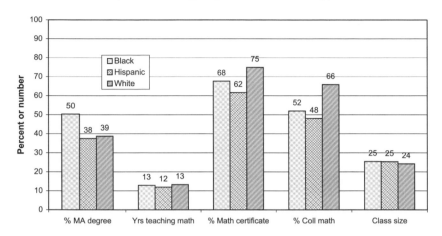

about the same years of experience teaching mathematics. All three groups also have very similar class sizes, averaging about twenty-five students per class. While the average class size for whites is one student smaller (twenty-four) than for the other two groups, this is not an educationally meaningful difference in class sizes.

There are, however, two differences in teacher quality that do favor white students: the percentage of math teachers with state certification for teaching junior high or middle school mathematics (which usually includes showing competence in algebra) and the percent majoring or minoring in mathematics in college. About 66 percent of black students and 62 percent of Hispanic students have math teachers with a junior high math certificate, compared to 75 percent for white students. A somewhat larger difference shows up in the percent of teachers who have studied math formally during their college education, either as a major or minor subject. Because having a college major or minor in mathematics is one way to obtain a junior high math certificate, the two characteristics are highly correlated in the NAEP data. Generally, about half of the minority students have math teachers who have studied math in college, compared to about two-thirds of the white students. Both of these teacher characteristics might contribute something to the achievement gap between minority and white students, the magnitude of which shall be investigated shortly.

It is widely accepted that one of the most important determinants of how much students learn in school is the amount of instructional time spent on a particular subject. Figure 4.16 shows that the average hours per week spent on math instruction is slightly higher for black and Hispanic eighth graders than

Figure 4.16
Hours of Math Instruction by Race of Student
(1996 NAEP Age 13)

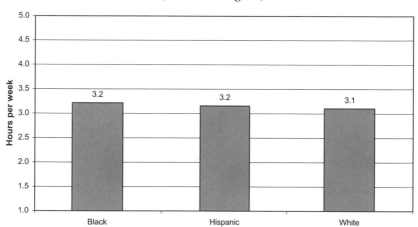

white students—3.2 hours compared to 3.1 hours. This translates into only about six minutes per week, which is probably not educationally significant.

What about the subject matter being taught? The NAEP teacher survey does not identify classes by name (such as general math, algebra, and so forth), but it does ask how much time is spent on various subjects. In particular, it asks how much time is spent in math classes addressing topics in "algebra and functions," which would be especially important for the NAEP math test since a score of 300 or higher requires being able to "evaluate formulas and solve simple linear equations."[13] About 56 percent of white students' teachers say they spend "a lot" of time on this topic, compared to only 44 percent of black students' teachers and 46 percent of Hispanic student's teachers. Most of the rest say they spend "some" time on these topics.

This difference must be interpreted cautiously, however, because in many schools eighth grade algebra is not a required course and may require a certain level of math skills as a prerequisite. Accordingly, many eighth grade students may not choose algebra or may not satisfy prerequisites if they have weak math skills, regardless of their race. Thus the percentage of students exposed to algebra concepts can reflect student proclivity and prior math skills as much as school policies.

In summary, only two school resource indicators show a difference in favor of white students, which are math-certified teachers and college math. Two other indicators favor black students—instructional expenditures and teacher education—and three others show no important difference by race—class size, teacher experience, and instructional time. Therefore, even if all of these characteristics benefited minority students' academic achievement, only certification and college math need to be investigated for a possible contribution to the achievement gap shown in Figure 4.3b.[14]

In the 1996 NAEP math assessment, both teacher certification in junior high math and studying math in college are moderately associated with a student's math scores, but they are also highly correlated. When both are entered into a prediction equation for eighth grade math scores, college math is statistically significant but certification is not. When each characteristic is analyzed separately, having a teacher with college math has the strongest effect on math achievement (11 points, controlling for student SES background). That is, students whose teachers studied math in college score about 11 points higher on the math test compared to students whose teachers are not so qualified, holding SES constant. This is a moderate effect, about one-third of a standard deviation.

To what extent does the difference in teacher's college math contribute to the national achievement gap? The maximum potential effect of college math on the eighth grade math gap would be 11 points, but this would occur only if all white students had teachers with college math while no black students had them. As shown in Figure 4.15, the difference between minority and white students with teachers who have college math is only about 16 percentage points. If this difference was eliminated by providing black students with same rate of certified junior high math teachers as white students (66 percent), then according to NAEP data black math achievement might rise by approximately 1.8 points (an increase of .16 times an effect of 11). Thus, only a small part of the 32-point math achievement gap might be explained by resource differences as documented by the NAEP data. Of course, some school reforms might offer black students more teachers with college math than white students, but the question here is whether inequalities in the allocation of school resources might explain, in part, the minority-white achievement gaps.

In conclusion, there is little evidence from the 1996 NAEP that there is any systematic inequality in school resources that could account for the black-white achievement gap. Only two interrelated school resources—teachers with college math and teacher certification—reveal modest disadvantages for black and Hispanic students, while two others show an advantage for black students. While teachers with college math also appears to influence student achievement, even if this resource was equalized it would close the current math achievement gap—now standing at about 32 points—by less than two points.

This is not the only study to find little inequality in the distribution of school resources among black and white students. Indeed, the famous Coleman report on Equal Opportunity found few inequalities in school resources for black and white students in 1966, when most black and white students were still attending separate schools. Since that time—during the 1970s and early 1980s—most school districts were desegregated so that black and white students were more likely to attend the same school. The Coleman report concluded that the allocation of school resources was quite "uniform" in American public education, and that resources were not correlated with the racial composition of a school. According to NAEP data, much the same conclusion can be reached today, with the main difference being that black and white students are more likely to attend the same schools.

School Desegregation

This brings up the potential role of school desegregation in the improvement of black achievement between 1970 and 1980. Since the timing of desegregation coincided with the reduction of the gap, some social scientists have argued that desegregation was one of the reasons that the achievement gap closed during this period.[15] The theory behind this argument is the "harm and benefit" thesis of school segregation: separate schools for blacks and whites, commonplace until 1970, harmed the self-esteem of black students, depriving them of the enriched environments provided by middle-class white classmates, and it led to lower academic standards. All of these conditions combined to cause lower black achievement. It was believed that placing black and white students in the same schools would undo these adverse effects, thereby improving black achievement and narrowing the achievement gap.

There is no question that the black-white gap narrowed during the 1970s and 1980s for all age groups and all subject matters tested, and also that school desegregation took place for the most part during the 1970s. But many other changes also occurred during this time period or just before, particularly improvements in black educational attainment as shown in Figures 4.6 and 4.7, and the onset of increased government compensatory programs like Head Start and Title 1. Therefore school desegregation is not the only possible explanation of improved black achievement.

One way to test for the potential effect of desegregation is by examining NAEP achievement trends for segregated and desegregated schools. Figure 4.17 shows the trends in black reading scores for thirteen-year-olds separated by schools that were majority black (segregated) or majority white (desegregated). The trend in age thirteen reading scores was selected because it revealed the greatest reduction in the achievement gap among all age groups and subject matters. Between 1971 and 1984, blacks in segregated (majority black) schools gained at the same rate as blacks in desegregated schools. There was a modest divergence between 1984 and 1990, when blacks in desegregated schools gained 9 points compared to 2 points for blacks in segregated schools. Of the total black gain of 20 points between 1971 and 1990 (see Figure 4.2), 16 points came from blacks in predominantly black schools. Thus school desegregation, in the sense of racially balanced schools, could

Figure 4.17
Black Reading Trends by School Type
(Age 13 NAEP)

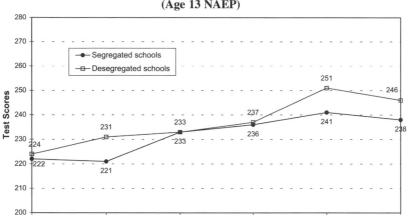

have accounted for a reduction in the NAEP reading gap for thirteen-year-olds of 4 points at most.

Another way to evaluate the effect of school desegregation on achievement is through case studies of desegregated districts. Most school districts that have been desegregated still show a large achievement gap between black and white students, which is prima facie evidence that desegregation by itself is not sufficient to eliminate racial differences in achievement. The important question is, if desegregation did not close the gap, what is the cause of the current gap? The case studies reviewed here attempt to explain the achievement gap in terms of students' socioeconomic status and their test scores when they entered school. Test score differences at the time students enter school must be attributed to the influence of family background factors rather than to school policies and programs.

Minneapolis, Minnesota was desegregated in several stages between 1974 and 1982, and by 1982 its schools had a very high degree of racial balance, certainly as good if not better than most of the larger cities that underwent desegregation during the 1970s. It also remained a majority white school system up through 1990, although demographic changes caused it to become about one-half black, one-third white, and one-sixth Asian by the late 1990s. Despite these demographic changes, Minneapolis schools remained well integrated throughout the 1990s.

Figure 4.18 shows the black-white achievement gaps in reading and math for the 1998 seventh grade class. Despite the history of successful desegregation, in the sense of racially balanced schools, Minneapolis black students scored 26 points below white students in both subjects (about one standard deviation). After adjusting these scores for family socioeconomic differences

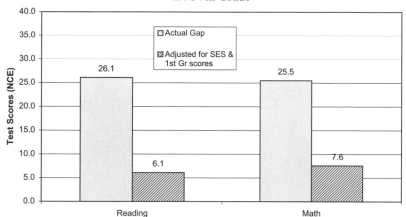

Figure 4.18
Black-White Achievement Gap in Minneapolis
1998 7th Grade

(poverty and number of parents at home) and first grade test scores, the achievement gap drops to about 6 or 7 points. In other words, between 70 and 75 percent of the achievement gap is explained by SES factors and achievement at the beginning of schooling, and therefore school policies and programs cannot be the cause of the achievement gap in Minneapolis.

A similar case study analysis was carried out for the Woodland Hills school district located in the suburbs of Pittsburgh, Pennsylvania. The district was created by a federal court order in 1978, which combined several smaller school districts that were racially and socioeconomically disparate into one larger, desegregated district. Its schools have been highly racially balanced for a long period of time, and it is still a majority white school system.

The achievement gaps are shown in Figure 4.19; the tests are different than those used for Minneapolis, so the scores are not directly comparable. Nonetheless, the math gap in Woodland Hills is about three-fourths of a standard deviation, and the reading gap is about one-half of a standard deviation. When this gap is adjusted for SES and first grade test scores, the gap nearly disappears. Virtually all of the black-white achievement gap in Woodland Hills is explained by a student's family SES and his or her test scores when school was started. Again, since the existing achievement gap is explained almost entirely by factors outside the school system, the gap cannot be caused by school policies and programs.

In conclusion, while desegregation may have closed the achievement gap by several points, a large achievement gap still exists between black and white students, whether one looks at national or local studies. Since inequalities in school resources do not explain the gap, and since desegregation has not closed the gap, the inescapable conclusion is that the gap is caused by in-

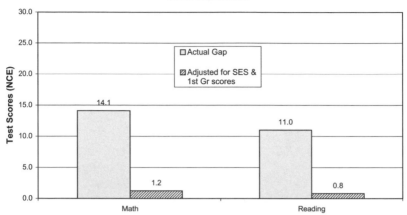

Figure 4.19
Black-White Achievement Gap in Woodland Hills
1999 6th Grade

equalities in the family risk factors analyzed in chapter 3. This is not to say that there is no school program that might reduce the achievement gap; the point is that existing school resources and policies are not the causes of the existing black-white gap. Chapter 5 will discuss the possibility that other educational policies and programs might be found that could overcome the adverse effects of family factors.

The remaining question in this chapter, then, is precisely which family factors are the strongest causes of the achievement gap, and especially the relative influence of parent IQ on the one hand versus environmental family characteristics on the other. That balance of influence will determine whether and how much the gap can be reduced in the future.

Reducing the IQ Gap

All the evidence discussed so far indicates that there are racial and ethnic differences between white and minority children's IQ and achievement scores, and that these gaps are associated most strongly with family risk factors. In order to explain the current gap and to understand how the gap can be reduced further, it is important to comprehend the role played by each of the family risk factors discussed in chapter 3. It is especially important to evaluate the relative contributions of those family factors that can be changed, like family size and parenting behaviors, and those that are very hard if not impossible to change once a woman decides to have a child, such as her IQ and education.

Chapter 3 identified the ten family risk factors that had the strongest independent associations with a child's IQ and achievement. Several of these risk factors also have very strong relationships with minority achievement and therefore offer the best explanations for the achievement gap. The risk factors

Figure 4.20
Simplified Model for a Black Child's IQ (not all risk factors shown)

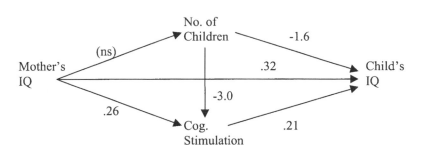

that have the strongest direct effects on an African American child's IQ, controlling for all risk factors in a multivariate analysis, include mother's IQ, father's education (as a surrogate for father IQ), number of children, family income, the parenting behaviors of cognitive stimulation and emotional support, breast-feeding, and birth weight. Although family structure does not have a direct effect on a child's IQ after controlling for the other family factors, it does have very strong influence on income and on the parenting behaviors. Thus family status has a strong indirect effect on IQ operating through income and the parenting behaviors. The details of the multivariate analysis are discussed in Appendix B.

The difficult problem is sorting out the independent effects of these different family characteristics, since they are all correlated with one another. For example, mother's IQ is correlated with a child's IQ, but it is also correlated with the parenting behavior of cognitive stimulation and number of children, both of which in turn influence a child's IQ. How do we separate out the effects of mother's IQ from the effects of cognitive stimulation, or the effects of family size from the effects of mother's IQ? It is especially important to sort out the effect of mother's IQ, because it is one of the family risk factors that is not likely to change during a child's developmental years.

One statistical technique for sorting out the effects of multiple factors is called "path analysis." This technique is useful for estimating the direct effect of one risk factor on IQ while statistically equalizing children on all the other risk factors ("controlling" for the other factors). Figure 4.20 shows a simplified path model for black children's IQ using only mother's IQ, number of children, and cognitive stimulation as the predictive factors (in actuality, there are more risk factors than this). The figure shows regular coefficients, not standardized coefficients, for ease of interpretation. For calculating indirect effects, the standardized coefficients are used (see Appendix B for the full regression and standardized coefficients).

This model demonstrates that the number of children in a family, the cognitive stimulation for a child, and the mother's IQ all influence a child's IQ. These relationships were established for all children in chapter 3, but the model also holds for black children when they are analyzed separately.

Note that the model also shows that mother's IQ and number of children influence cognitive stimulation scores, in that mothers with higher IQs and fewer children also tend to have higher cognitive stimulation scores. This gives rise to two "indirect" effects on IQ. First, the number of children has an indirect effect on IQ by reducing cognitive stimulation scores (probably through dilution of parenting resources). Mother's IQ also has an indirect effect on a child's IQ by increasing cognitive stimulation scores. The numbers next to each of the causal arrows are the estimated effects of each risk factor on a child's IQ or on the intermediate variables. For example, controlling for mother's IQ and cognitive stimulation, having one less child increases a black child's IQ by just over 1.5 points. Controlling for mother's IQ and number of children, a 1-point increase in the cognitive stimulation score increases a black child's IQ by .21 points; a 10-point increase would increase a black child's IQ by just over 2 points. Controlling for number of children and cognitive stimulation, a black mother whose IQ is 10 points higher than another black mother will have a child whose IQ is 3 points higher on average.

Indirect effects are calculated by multiplying the standardized coefficients for each arrow in the causal chain (see Appendix B for standardized coefficients). For example, the indirect effect of one less sibling on a child's IQ, operating through cognitive stimulation, is about .5 points. Thus the total effect of one less child on a black child's IQ is estimated at about 2 points. The indirect effect of being 10 points higher on mother's IQ, operating through cognitive stimulation, is also estimated to be about .5 points.

The full causal model for black children is more complex than what is shown in Figure 4.20. It adds the risk factors of father's education (surrogate for father IQ), emotional support, income, birth weight, and breast-feeding to the four risk factors shown in Figure 4.20 (see Appendix B). Family structure (two parents, mother with husband not in the home, or mother never married) does not have a significant direct effect on a child's IQ, but it does have a strong indirect effect because of its influence on income, cognitive stimulation, and emotional support. Having two parents in the home not only means greater economic resources, it generates more parenting resources and means more time spent teaching children (cognitive stimulation) and more nurturing and attention for each child (emotional support), as compared to a family with only a single, never-married mother.

Table 4.1 summarizes the potential effects on a black child's IQ of changing each of the risk factors in the full causal model. The risk factors are separated according to their potential for change. Mother's IQ and father's education are considered very hard to change after a child is born, while the other family risk

Table 4.1
Estimated Effects of Risk Factors on a Black Child's IQ

	Amount of Change	Effect
DIRECT EFFECTS		
POTENTIAL GENETIC		
Mother's IQ	+10 points	2.2
Father's Education (for IQ)	+ 2 points	1.2
TOTAL DIRECT		3.4
ENVIRONMENTAL		
Cognitive Stimulation	+10 points	1.2
Emotional Support	+10 points	0.8
No. of Children	- 1 child	1.4
Breast-fed	Yes vs. No	1.7
Birth Weight	+ 1 lb.	0.4
Family Income	+$10,000	0.7
TOTAL DIRECT		6.2
INDIRECT EFFECTS[a]		
Family Structure[b]	2 vs. mom never married	1.9
TOTAL ENVIRONMENTAL		8.1

[a] Through cognitive stimulation, emotional support, and income
[b] Two parents=2; one parent married=1; mother never married=0

factors have the potential for being changed at the time or shortly after a couple has their first child. Mother's IQ has the single strongest effect of any of the risk factors taken alone, which is over 2 points in the child's IQ for a 10-point increase in mother's IQ. The combined effects of mother's IQ and father's education are about 3.5 points. But the combined direct effects of increasing parenting behaviors, reducing the number of children, increasing annual income, breast-feeding, and increasing birth weight (by the indicated amounts) are estimated to be somewhat greater than 6 points. Further, if the indirect effect of a change in family structure is included, the total benefit of these changes in environmental risk factors rises to 8 points for black IQ scores.[16]

Recall that the black-white IQ gap in the Youth Study is 17 points. This analysis suggests that children who are most at risk (with never-wed mothers, low income, three children in the family, not breast-fed, and low parenting scores) might have IQ scores 8 points higher if they had two-parent families, one fewer sibling, family income increased by $10,000, and stimulation and support scores that are 10 points higher.

Are these degrees of change attainable? Increasing annual income by $10,000 is a lot of money, and 10 points higher in both of the parenting

Table 4.2
Effect of Family Status on Income and Parenting Behaviors
for Black Families, 1994 (effect of mother's IQ removed)

Family Status	Family Income	Cognitive Stimulation	Emotional Support
Never married	$18,000	95	91
Father absent	$21,000	97	94
Both parents	$31,000	100	100

behaviors represents a lot more time and attention given to children. But the Youth Study shows that black families with both parents at home, as compared to never-married mothers, actually come close to these higher levels of income and parenting behaviors.

To show that changes of these magnitudes are possible, consider the information in Table 4.2. After removing the effects of mother's IQ (because it is also correlated with both income and family status), a never-married African American mother earns only $18,000 per year, and her children score 95 on cognitive stimulation and 91 on emotional support. In contrast, two-parent black families, on average, earn $13,000 more and their children score 5 and 9 points higher, respectively, on stimulation and support, showing that a change in family status alone is sufficient to make significant improvements the other three risk factors. This is not to say that a single mother could not find a way to match these higher levels of income and parenting behaviors, but it would be a very difficult challenge given her limited resources. The two-parent family represents a reasonable pathway for improving these important family environment risk factors and, in turn, for raising black achievement.

Of course, even if all the changes in Table 4.1 were made for black families today, there would still be an achievement gap. But consider a two-generation scenario assuming the path model is valid. If the family changes in Table 4.1 could be made for the coming generation of black parents, and if the effects of the risk factors are approximately correct, then we would see a substantial increase in the IQ of the next generation of black children. When these children become parents, we can then calculate an additional effect from the higher IQ of the parents, in addition (hopefully) to the continued positive effects of the other family risk factors. Over a time span of two or three generations, then, this model would predict a near elimination of the IQ gap.

This intergenerational scenario assumes that the family environment factors can be changed, such as increasing the rate of two-parent families, or finding other ways to improve parenting resources, which in themselves represent major challenges. Having established that there is a potential for improved intelligence levels for minority children through changes in family environments, it now remains to discuss just how these changes might take place.

Notes

1. S. J. Gould, *The Mismeasure of Man*, New York: W. W. Norton, 1996, chapter 5.
2. James Coleman et al., *Equality of Educational Opportunity*, Washington, DC: U.S. Government Printing Office, 1966.
3. Christopher Jencks and Meredith Phillips, eds., *The Black-White Test Score Gap*, Washington, DC: Brookings Institute, 1998.
4. During the elementary grades, students usually gain about 1 standard deviation in raw scores on most standardized tests. A gap of 1 standard deviation can be interpreted, roughly, as a one grade-level difference.
5. As children get older, the gap generally decreases in terms of sd units.
6. The standard deviation of both the IQ and the math achievement scores have been set to 15 points.
7. These annual surveys are called Current Population Surveys (CPS) and are reported in a series called Current Population Reports.
8. Michael T. Nettles, *Statement on the NAEP 1999 Trends Report*, Washington, DC: National Assessment Governing Board, 2000 (August 24).
9. D. P. Moynihan, *The Negro Family: A Case for National Action*, Washington, DC: Department of Labor, March 1965.
10. A proponent of this view was Charles Murray, *Losing Ground*, New York: Basic Books, 1984; a critic of this view is Christopher Jencks, *Rethinking Social Policy*, Cambridge, MA: Harvard University Press, 1992.
11. See *Campaign for Fiscal Equity v. New York*, 86 N.Y.2d 307 (1995).
12. Educational adequacy lawsuits have been brought against state governments in Connecticut, Minnesota, Florida, and South Carolina, to name just a few.
13. J. R. Campbell, C. M. Hombo, J. Mazzeo, *NAEP 1999 Trends in Academic Progress*, Washington, DC: U.S. Department of Education, 2000, p. 56.
14. The amount of algebra taught in the student's math class is excluded because it is not necessarily a school policy and might also be confounded with the math test results, since students with low math skills may not be taking algebra or even pre-algebra. In addition, in the 1996 NAEP data none of the other school resource measures was correlated significantly with eighth grade math achievement scores.
15. D. Grissmer, A. Flanagan, and S. Williamson, "Why Did the Black-White Test Score Gap Narrow in the 1970s and 1980s," in C. Jencks and M. Phillips, eds., *The Black-White Test Score Gap*, Washington, DC: Brookings Institution, 1998.
16. Note that the estimated 8-point benefit of the indicated environmental changes is for black children with none of the changes compared to a group with all of the changes.

5

Agents of Change for Intelligence

The evidence presented in chapter 2 demonstrates that IQ and academic achievement can and do change for societies as a whole, for subpopulations within societies (e.g., minority groups in the United States), and for individuals. The magnitude and timing of these changes strongly suggest environmental influences that operate primarily during the early years of a child's development. Chapter 3 established a framework for explaining intelligence levels of young children based on a series of risk factors and showed that these risk factors were strongly related to IQ and achievement. Two of the risk factors, parent IQ and birth weight, may be classified as partly genetic or physical influences, but the other eight were clearly environmental effects that offer the potential for conscious, intentional change.

Taken together, this evidence supports a conclusion that specific environmental influences can and do make a difference for a child's IQ, and it provides a basis for arguing that a child's IQ could be maximized if these environmental risk factors can themselves be optimized in appropriate ways. This is a very big "if," however, and it raises a host of complex issues about the most effective and most feasible ways to change any of the environmental risk factors that impact a child's intelligence. It is one thing to know, for example, that specific parenting behaviors influence a child's IQ, but it is quite another matter to actually change the parenting behavior or to find ways to supplement it with programs outside the family.

The Timing of Changes

This chapter addresses these implementation issues by attempting to identify some of the more promising as well as less promising pathways for maximizing a child's intelligence. The discussion of timing in chapter 2 and the risk factors in chapter 3 established that the effectiveness of environmental influences on intelligence depends heavily on the age of the child. Clearly, if the timing of environmental influence is a critical consideration, then both the locus and the types of change agents are subject to major constraints. If environmental influences arc strongest at very young ages, then formal school programs may be too late for optimal benefits for IQ. If environmental influences are equally effective at all ages, at least through the teen years, then many more agents of change come into play.

The first implementation question is whether environmental risk factors can be changed effectively using existing agencies, such as formal school and preschool programs. At the present time, of course, the major pathway for helping disadvantaged, low-achieving children is through such programs as the federal Head Start and the Title 1 Compensatory Education programs. Unfortunately, there are serious questions about the long-term effectivness of these programs for the purpose of raising IQ and academic achievement, perhaps because these interventions come too late.

If existing agencies and programs are not effective for maximizing IQ, are there new intervention strategies that might be developed for optimal change of the risk factors? One approach is very early childhood programs, where children and parents receive education and training in childcare centers or through home visits. There are a number of experimental and demonstration programs that offer some evidence on the effectiveness of very early childhood interventions. Aside from the obvious problem of cost, there are serious implementation issues surrounding any type of early childhood intervention program, particularly getting cooperation from parents who may not want their children in educational programs at very young ages.

A second approach consists of trying to change all environmental risk factors at once; this can be called the whole family approach. Since all of the environmental risk factors discussed in chapter 3 are imbedded in parent characteristics and behaviors, it makes sense to focus on making parents and families the major agents of change. This approach has not been fully implemented as a matter of public policy, but under welfare reform states have been encouraged to experiment with various family policies that are similar to the whole family approach. Although embryonic in its current state of implementation, the whole family approach may hold the greatest potential for maximizing children's intelligence.

Schools and Preschools

Major studies of school effects on IQ and achievement can be grouped into several broad classes according to certain conceptual and methodological criteria. Understandably, some types of studies are more relevant to this review than others.

The first class of study might be called gross or total effects of schooling on IQ. These studies focus on the relationship between IQ and the total amount of schooling, for example the total years of formal schooling completed through high school. These studies are least relevant to the propositions being studied in this book, because there is no question that the total amount of schooling influences the absolute level of academic knowledge and skills acquired. Several of these studies are reviewed here primarily to clear up any misunderstanding about the role that schools play in learning.

The second class of study is the input-output (or production function) design that attempts to model academic achievement (output) as a function of any number of school program and resource measures (inputs). This class contains by far the greatest number of studies of school effects, simply because there is so much data available. Many states and larger school districts maintain data files that permit this type of study. Since these studies use cross-sectional designs rather than experimental or longitudinal designs, the more rigorous studies in this group also include at least some measures of family socioeconomic status (e.g., poverty) in order to eliminate the possibility that SES may be responsible for correlations between resources and achievement. In many states, more affluent communities may commit more resources to schooling, and if they have higher test scores it may be the higher family SES, not the greater school resources, that may be responsible for higher achievement test scores. The classic study headed by James Coleman mentioned earlier is a good example of this type of study.[1]

A third group of studies will be called "special studies," and this group includes experimental and longitudinal designs that examine the effects of particular programs or interventions. Generally, the achievement of students who receive the intervention is compared to achievement of students who do not receive the intervention. The most rigorous of these studies use randomized procedures to assign students or schools to "treatment" and "control" groups, to help rule out the possibility that extraneous differences between the groups (like SES) cause whatever achievement differences are observed. Other studies of ongoing interventions use longitudinal designs that compare achievement gains for students receiving the intervention to gains of those who do not. These "quasi-experimental" designs must also control for SES factors to eliminate the possibility that achievement gains might be caused by SES differences between the two groups of students. A good example of an experimental design is the Tennessee Star study of the effects of classroom size on achievement, and a good example of a longitudinal design is the Prospects study, which evaluated the federal Title 1 compensatory education program for disadvantaged students. Some of the evaluations of federal Head Start programs also use well-designed experimental designs.

A final group of studies will be called "new" input-output studies. These are studies that I have conducted but that have not been published in full. These studies are similar to existing input-output studies, but each of them illustrates various issues that arise when interpreting the results of input-output studies. In particular, each of the new studies compares the size of SES effects to the size of school resource effects, a feature that is missing in many existing studies.

It might appear at first glance that experimental designs would produce the most rigorous evidence about the effects of school programs on IQ and achievement, but that is not necessarily the case. Randomized designs can have two problems that reduce confidence in generalizations. One is that the randomization can be undermined by inadvertent administrative errors or by students who drop out of a program before completion, thereby causing potential differences between the experimental and control groups. Another is the possibility that people involved in the experimental group—students, parents, teachers, and administrators—are so enthusiastic about participating in the intervention that they work harder than they normally would without the experiment. This so-called "Hawthorne Effect" can produce results in an experiment that cannot be replicated when the intervention is routinely introduced throughout a school district or a state.[2]

While an input-output model is less rigorous for testing the effects of a new intervention, its most important advantage is that school programs are evaluated "as implemented" in the field, with little chance of spurious effects due to the temporary and sometimes artificial conditions of an experiment. The key to sound conclusions is availability of sufficient SES measures to estimate a credible model. Hopefully, carefully done studies will converge on similar findings regardless of the type of design.

Total School Effects

In chapter 2, the discussion of the importance of IQ presented a very strong correlation between teenage IQ and ultimate educational attainment sixteen years later. This relationship is turned around here to consider the effect of schooling on IQ. Given the explanation above about how standardized IQ and achievement tests are constructed and scored, it should not be surprising that the reverse is also true, that the amount of schooling influences the level of IQ.

Since raw scores for both IQ and achievement tests increase with age and grade level, in order for an average child to maintain an IQ score of 100 or an achievement test score of 50 that child must continue to acquire knowledge and skills each year corresponding to the gains of children nationally. Since most children attend school where they acquire a great deal of new information and skills each year, the average child must do the same if he or she is to remain "average."

Studies of total school effects show that children who receive less schooling than "normal" through a variety of circumstances (not of their own or their parents' doing) generally score lower than children who are not so deprived. The reverse is also true: children who get more than the normal amount of schooling during the K-12 years score higher, controlling for SES and other factors that might also be related to finishing high school.

One of the more comprehensive and recent reviews by Ceci and Williams cites seven types of evidence (studies) that demonstrate an effect of amount of schooling on IQ scores.[3] The seven types of studies include intermittent school attendance, delayed school starts (due to school resources deficiencies), remaining in school longer, discontinuing school prematurely, effects of summer vacations, and the amount of schooling attained as a result of early versus late birth dates for a birth cohort (delayed entry). Timing of birth date determines when a child can enter school, and it leads to two groups of students with the same ages but with a year difference in schooling. All of these studies found that students with greater amounts of schooling had higher IQ scores, and sometimes the differences were striking. Many of these studies showed an average of 2 or 3 IQ points gained (or lost) per year of schooling.

For most of the studies cited there are no detailed descriptions of the type of test or scoring used, so it is hard to determine whether these changes reflect gains in absolute knowledge or gains relative to a national norm. To the extent that these studies administered the same IQ test using the same norms, we would conclude that the gains would be expected. Children who attend school for five years (900 days if 180-day years) would be expected to gain more knowledge than same-age children who attend school for only four school years (720 days), whether the difference in days is due to illness, starting school late, closure of schools, or so forth.

One thorough study of the effect of delayed school entry showed that the amount of schooling affects both crystallized and fluid intelligence. Cahan and Cohen administered twelve cognitive ability tests to about 12,000 fourth, fifth, and sixth graders in Jerusalem.[4] The twelve types of tests are similar to those in many IQ tests, including tests of verbal skills (the most crystallized), numeric skills, and figure skills (the most fluid). On the verbal tests, one year of additional schooling for same age children was worth about 1/3 of an sd increase in raw scores, compared to 1/6 of an sd increase in raw scores for one more year of age for the same grade children. In contrast, the figural tests yielded about 1/6 of an sd increase in raw scores for one additional year of schooling and one more year of age. Although the more crystallized verbal tests were the most responsive to the amount of schooling, the more fluid tests were also influenced by schooling. Again, since the criterion used in this study is absolute skill levels, additional time in school would be expected to increase absolute IQ scores.

It is tempting to infer from these studies that one could design a school intervention program that could increase the IQ scores of a disadvantaged group of students simply by providing more instructional time than was available to the average student. Indeed, this is the conceptual assumption of many compensatory programs, such as Head Start and Title 1. But the total effect studies do not necessarily support such an inference, for several reasons. First, since most of these studies track absolute changes in total populations, all inferences would apply to absolute gains in a total population rather than relative gains of a disadvantaged sub-population. Second, some of the studies may reflect the effects of unmeasured risk factors, in that students who did not complete as many years of education might have been more disadvantaged than those who did (often only a single SES measure was controlled). Finally, some studies of delayed entry like the Cahan and Cohan study used raw IQ scores, and raw score increases should be expected over the course of a school year; they do not mean that students increased their scores relative to national norms. Nonetheless, several studies of compensatory school programs will be reviewed in a subsequent section.

Existing Input-Output Studies

One of the earliest and most comprehensive input-output studies was the Coleman report, commissioned by the Civil Rights Act of 1964. Since that time a great number of similar input-output studies have appeared, many of which have utilized the growing number of national education data bases that have been created since the Coleman report. There are far too many studies to review all of them here; instead, a representative selection of some of the more comprehensive studies are discussed. Some are meta analyses which are themselves consolidations of many smaller studies, others are based on large national education data bases including NAEP, and yet others are original analysis of large state data bases.

Most input-output studies address the question of whether specific school resources affect achievement scores. In most studies, the school resource measures are rather broad and include such items as per pupil expenditures, class size or pupils per teacher, teacher experience, teacher education, and teacher salary (as a surrogate for teacher quality). A smaller number of studies include more measures of teacher quality characteristics, such as certification status, whether teaching in one's certification field, college major, and teacher scores in skill tests. In more rigorous studies, additional variables are introduced to control for family SES factors. Since affluent families tend to settle in wealthier school systems, and wealthier systems may provide more school resources, the correlation between school resources and student test scores might simply reflect a relationship between family SES and student achievement.

The potential policy implications of these studies are clear. If it can be shown that certain school resources benefit academic achievement more than others, then improved outcomes can be attained by increasing those resources, either system-wide or just for disadvantaged students.

From purely theoretical grounds, it is by no means clear why the school resources on this short list should have a significant impact on academic achievement. For example, while many educators claim that higher funding is needed to raise the quality of education, there is no intrinsic reason why more money per se should raise test scores unless it is spent on the right things—such as hiring better-trained classroom teachers rather than more guidance counselors. Further, while it might seem reasonable to assume that more experienced and educated teachers would be more qualified and therefore better teachers, this assumption may not hold if teachers are assigned to subjects outside their areas of expertise. Finally, pupil-teacher ratios would seem to have the greatest prima facie basis for having an effect on achievement, because a smaller ratio would indicate greater instructional effort per student, assuming no change in teacher quality as the ratio declined. However, even here improved achievement might not materialize if lower quality teachers are hired to bring the ratios down, as was reported in California following a state-wide initiative to reduce class sizes.[5]

These caveats about school resources should be kept in mind as the major input-output studies are reviewed. The absence of a significant relationship between a particular school resource and academic achievement in a given study does not necessarily mean the resource is not important, but rather it could mean that the data in that study failed to assess the true meaning of that resource.

The Coleman study was classic in more ways than one. It was the first national study of the relationship between school resources, family characteristics, and academic achievement; it drew a very large sample of students of all races, in all sections of the country, and in five grade levels; and it had more measures of school resources and family characteristics than any prior study. And its conclusions were as big and controversial as the act of Congress that spawned it. The Coleman conclusions can be summarized in several statements: (1) Most of the variation in achievement test scores occurred within schools while only a small fraction was between schools, thus indicating that most of the variance in achievement was explained by individual student background rather than school program differences. (2) Family background characteristics such as parent education, household economic status, and family structure had large correlations with academic achievement. (3) After controlling for student SES background, none of the school resource measures had as much association with achievement as SES measures, and the strongest correlates were teachers' verbal ability and teachers' education level. (4) The only school-level variable that had a large correlation with individual achievement was school SES, although subsequent analysis found a simple data processing error that apparently exaggerated this correlation.[6]

It is important to emphasize that the Coleman team did not interpret these finding as meaning that school resources had no effect on student achievement. Rather, they concluded that school resources were similarly distributed within most regions of the country (there were some differences between northern and southern regions), and therefore that the effect of resources on achievement was relatively uniform in most American school systems within regions.

In their own words:

> [T]he schools are remarkably similar in the way they relate to the achievement of their pupils when the socioeconomic background of their students is taken into account. When these factors are statistically controlled, however, it appears that differences between schools account for only a small fraction of differences in pupil achievement.[7]

There were many follow-up studies that reanalyzed the Coleman data, including a comprehensive reassessment by a special seminar at Harvard University and yet another by Christopher Jencks et al., but the Coleman findings survived relatively unscathed, except for conclusion (4).[8] After the reanalyses were published, most of the remaining criticisms were that school resources and programs were too narrowly defined, that the study was cross-sectional instead of longitudinal or experimental, and that the standardized tests used were more measures of academic aptitude than academic achievement. Despite these criticisms, the Coleman report remains a landmark study, and most subsequent national studies have confirmed its seminal finding that family characteristics have much stronger influences on academic achievement than school resources and programs.

For twenty-five years after the Coleman report there were many smaller-scale studies of the relationship between school resources and achievement, but nothing comparable to the scope of the original Coleman study. Accordingly, the next major set of studies reviewed here use meta-analysis techniques, which synthesize large numbers of smaller studies in order to arrive at conclusions about the impact of school resources. The best-known meta-analyses are those conducted by Eric Hanushek on the one hand, and Larry Hedges et al. on the other.[9] Although these researchers use much of the same raw research data for their syntheses, they used quite different methodologies and, perhaps not surprisingly, they came to different conclusions about the relationship between resources and achievement.

The most recent Hanushek meta-analysis summarized results of 377 studies and finds no consistent impact on student performance for pupil-teacher ratio, teacher education, teacher experience, teacher salary, and per pupil expenditures.[10] The percentage of statistically significant *positive* effects for a given resource, based on all estimates, was as follows: 15 percent for pupil-teacher ratio, 9 percent for teacher education, 29 percent for teacher experience, 20 percent for teacher salary, and 27 percent for per pupil expenditures. Moreover, he also found 13 percent significant *negative* effects for pupil-teacher ratio and 5 percent significant negative effects for teacher experience, thus indicating a nearly total wash with respect to significant positive and negative effects for these two resources. The percentage of significant negative effects was smaller for teacher experience and per pupil expenditures (5 and 7 percent, respectively), so these two resources have a higher rate of net positive effects. Nevertheless, the majority of studies reviewed found no significant effects either way for these two resources.

After reviewing these studies, Hanushek concludes that there is "no strong or systematic relationship between spending and student performance."[11] He also says that the existing research literature provides little basis for making policy decisions based on the research. Because so many studies had non-significant or even negative effects, he believes there is no reliable basis for believing that, if a given resource is increased, one could count on improved performance in most cases. Further, Hanushek says:

> [T]he results do not say that school resources *never* have an impact. They say only that there is no reason to expect that added resources will have any consistent effect across typical schools.... Knowing that resources could and sometimes do affect student performance is not, however, helpful from a policy perspective. The existing research does not indicate under which circumstances resources are likely to be used effectively.[12]

The Hedges et al. meta-analysis reanalyzed the Hanushek studies using a different methodology. They criticized the simple counting procedures used by Hanushek on the grounds it does not utilize all of the information available in the research. For example, if one ignores significance levels in Hanushek's studies of per pupil expenditures, one finds 61 percent of the studies with positive impact and only 26 percent negative (and 13 percent unknown direction). Applying a different type of statistical test for all studies except those with no direction reported, Hedges et al. conclude that "there are at least some positive relations between each of the types of educational resource inputs studied and student outcomes."[13]

Hedges et al. also estimated the size of the effects for each school resource, which is generally more important to policymakers from the standpoint of cost-benefit assessment, and he did this for achievement test outcomes as well as for other student performance measures. They found substantial effects for both expenditures and teacher experience, but they also found small or inconsistent effects for teacher education, teacher salary, and pupil-teacher ratios. The effect for per pupil expenditures is remarkably large, such that an increase of only 10 percent in school expenditures would supposedly generate 1 standard deviation increase in achievement scores. No recent national or statewide study has reported such a large effect for any school resource, and even Hedges et al. questions the validity of this estimate.[14] Thus the Hedges et al. findings are not that different than Hanushek's.

David Grissmer and colleagues at the Rand Corporation have carried out a series of comprehensive studies on the relationship between school resources and achievement. One of these is a study of achievement in the states of Texas and North Carolina, which is especially significant because Texas and North Carolina are two states that have shown large achievement test gains after initiating a series of education reforms. These achievement gains have been confirmed by both a state testing program as well the NAEP testing, and while their NAEP gains are smaller than those shown by the state tests, their gains in math between 1990 and 1996 are the largest in the nation. Another noteworthy study by the RAND group is a national study of the relationship between school resources and achievement using NAEP state testing results.

In the earlier study of Texas and North Carolina, Grissmer and Flanagan reported that there were no statistically significant relationships between achievement test scores and standard school resource measures, including expenditures, pupil-teacher ratios, teacher experience, and teacher education.[15] Instead, they credit overall state education reform efforts in the area of accountability, which consisted of specific state education goals, explicit academic standards, and a mandatory state testing and assessment system. This is an intriguing conclusion, because rather than finding that achievement gains require additional school resources, they find that gains can occur when specific achievement standards are established and when school districts are held accountable for meeting those standards. The result of turning the spotlight on the process may simply cause everyone to work harder to meet specific objectives, much like the Hawthorne Effect mentioned earlier.

A more recent national study of school resources by Grissmer et al. differs from many others in that the state is the unit of analysis, and the outcome measures are state gains in NAEP test scores between 1990 to 1996. The study used several different sources for family background measures, including Census data, NAEP surveys, and surveys from the National Educational Longitudinal Study (NELS). The study also included most of the major school resources mentioned in other major studies: per pupil expenditures, teacher salary, teacher experience, teacher education, pupil-teacher ratio, availability of public pre-K programs, and teachers' assessments of whether they have sufficient resources. They did not, however, include measures of teacher certification or teacher's college majors.

While the methodology of this highly aggregated study is quite complex, the findings are not too different from other input-output studies, with one important exception. Like most other studies, the Rand team concludes that family background is more important than school resources in explaining achievement scores: "The pattern of achievement across states from 1990 to 1996 suggests that family variables explain most of the variance in scores across states."[16] The socioeconomic factors that have the strongest impact on achievement are parent education, family income, and race/ethnicity, but important effects are also found for single-parent families, number of children, and age of mother when child was born. This set of family characteristics (based on the NELS survey) is quite consistent with the risk factors discussed in chapter 3, and it is missing only the risk factors of mothers' IQ, nutrition, and parenting behaviors.

With respect to school resources, the Rand study finds that only two school resource variables have statistically significant effects on achievement using conventional levels of significance: per pupil expenditures and pupil-teacher ratios for grades one to four (pupil teacher ratios at grades five to eight are not statistically significant). Actually, these two effects are probably not independent, because smaller class size is a major determinant of higher expenditures (holding constant teacher salary, which did not have significant effects on achievement).

The study also claims statistical significance for having more pre-K programs and higher proportions of teachers saying they need more resources (of unknown type), but the significance level is only 10 percent, meaning there is a one in ten chance that there is no effect for these resources. The conventional significance level for policy decisions is 5 percent, or one in twenty, to be relatively certain that effects really exist before asking for more public funds. No clear rational is articulated in this study for changing this long-standing policy practice.

The Rand study also found that the proportion of teachers with three to nine years experience has a significant effect on achievement when compared to the proportion with less than three years experience. The meaning of this finding is not clear, however, since the effect of teachers with ten to nineteen years of experience is not significant when compared to the lower experienced group. Again, there is no clear mechanism offered for this nonlinear effect, and it could be some sort of idiosyncratic effect of teacher experience in certain states.

Aside from significance tests, the magnitude of the effects for all of the school resource variables are quite modest. For example, using what they called their "best" estimate of school resource impacts, the effect of increasing a state's annual expenditure by $1000 per student (a sizeable sum in 1993-94 dollars) would be to increase a state's average achievement level by only 1 percentile point. Likewise, a sizable reduction of five students per teacher in grades one to four would be expected to increase a state's average achievement by only 3 percentile points. The effects of all the other school resources with significance levels below the 10 percent threshold are even smaller.

The most controversial conclusion of the Rand study pertains to "interaction" effects, whereby it is claimed that the effect of additional resources is stronger for lower SES families (more accurately, states) and those starting with higher pupil-teacher ratios. By imposing a non-linear model on their data, they claim that a reduction of three pupils per teacher for low SES families in schools that have an average of twenty-seven students per teacher could raise average test scores by 5 to 6 percentile points. The problem with this conclusion is that the Rand data is aggregated to the very highest level, states, and even if family poverty and pupil-teacher ratios have nonlinear effects on achievement, these nonlinear effects are lost when data is aggregated to the

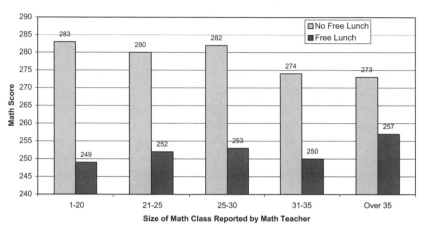

Figure 5.1
Class Size, Poverty, and National Math Achievement
(1996 NAEP Grade 8)

state level.[17] For example, in a low SES state like Louisiana, it cannot be assumed that low SES students are in schools with high pupil-teacher ratios, and vice versa; in fact, the opposite might be true, with most low SES students in schools with low pupil-teacher ratios.

The hazard of making inferences about nonlinear interactions with aggregate data is illustrated in Figure 5.1, which shows the relationship among size of math class, poverty, and NAEP math achievement for individual eighth graders in 1996. Both free lunch status and math scores are measured for individual students, and class size is reported by the students' math teachers. The numbers in the figure are actual math achievement means for each category; no adjustments or controls for other variables are made in this chart. Interestingly, the data does reveal an interaction, but for individual students it is in precisely the opposite direction to that claimed in the Rand study. Smaller classes generate a modest benefit for non-poverty students, with a 10-point advantage for students in the smallest classes compared to those in the largest classes. But the relationship reverses for students in poverty, so that free lunch students in the smallest classes have an 8-point disadvantage compared to those in the largest classes.[18]

The class size-achievement relationship in Figure 5.1 does not necessarily mean that low-income students learn more in larger classes. Rather, it probably means that many school districts reduce class size for low-achieving, low-income students who continue to score lower because of their poverty, thereby giving rise to a spurious relationship. In a later section, the class size variable in Figure 5.1 is shown not to have a significant relationship with achievement once other school and family factors are taken into account.

One of the criticisms of input-output studies is that they often lack more detailed measures of teacher quality, a school resource judged by many experts as critical for maintaining high achievement levels. Most state and national studies include such variables as teacher education, experience, and teacher salary. It is less common to see more specific indicators of teacher quality such as certification status, teaching in the certification field, whether college major is in the teaching field, measures of teaching skill, and teacher attitudes (e.g., efficacy). For this reason it is important to consider studies of school resources that include more specific measures of teacher quality, such as a 1999 study carried out by Linda Darling–Hammond.

The Darling-Hammond study collected measures of specific teacher characteristics from the NCES Schools and Staffing Survey of 1994, including certification status, college major, and education level; other school resource measures included class size, pupil-teacher ratio, and per pupil expenditures. No mention is made of years of experience in teaching. A summary measure of "fully qualified teacher" was defined as teachers who were fully certified and had a college major in their field of teaching. All of these measures were correlated with state NAEP scores including grade four math (1992, 1994), grade eight math (1990, 1996), and grade four reading (1992, 1994). Student SES was controlled using student poverty rates and the percentage of students with Limited English Proficiency (LEP); percent minority was also available but was not used in the multivariate analysis. Like the 2000 Rand study, all analyses were aggregated at the state level; no individual analyses were conducted.

Examining simple correlations, partial correlations, and multivariate regression, Darling-Hammond found that the strongest correlate of state test scores was the percent of fully qualified teachers (certified and a college major in their field). Student poverty, percent minority, and LEP status were also correlated with NAEP scores, but in her multivariate analysis fully qualified teachers had a stronger effect on achievement than either student poverty or LEP status. With respect to other teacher and resource characteristics, the multivariate analysis found no significant relationships for the percentage of teachers with MA degrees, percent of new teachers that were uncertified, and average class size after controlling for student poverty and LEP status. In the partial correlation analyses, significant correlations were found for several measures of certification status, but there were no significant partial correlations for class size, pupil-teacher ratio, or per pupil expenditures.

Darling-Hammond concludes from this analysis that teacher quality variables, in particular having certification and a college major in one's teaching field, are more important for raising student achievement than other school resources such as teacher education, pupil-teacher ratios, class size, and per pupil expenditures. She also argues that teacher quality variables are more important than student demographic characteristics, but because this study is highly aggregated, and only poverty and LEP status are used as control variables, this generalization is not valid. Aggregated studies can give biased estimates whenever key predictor variables are omitted, such as parent education, income, and family size and structure.

For example, the 2000 Rand study assessed a full range of family background measures, and they found that SES explained most of the variation in state test scores, exactly the opposite conclusion of the Darling-Hammond study. Nevertheless, while the absence of more SES controls might inflate the impact of teacher quality, Darling-Hammond does present some evidence that teacher certification and field of study might impact student achievement. An analysis of NAEP data presented below also finds that teacher major or minor in college math is a significant correlate of math scores, although the effects are small and much smaller than the effect of family SES.

Studies of Special Interventions

Comprehensive evaluations of four major school interventions are selected for review here; together they represent some of the most ambitious experimental and longitudinal designs for studying school resource effects. One of these interventions is the Tennessee STAR project, a large experimental trial designed to assess the effect of reduced class size on academic achievement. The other three interventions represent the largest efforts ever undertaken to improve the academic achievement of disadvantaged students, generally defined as children who are below the poverty line and who have low achievement test scores. These interventions are the Head Start preschool program, the federal Title 1 compensatory education program, and a subgroup of Title 1 programs called "Special Strategies," which include the *Success for All* program and the "Comer" model.

Tennessee STAR. The Tennessee STAR experiment was one of the largest and most carefully designed studies of an educational intervention ever undertaken.[19] The design included seventy-nine schools in forty-six school districts, 329 classrooms, and more than 6000 students in the initial kindergarten cohort. Incoming kindergarten students in these classrooms were assigned to one of three conditions in each school: small class size (median fifteen students), regular class size (median twenty-four), and regular class size plus a teacher aide. The reduced class sizes continued for four school years, until students completed grade three, and then all students returned to regular class sizes.

The apparent effect of smaller class sizes started in kindergarten. At the end of kindergarten, smaller classes outscored larger classes by nearly .2 standard deviations in reading and .15 in math. By the end of first grade, these differences had increased to .24 and .27 standard deviations, respectively, and the effects remained on the order of ¼ standard deviations until the end of grade three. After the experiment ended and students were returned to regular classes, the small class advantage declined appreciably, to about .13 sd for fourth grade and .15 sd at the end of seventh. It is not uncommon for effects of an educational intervention to decline after students return to regular school program conditions. Whatever the long-term effects of smaller classes in grades K-3, it is especially noteworthy that these effects are larger than those found by the typical input-output study reviewed above. As such, it is not unreasonable to ask whether the sizes of these effects are credible.

Although the Tennessee study is one of the better-conceived and more rigorously designed studies in the history of education policy, it is not free of criticisms.[20] Perhaps the most important is lack of a baseline measure of IQ or readiness, to make sure that the experimental and control groups were identical in academic ability before the experiment began (that is, to demonstrate that the random assignment worked). Also, the fact that the effect on achievement reached its maximum after first grade raises a legitimate question as to whether smaller classes were necessary in grades two and three in order to obtain the same longer-term effects; this issue has substantial cost implications. Finally, some critics have expressed concerns about possible expectation effects, a self-fulfilling prophecy similar to a Hawthorne Effect, where the teachers (and perhaps students) in the smaller classes worked harder because they believed that the smaller classes were superior. This phenomenon can be responsible for at least part of the shrinkage of effects after students went back to regular classrooms.

One should also evaluate the validity of the Tennessee STAR results in light of the subsequent adoption of small classes for the entire state of California, based largely on the Tennessee results.[21] California gave school districts sufficient funding to reduce virtually all full-day kindergarten through third grade class sizes to below twenty students, from an average of close to thirty students. Yet this massive infusion of state funds ($1.5 billion per year) and these dramatic reductions in class sizes led to only a .1 standard deviation increase in achievement levels by the third year of the program. This much smaller benefit of class size reduction may well reflect the differences between an experiment and a real, statewide (or even district-wide) policy implementation, and it raises questions about the cost effectiveness of class size reduction versus other educational reforms, such as raising academic standards or improving teacher quality. At the very least, the California experience should place the Tennessee results in perspective and serve as a caution to policymakers that the magnitude of the Tennessee results may not be replicated in state- or district-wide implementations.

Head Start. The federal Head Start program is the largest educational intervention aimed at the preschool child. The program started in 1965 as part of the war on poverty; it began as a six-week summer program, but it expanded in 1966 and soon became a full-year program. Eligibility requires that the family be low income or on public welfare, although a small percentage can be above the poverty line. The program has multiple goals, including improving children's physical health and abilities, bolstering self-esteem and self-discipline, and enhancing a child's cognitive skills. The program currently serves over 850,000 children at an annual cost of about $6 billion (up from 540,000 and $1.5 billion in 1990). Most children are between the ages of three and four (33 and 56 percent), although a new Early Head Start program focuses on birth to age three (6 percent). The racial and ethnic breakdown for FY 2000 is approximately 35 percent black, 29 percent Hispanic, and 30 percent white.

The most thorough evaluation of the Head Start program was a meta-analysis of seventy-six individual studies carried out by the Head Start Bureau in 1985. These studies provided sufficient quantitative data to allow calculation of effect estimates for cognitive performance (in standard deviation units), where the Head Start children were compared to similar low income children who had not been in Head Start. The studies also allowed comparisons of effects up to three years after Head Start, when most children would have completed second grade. Basically, the meta-analysis concluded that Head Start had immediate effects on cognitive skills, but they decayed rapidly and therefore Head Start did not produce lasting effects:

> "One year after Head Start, the differences between Head Start and non-Head Start children on achievement and school readiness tests continue to be in the educationally meaningful range, but the two groups score at about the same level on intelligence tests. By the end of the second year there are no educationally meaningful differences on any of the measures."[22]

The evaluation also found evidence for some positive effects on grade retention and avoidance of special education assignment, but this finding is based on a smaller number of studies. The study also found short-term effects of Head Start on socio-emotional outcomes like self-esteem and motivation, but again the effects were not lasting. In summary, Head Start produced significant educational and social benefits during the course of the intervention, but few of the benefits persisted into the second year of grade school.

To illustrate these conclusions, it is useful to examine the Perry Preschool Project, which was one of the early Head Start programs to be included in the meta-analysis. The Perry Project is especially interesting because it has one of longest follow-up studies in the research literature; about 120 children in the preschool and control groups were followed until they reached the age of twenty-seven.[23]

Perhaps the most significant educational benefit established by the Perry studies is educational attainment: about 66 percent of the Perry program students graduated from high school, compared to only 45 percent of the control group. But this educational advantage is not reflected in either IQ or achievement test scores. Consistent with the meta-analysis, at the end of preschool the

Perry program children had IQ scores 10 points higher than the control group, but this highly significant difference began shrinking by age six and dwindled thereafter until there was no significant IQ difference by the age of seven and thereafter. On the achievement tests there were no statistically significant differences in reading or math scores between ages seven and eleven (sixth grade), although the program students scored consistently higher. Inexplicably, an achievement test administered at age fourteen (using a different form) did show a statistically significant difference, although the scores for both groups were very low.

The Perry project evaluations are quite consistent with the larger meta-analysis, and it reinforces and even extends the meta-analysis findings about long-term effects. The Perry Preschool program produced short-term but not long-term gains in IQ scores, and it produced small but not statistically significant short- and long-term improvement in academic achievement during the elementary grades. The higher graduation rate in the absence of clear gains in IQ or academic achievement suggests rather strongly that the Perry program may have improved motivation and self-discipline but not necessarily intellectual skills. This conclusion is consistent with other significant behavioral differences observed at age twenty-seven, including fewer arrests, fewer social services, higher marital status, and greater home ownership.

Title 1. The federal Title 1 program is the largest educational intervention aimed at raising the academic skills of disadvantaged students during the early elementary grades. Like Head Start, it began in 1965 as part of the war on poverty, and it targeted high poverty schools and low-achieving students. The primary objective of Title 1 (similar to the former Chapter 1) is to improve basic academic skills through various methods of supplemental instruction, primarily in the areas of reading and math. A major restructuring occurred in 1994, whereby more flexibility was given to the states to fashion programs most appropriate to their poverty-level populations. One of the innovations is that an entire school could be designated as a Title 1 school, so that all low-achieving students—not just those in poverty—could receive compensatory services. In FY 2000, more than 6 million students in early elementary grades received Title 1 benefits, at a total cost on the order of $7 billion.

The most comprehensive evaluation of Title 1 took place during the school years 1991 to 1994 (Chapter 1 at that time), where a very large national sample of nearly 40,000 students in 400 schools were evaluated with respect to their participation in Chapter 1 and changes in achievement test scores.[24] Perhaps the most important subgroup evaluated was 10,000 students whose achievement scores were tracked between first grade in the fall of 1991 to the end of third grade in the spring of 1994.[25] This group represents the largest and longest-term evaluation ever carried out for an entry-level cohort of students receiving compensatory education. Not surprisingly, the Prospects study found a large achievement gap between Chapter 1 students and non-Chapter 1 students, a situation they attributed to the successful targeting of a low-income, low-achieving population. Over the three school years of evaluation, however, the scores of Chapter 1 students did not improve in comparison to non-Chapter 1 students with similar poverty rates:

> "Chapter 1 did, on average, serve those students who were clearly most in need of supplementary assistance. However, Chapter 1 assistance was, on average, insufficient to close the gap in academic achievement between advantaged and disadvantaged students."[26]

The authors point out that Chapter 1 was restructured in significant ways in 1995 (now Title 1), so the findings of this evaluation may not apply to the new program. However, there has been no comprehensive evaluation of the new Title 1 program that compares the achievement levels of Title 1 students to those of non-Title 1 students to verify whether the program is closing the achievement gap. The Prospects study remains the most recent comprehensive and rigorous evaluation of Chapter 1 or Title 1 to date.

Exemplary Programs. When the Prospects study was initiated, the Department of Education also initiated a companion study that would carry out intensive case studies of "special strategies" used in Title 1 schools to educate disadvantaged children. The special strategies selected by the study team represent most of the well promoted and widely implemented special interventions aimed at raising achievement of low-income children.[27] The strategies evaluated included the Comer School Development Program, *Success for All*, the Padeia program, Sizer's Coalition of Essential Schools, Reading Recovery, Extended Year Schools, METRA tutoring programs, Extended Day programs, and two total school reform projects in urban and rural settings (reduced class sizes, site-based management, etc.).

For each of these special ten strategies, the study team then requested nominations for two "exemplary" schools to represent each strategy. Nominations usually came from people familiar with the programs, usually a developer or disseminator, and these nominations were then passed to state and local Chapter 1 directors who had to confirm their exemplary status. This nomination process led to twenty-five schools that were supposed to be exemplary examples of ten of the most promising strategies for raising achievement levels of disadvantaged children. Most of these schools were high poverty and predominately minority (mostly African American). The evaluation process called for the same data collection as for the national Prospects study. Six programs were evaluated from grades one to three, and four programs were evaluated from grades three to five. The primary criteria for evaluation were gains in achievement test scores as compared to gains in the larger Prospects study.

Tests of statistical significance were reported only for reading gains.[28] Of the six intervention programs followed from grades one to three, four strategies showed no significant reading gains compared to the national Prospects gains (which were 0). The only two strategies with significant reading gains compared to Prospects (6 points) were the two Comer schools and the two *Success for All* schools. Of the four intervention strategies followed from grades three to five, three did not show statistically significant reading gains compared to Prospects (which showed a -3 point loss). The only significant reading gain was for an urban site-based management reform), but the educational significance here is questionable, because the gain was only +1 point.

With only two out of ten strategies, or four out of twenty-five schools, showing meaningful gains compared to national Chapter 1 students, it is instructive to examine these four schools in greater detail, looking at both reading and math. Although no significance tests are offered for math gains, it appears that neither of the Comer schools produced significantly higher math scores than the full Prospects sample, and only one of the *Success for All* schools did so. For reading achievement, one Comer school showed significant gains and one did not; likewise, one *Success for All* school showed *very* large gains—the same one showing math gains—but the other school showed no gains. Moreover, it turns out that the one *Success for All* school with significant reading and math gains was predominately Asian American; this makes the comparison with Prospects data problematic, since Prospects low-poverty students are predominately black and Hispanic. Generally, Asian American students perform better on achievement tests than either black or Hispanic groups. The other *Success for All* school was predominately African American, as were both Comer schools.

Despite the fact that the selected strategies are among the most promoted school reforms in the nation for helping disadvantaged students, and despite the fact that the schools used to evaluate these strategies were chosen intentionally to represent "exemplary" programs, the Special Strategy study boils down to a remarkably weak finding. Only a single school serving a predominately black or Hispanic population, a Comer program, was found to have significant effects on reading (but not math). One other school, a *Success for All* program, showed large gains in both reading and math, but since it is predominately Asian American, its comparison to the Prospects low-poverty sample is inappropriate. The conclusion of the study team, that "the ability of disadvantaged students to achieve academically was clearly demonstrated at *some* of the Special Strategies sites" is clearly a very generous summary of the exemplary study findings (emphasis added). A more objective statement would be that only a few schools out of twenty-five were found to raise achievement significantly compared to all Prospects students.

New Input-Output Studies

Despite the number of school resource studies completed since the original Coleman report, it is by no means clear that any significant advances have been made, or any drastic new findings have emerged, that would overturn Coleman's original conclusions, with the possible exception of pupils per teacher or class size. There is a presumption that good science builds on previously established findings, but in the field of education that presumption often goes wanting. For example, despite the many and repeated criticisms of the original Coleman study, there has never been a replication of that classic study aimed at fixing its well-known methodological limitations. For example, the Department of Education has never conducted a comprehensive longitudinal study of student achievement, starting from kindergarten or first grade, following students over their school career with the detailed measurements of school resources and student background employed in the Coleman study. The Prospects study comes closest to this kind of study, but that study was terminated when the first grade cohort finished third grade, perhaps because the results were not favorable.

Lacking comprehensive longitudinal data, education researchers have had little recourse but to conduct one of two types of studies: (1) meta-analyses of many small-scale studies, such as those of Hanushek or Hedges, or (2) highly aggregated studies using state-level data, such as those of Grissmer and Darling-Hammond. It is perhaps not surprising, given the very different types of data and different methodologies used, that the results of these major studies lack convergence. Hanushek finds no significant and consistent effects for any resource, but he acknowledges that significant effects occur in some studies. Hedges finds significant effects for expenditures and teacher experience but not pupil-teacher ratios, but the size of the expenditure effect is not credible. Grissmer finds significant but small effects for expenditures and pupil-teacher ratios but not teacher experience. Darling-Hammond finds no significant effects for expenditures, pupil-teacher ratios, or teacher education, but does find strong effects for teacher certification and college major (which none of the other studies measured).

One explanation for these inconsistent findings is that school resources tend to have small effects on achievement, especially when compared to (and after controlling for) family SES and other background factors. Therefore, researchers using different data and different analytic methodologies can arrive at different conclusions, particularly if they use different SES measures for controls. Given the strong impact of family variables on IQ and achievement, which all of these studies acknowledge, any variation in the number and quality of the available SES measures will undoubtedly affect the results. This may be particularly true for the meta-analyses, where the only requirement is that at least one measure of SES is used as a control variable. The level of aggregation may further complicate matters, since omitted SES variables can create biased estimates of school resource effects.

To further illustrate these issues, I will present the results of three new studies of the relationships between school resources and achievement. Two are studies of state achievement test results, conducted at the school district level for the states of Michigan and New York. The other is a national study using the 1996 NAEP test scores for individual students. These studies illustrate the discussion here by showing how academic achievement is affected by both family SES factors and school resources, how the level of aggregation can affect outcomes, and how SES factors consistently produce stronger effects on achievement than school resources.

Michigan Study. For many years Michigan has maintained a statewide testing program known as MEAP, where tests are administered at grades four, seven, and eleven. Although the test is voluntary, nearly all school districts administer the test and a very high percentage of students in each district take the tests each year. The State Department of Education maintains comprehensive data bases of individual test scores, teacher characteristics, and a number of measures aggregated to the school district level including percent of students on free lunch, expenditures, and pupil-teacher ratios.

This study is based on individual test scores in reading and math for about 92,000 seventh graders from the 1999-2000 testing cycle. The analysis selected about 380 medium and larger districts with enrollments over 1000. Analyses were run with and without Detroit (because of its size) and results were similar for school resource measures.[29] School resources measured at the school district level included teacher experience, percent of teachers with higher degrees, teacher salaries, pupil-teacher ratios for regular students, and per pupil instructional expenditures for regular students. SES measures were percent of district students on free/reduced lunch and percent of children at risk from the 1990 U.S. Census.[30]

The results of correlation and multiple regression analyses are shown in Table 5.1. The two SES measures have much stronger correlations with achievement than any of the school resource measures. The highest resource correlation is observed for pupil-teacher ratios, but it has the wrong sign, probably reflecting policies and programs (e.g., Title 1) that place more instructional staff in high-poverty schools. Indeed, the simple correlation between free lunch rate and pupil-teacher ratio is -.45, suggesting precisely that conclusion. In the multivariate analysis, both SES measures show strong effects on achievement, while none of the school resources are statistically significant except instructional expenditures and pupil-teacher ratio (which now has the correct sign after controlling for SES). The effects for expenditures and pupil-teacher ratios are probably not independent, because the ratios are a major determinant of instructional expenditures (the correlation is .62). Although the effect of pupil-teacher ratios is statistically significant for both reading and math, the magnitude of the effect is quite small when compared to the effect of SES. For example, if a district lowered its average pupil-teacher ratio by one standard deviation (two students per teacher), the regression in Figure 5.1 suggests an

Table 5.1
Effect of School Resources on Michigan Achievement Scores.

	Correlations		Standardized Regression Coefficients	
	Reading	Math	Reading	Math
STUDENT SES				
% Free lunch	-.28	-.37	-.19 (<.001)	-.28 (<.001)
% At risk (Census)	-.26	-.34	-.11 (<.001)	-.08 (<.001)
SCHOOL RESOURCES				
Teacher Experience (yrs)	-.04	-.07	.00 ns	-.01 ns
% Teachers MA+	-.02	-.04	.00 ns	-.02 ns
Pupils per teacher	.09	.11	-.05 (<.001)	-.07 (<.001)
Teacher Salary	.03	.03	-.02 ns	-.01 ns
Per Pupil Expend.**	-.01	-.01	.02 ns	.05 (.02)

*   N=383 districts; excludes Detroit and districts <1000; excludes special ed. students & teachers
** 1999 instructional expenditures for regular students; regression run separately

increase of only 1 point in state reading scores and 2 points in state math scores in that district.[31] An increase of $500 per student in instructional expenditures, compared to the 1999 state average of $3600, would translate to only a 1.5 point gain in math achievement (assuming it was spent on effective resources like lowering pupil-teacher ratios). For comparison purposes, a 1 standard deviation decrease in student poverty rates yields an estimated 8-point gain in seventh grade math scores. To put these gains in perspective, the 1999-2000 black-white achievement gap in Michigan is about 15 points in reading and 28 points in math. Clearly, even with the limited number of SES factors measured here, the SES factors are far more important than school resources in determining student achievement in Michigan.

New York Study. Like Michigan and a number of other states, New York also has a state testing program; unlike Michigan, the New York tests are mandatory. Both reading and math tests are administered at grades three and six, and several other special achievement tests are administered at other grades. Accordingly, this New York study is based on sixth grade reading and math scores for about 520 school districts with enrollments over 1000, which represents about 192,000 sixth graders. The State Department of Education maintains data bases for individual test scores and for school district resources, including teacher and expenditure characteristics. New York City (NYC) has thirty-two community school districts serving grades K-8, and each of these is counted as a separate school district in the state data base except for per pupil expendi-

Table 5.2
Effect of School Resources on New York Achievement Scores,
Medium and Large Districts, 1998 Grade 6*

	Correlations, excluding New York City		Correlations, including New York City		Standardized Regression Coefficents excluding New York City	
	Reading	Math	Reading	Math	Reading	Math
STUDENT SES						
% Free lunch	-.55	-.56	-.74	-.65	-.28 (<.001)	-.31 (<.001)
% Limited English	-.24	-.14	-.62	-.36	-.14 (<.001)	-.07 ns
% At risk (Census)	-.49	-.46	-.70	-.54	-.16 (<.001)	-.12 (<.01)
% BA degree (Census)	.41	.46	.37	.46	.29 (<.001)	.29 (<.001)
SCHOOL RESOURCES						
Teacher experience (yrs)	.07	.06	.32	.22	-.05 ns	-.07 ns
% Teachers MA+	.13	.23	-.06	.11	-.04 ns	.04 ns
Pupils per teacher	-.01	-.04	-.19	-.13	.10 (.01)	.10 (.01)
% Teach. turnover	-.03	.02	-.39	-.21	-.05 ns	-.01 ns
% Permanent License	.08	.06	.48	.33	.03 ns	.02 ns
Per pupil expenditures**	.07	.18	N/A	N/A	-.22 (<.001)	-.10 (.04)

*   N=491 districts; excludes NYC and districts <1000
** Expenditures regression run separately

tures, which is a single number for all NYC districts. As for Michigan, analyses were run with and without NYC districts.

For this analysis, state test raw scores were aggregated to the district level and merged with the other district data, which included four SES measures and six school resource measures. In addition to having the resource measures used in the Michigan study, New York also had the percent of teachers with permanent licenses (certified teachers) and the annual teacher turnover rate. New York data also included teacher salaries, but nearly 100 school districts were missing salary data, so salaries were not included in the final analyses shown here.[32] In this case expenditures are total operational expenditures rather than instructional expenditures, so administrative expenses are also included.

The results of correlation and regression analyses are shown in Table 5.2. Like Michigan, the student SES variables are much stronger correlates of achievement than the school resource variables, with some correlations exceeding .5 (excluding NYC). The correlations including NYC are larger, mainly because NYC has some of the lowest SES rates while at the same time having relatively high rates of teacher turnover and provisionally licensed teachers. Although the regression coefficients for school resources are about the same with and without NYC, Table 5.2 shows regression results without NYC.

The regression coefficients for the four SES measures are both statistically significant and large in magnitude; some of the standardized coefficients exceed .3, meaning that a 1 standard deviation decrease in a SES factor would increase test scores by nearly a third of a standard deviation of the test scores. In contrast, four of the six school resource coefficients are small and not statistically significant. Of special interest here are the near-zero effects of teacher licensure (certification) rates, which was not available in the Michigan data. The only statistically significant effects for school resources in New York are pupil-teacher ratio and expenditures, but the effects are opposite from what one would expect. After controlling for SES factors, lower pupil-teacher ratios and higher expenditures are associated with lower achievement; these are probably not independent effects given a correlation of -.45 between expenditures and pupil-teacher ratios. This inverse relationship probably reflects state policies that give more money to school districts with high concentrations of low-achieving, low SES students. This condition weakens the normally small relationship between resources and achievement and reverses it when SES controls are applied.

The NAEP Study. In more recent administrations, the NAEP project has been collecting increasingly detailed data on classroom data and teacher characteristics and linking it to individual student data. These efforts create a unique set of data, a representative national sample of students with individual test scores, SES measures, and school resource measures that include the characteristics of those students' teachers. Since the classroom is the lowest level of study for the impact of school resources and teacher quality, this NAEP data eliminates some of the problems of inference that can occur in aggregations to the school, district, or state levels.

The study presented here examines math scores for eighth grade students in the 1996 NAEP administration (see Appendix C for details of the analysis). This test and grade level is chosen primarily because of better-delineated measures of teacher quality for the teaching of eighth grade math. By the eighth grade more complex math topics such as algebra and functions are being introduced, sometimes for the first time, and effective teaching is going to require higher math skills on the part of the teacher. Moreover, at this grade level a teacher's math skills may be better aligned with his or her certification status and college major as compared to the skills required for teaching reading or other subjects. Many states require a specific certificate for teaching junior high math, and college major or minor may be more critical for a math certificate than it is for certification in other subject matters.

The SES measures available at the individual student level are race or ethnicity, free lunch status, education of parents, family structure, and an index of household reading materials. Race/ethnicity is used here as a surrogate for unmeasured family risk factors such as family size and parenting behaviors (see chapter 4). Teacher characteristics include years of teaching math, having a Master's degree (or higher), holding a certificate in junior high math, and having a college major/minor in math (either undergraduate or graduate). Other school characteristics included are size of the math class (as reported by teacher) and instructional dollars, which is measured at the school level. Approximately 6800 students and 560 teachers are included in the study (about 5300

Table 5.3
Effect of School Resources on NAEP Math Achievement, 1996 8th Graders

	Correlations	Standardized Regression Coefficients
STUDENT SES		
Black	-.37	-.31 (<.001)
Hispanic	-.18	-.13 (<.001)
Free Lunch	-.34	-.11 (<.001)
Parent Education	.29	.19 (<.001)
Two-Parent Family	.22	.12 (<.001)
One-Parent Family	-.17	.07 (.003)
Reading Items in Home	.28	.12 (<.001)
SCHOOL RESOURCE[a]		
Years Teaching Math	.09	.05 ns
Masters Degree or Higher	.00	.00 ns
Certified for JH Math	.11	.02 ns
College Major/Minor in Math	.16	.09 (.003)
Math Class Size[b]	.01	-.03 ns
Instuctional Expenditures[b]	-.05	.02 ns

[a] N=5400 students and 565 teachers; students with IEP (special ed.) excluded
[b] Separate regressions; class size N=3500, expenditures N=3800

have data on all variables except class size and instructional expenditures). Special education students with Individualized Education Plans (IEP) have been excluded.

The results of correlation and regression analyses are presented in Table 5.3. Again, as with the Michigan and New York studies, the simple correlations for all of the SES measures are much stronger than any of the teacher and school resource measures, generally by a factor of two or three. All of the SES factors also have highly significant effects in the regression analysis, with race and parent education standing out as especially strong, followed by two-parent families, reading items in the home, and poverty. After controlling for SES, only one of the school resource or teacher quality measures has a significant effect on achievement: teachers with college majors or minors in math. Students with teachers who have studied math in college score about 7 points higher than students whose teachers have not studied math, everything else being equal.[33] This effect is quite modest, however, when it is compared to the 30-point advantage that higher SES students have over lower SES students.[34]

Regarding the importance of studying math in college, it should be noted that if college math is deleted from the regression equation in Table 5.3, then teacher certification in math becomes statistically significant, although the magnitude of the effect is smaller—just 5 points (the two characteristics are highly correlated). For this national sample of eighth grade students, then, teacher certification appears less important than subject matter mastery as indicated by having a major or minor in mathematics. For studies that do not assess a teacher's degree status, certification might be a reasonable surrogate for mastery.

One caution is necessary when interpreting the relationship between teacher's college degree and student math achievement. It is possible that the causal direction between teacher's college math and student achievement runs in the opposite direction. That is, teachers with less mastery of eighth grade math may be teaching more general math courses rather than algebra or pre-algebra, and students with lower math skills may be more likely to select or be assigned to these less difficult math courses. In that case, we would not necessarily expect to see a rise in test scores if the percentage of teachers with college math was increased. That percentage happens to be 75 in the NAEP study, indicating that it might be difficult to raise it much higher.

In conclusion, the three new studies reviewed here are representative of the vast body of research on the relationship between school resources and academic achievement. Like most of the research literature and the discussions in chapter 3, the three new studies find that family SES factors have large and consistent effects on academic achievement. The evidence for school resource effects is much weaker and inconsistent; the Michigan study finds significant but modest effects for pupil-teacher ratios but the other two do not. If the underlying relationships between school resources and achievement are generally weak, it is not surprising to find some studies with positive effects and others with zero or even negative effects. This is basically what Hanushek found when he reviewed 377 studies.

One of the few school resource measures that was not included in the Hanushek, Hedges, and Grissmer studies, but that figured prominently in the Darling-Hammond study, is teacher's college major or minor in the area being taught. This teacher characteristic undoubtedly relates to subject matter mastery, as would teacher certification (in the absence of college major) or teacher skill level as measured by standardized tests. In this sense, the NAEP finding is similar to the Coleman finding about the relationship between teacher verbal ability and student achievement. Although the effect of college major in the NAEP data is much smaller than that found by Darling-Hammond, it nonetheless represents a school resource area where improvements might have modest benefits for raising a student's IQ and achievement. Even here, however, the size of the effect of teacher's college major pales in comparison to that for student's socioeconomic status.

Summary of School Effect Studies

This review of research on the relationship between school resources and student achievement is not intended to do full justice to the massive body of research that exists on this topic. I do claim that the review is representative of the major studies in this area, including some of the most sophisticated and more important, that more inclusive reviews will yield the same pattern of findings. The following points summarize the relationship between school resources and student achievement:

(1)   Schools increase the *absolute* (as opposed to relative) level of knowledge for nearly all children, but the effects are relatively uniform across various groupings of students;

(2)   Where SES is properly measured, a nearly universal finding is that students from lower SES families have lower achievement in school, starting in the earliest grades;

(3)   The impact of SES factors on *relative* achievement (normed test scores) are much stronger than school resources;

(4)   School resource effects are inconsistent from one study to another, and they are generally small in magnitude;

(5)   Whether or not a given school resource raises relative achievement appears to depend partly on study methodology and partly on idiosyncratic characteristics of particular schools or programs.

It is important to emphasize that these findings do not add up to a conclusion that schools or school programs have no affects on academic achievement or IQ. Schools do produce overall achievement growth for nearly all children, but the effects are sufficiently uniform that whatever skill gaps children bring to school tend to be perpetuated throughout the school career, despite special interventions. Moreover, while certain school programs and policies *can* have a positive impact on the achievement of low-achieving students, it is very difficult if not impossible to specify the exact conditions under which those benefits will take place and how large they will be. This lack of reliable and predictable outcomes renders school interventions uncertain for the purposes of maximizing children's intelligence.

A second general caveat concerns outcomes for other social and behavioral characteristics, particularly for preschool programs like Head Start. Like the Perry project, many special interventions for disadvantaged children have found beneficial effects on a variety of behavioral problems, attitudes, and motivation, in many cases leading to long-term outcomes such as greater educational attainment and reduced delinquency rates. The fact that school and preschool programs do not have reliable records for raising academic achievement does not mean they are having no effects whatsoever on the behavior of children. In view of the importance of intelligence for future success, however, it is worth investigating the feasibility of other potential agents of change.

Families and Early Intervention Strategies

The findings from the review of schools as agents of change generally reinforce the conclusions of chapter 3, which found that family SES and parenting behaviors have significant impacts on children's intelligence. The school research also tends to support the viewpoint that the most important environmental influences on children's intelligence must come earlier than the normal school or preschool ages if they are to have maximum benefit. This does not mean that regular school and preschool programs have no effects on IQ or achievement, but simply that there are diminishing returns to intervention as children get older. The policy challenge becomes how to utilize the great potential of the family characteristics so that they might have maximum effect on a children's intelligence and academic achievement.

Conceptually, there are three approaches for raising children's intelligence using the potential influence of family and parenting risk factors during the early childhood years. Two of these approaches focus on critical parenting behaviors (such as cognitive stimulation and emotional support), and they have already been implemented and tested in various formats, although none are yet as widespread as Head Start or Title 1. The first and most direct method is intensive childcare for infants and very young children, where a trained staff aims to provide additional instruction and positive interaction (cognitive stimulation, emotional support) to whatever the child receives at home. There have been a number of such programs implemented over the past twenty years or so, the largest of these being a relatively new federal government project called Early Head Start.

A second and slightly less direct method is the home visit approach, where professionals and paraprofessionals visit families periodically with a goal of training one or both parents in various parenting skills such as cognitive stimulation, nurturing and discipline, and health practices. In effect, rather than supplementing parenting behaviors, the home visit approach aims to improve parenting skills. The typical home visit intervention is somewhat less intensive (and less costly) than the full-time child care interventions, and therefore more implementations are available for evaluation. Some early intervention experiments actually combine the two approaches, so that home visits and parent training are offered at the same time as centralized childcare services. Both the educational childcare and the home visit interventions have usually been targeted towards at-risk children and families not unlike the Head Start program.

A third approach is even less direct but potentially more comprehensive. It has been called a "whole family" approach and it attempts to change overall family SES and structure, so that parenting behaviors might improve because of the improved family characteristics. A whole family approach that builds on the risk factors described in chapter 3 would try to improve parent education levels (e.g., dropout prevention), increase the number of two-parent families, increase income, reduce births to unmarried teenagers, limit the number of children, and improve parenting skills. While there is no single whole family program or policy that covers all of the environmental risk factors, there are many experimental and demonstration programs that target many if not most of these risk factors. The most comprehensive of these programs have been implemented by states as part of welfare reform. There are many other initiatives that address one of the risk factors, such as high school drop out prevention, laws that make it harder to get a divorce, and programs to locate and compel "deadbeat dads" to contribute financially to their children.

There are three major issues to consider when evaluating any of these policy or program strategies, at least for the purpose of this book. Obviously, the first is their impact on raising IQ or achievement test scores; this is often a primary but not an exclusive goal of the program. Many family intervention programs aim to improve a whole cluster of cognitive, behavioral, and health outcomes for children. A second issue is cost, which has not been discussed much up to this point. Family interventions, especially intensive childcare, can be far more costly on a per capita basis than school interventions. A third is ethical and moral considerations, because some family interventions raise sensitive issues about separating children from their parents or intruding into decisions about marriage and childbearing often thought to be strictly private matters.

The considerations of benefit, cost, and ethics should be considered for any new policy, although unfortunately this is not the way most social policies evolve. Because of political pressures to "do something" about a social problem of some type, legislatures more often than not implement a program first and evaluate it later. For example, both Head Start and Title 1 were already very large programs before the first comprehensive evaluations were carried out. By the time it was discovered that neither of these programs produced lasting benefits for children's IQ and academic achievement, the programs were so well institutionalized that they were very hard to modify.

Given that Head Start and Title 1 are so well established, new intervention strategies will have do demonstrate greater measurable benefits than existing programs, and the costs would probably have to be no more than existing programs on a per pupil basis. For some types of interventions, such as changing a law or a regulation, monetary costs may be inconsequential but there may be heavy social and political costs, such as controversies that might erupt over the wisdom or fairness of imposing an unpopular policy.

Early Childhood Programs

Some of the early childhood interventions have been in existence as long as Head Start (and even longer), and in fact many are designed as extensions of Head Start and utilize some of the staff and services of Head Start programs. Other early intervention programs are more recent, particularly some that have been implemented on a nationwide scale. Unlike the regular Head Start program, early childhood programs vary widely on many parameters such as intensity and location of services; age of child and socioeconomic criteria for eligibility; focus on parent, child, or both; and program objectives in terms of desired outcomes for both children and parents.

The most intensive programs offer center-based, full-day educational childcare from early infancy to the start of regular school, with additional parent training in the home, and a primary objective is to improve cognitive and school outcomes for children. The least intensive programs offer only home visits with parents once or twice a month, with no independent services offered to children, and goals are sometimes aimed more at children's physical health than cognitive development. The largest and most ambitious of the early childhood programs is the Early Head Start program, which started in 1995 as a special component of the regular Head Start program in the Department of Health and Human Services. These programs offer a comprehensive set of social and educational services, delivered in a variety of modes, to infants and young children from low-income families.

The variation in program features coupled with the usual challenges of field research substantially complicate the evaluation process, and accordingly there is wide variation in the quality of program evaluations. This review builds heavily on four comprehensive evaluations of early interventions that appear to be among the most promising. These four evaluations provide ample information about program characteristics, methodology, and outcomes for individual studies. Two of these evaluations were carried out by the Center for the Future of Children in 1995 and 1999 (David and Lucile Packard Foundation), one was carried out by the Rand Corporation in 1998, and the fourth—an evaluation of Early Head Start—was done by the Mathematica Policy Research Corp.[35] In addition, a subset of the intervention programs reviewed in these studies will receive special attention because of their unusual programmatic or methodological features.

Outcome Impacts. The first Future of Children study selected fifteen model programs for early childhood intervention. Eight of these were Head Start programs targeting mainly four-year-olds, and this type of preschool program has already been reviewed (e.g., the Perry Preschool). The main interest here are the other seven model programs that targeted much earlier ages, usually from six months to three years or less.[36]

Of the seven programs for very young children, six evaluations assessed IQ and six assessed academic achievement sometime after the start of regular schooling. The IQ gains attributed to these programs ranged from a little over 3 points to a high of 10 points, with an average of nearly 5 points. While only three of these differences were statistically significant in the original studies, all of them were in the positive direction. Since IQ tests are normed with a standard deviation set at 15, this represents an average effect size of one-third (.33) of a standard deviation. In addition, four of the achievement outcomes were statistically significant favoring the treatment group, while two others were positive but not statistically significant. Although these IQ effects may seem small, they are much larger than the average effect sizes for 1985 Head Start evaluation and the effect sizes associated with many school resource programs discussed earlier. This IQ effect is also larger than the post-treatment achievement effects of the Tennessee STAR class room size experiment, which average about one-sixth (.15) of a standard deviation. The effects of early intervention on academic achievement are also more consistent than any of the school program evaluations reviewed above.

Some of the individual studies in the 1995 Future of Children report have a variety of methodological problems, such as lack of a randomized control group, high attrition, and different intervention intensity. The report also omits two other important studies, one of which was not completed in time for inclusion. These are the North Carolina Project CARE, a replication of the Abecedarian project, and the national Infant Health and Development Program for low birth-weight infants. These two projects were reviewed in the Rand evaluation and should be included in any review of the more comprehensive and well-designed early intervention projects. These two projects, when added to the Abecedarian project and the Milwaukee project, provide a small sample of the most intensive early childhood interventions and the most rigorously designed evaluations. All four programs provided full-day educational childcare lasting from two to five years, and three of the programs also had regular home visits for parent training and education. All programs utilized randomized assignment to treatment and control groups, relatively low attrition from the program over the course of study, and at least one evaluation when the child reaches school age.

The impact of these four "exemplary" early interventions on IQ scores is summarized in Table 5.4. The effects on IQ range from 4.4 to 13.2 points, with an average size of just over 8 points. All of the individual effect sizes were statistically significant in the original studies with the exception of the Abecedarian project, but a similar effect of 5.3 points at age twelve was statistically significant. The average standardized effect size is one-half of a standard deviation. The three studies that administered achievement tests (Project CARE did not) also found significant gains in academic achievement.

Table 5.4
Effects of Selected Early Intervention Programs on IQ

Intervention	Entry Age	Exit Age	Age at last followup	Experimental IQ	Control IQ	Difference	Effect Size (sd)*
NC Abecedarian	3 months	5 years	15 years	95.0	90.3	4.7	.31
NC Project CARE	3 months	5 years	5 years	103.1	89.9	13.2	.88
Infant Health (IHDP)	1 month	3 years	8 years	96.5	92.1	4.4	.29
Milwaukee Project	6 months	5 years	13 years	101.0	91.0	10.0	.67
Averages				98.9	90.8	8.1	0.5

* Assuming IQ sd=15

In view of these results, it may be instructive to review the Abecedarian and CARE projects in more detail. Researchers at the Frank Porter Graham Child Development Center of the University of North Carolina began an early intervention project to determine if the mild mental retardation often associated with disadvantaged children could be prevented through early daycare, school-age intervention, or both.[37] The Abecedarian project recruited 111 mostly African American children born between 1972 and 1977 who scored high on a High Risk index, and they were then randomly assigned them to either a full-time educational childcare center or a control group. At age five all of the children were then reassigned to either a school-age intervention group or a control group. The school-age treatment provided a home/school resource teacher that visited the home approximately every two weeks and provided supplemental curriculum materials to the parents. The childcare program produced significant IQ effects of 7 points at program completion, 5.3 points at age twelve, and 4.7 points at age fifteen (shown above). The school-age intervention (alone) did not produce significant IQ effects, thereby strongly suggesting that the early childcare component was more critical than a school-age intervention.

Project CARE was a follow-up to the Abecedarian Project to determine if home-based intervention could produce the gains made by center-based intervention.[38] The project began in 1978 and recruited sixty-five families whose children were 90 percent black and scored high on the High Risk index. The participants were then randomly assigned to a home-visit-only group, a childcare group, or a control group. The home visit group received weekly visits from a trained family educator for the first three years and monthly visits during the last two years; the visits were about an hour long and focused on educating the mother in child development issues and training her in parenting skills. The childcare group received a year-round, full-day educational childcare similar to the Abecedarian Project, and in addition received home visits just like the home-visit-only group. The control group received no treatment. The children were evaluated at the end of the program period (age five), and the results showed that the childcare center group had significantly higher IQ scores (shown above), while the home-visit-only group showed no significant difference from the control group.

The combination of findings from the Abecedarian project and Project CARE suggest that the full-time childcare component plus home visits—rather than home visits alone—generates benefits for IQ and academic achievement. These results may not be surprising, because home visits do not offer direct instruction to children. Rather, the home visits rely on changing parenting behaviors which would in turn deliver more instruction and nurturing to the child, but this obviously did not happen in Project CARE. In contrast, full-time educational childcare delivers direct instruction to children over a substantial period of time; it is like giving two to five years of additional formal schooling (or preschooling) to the children in these programs.

What about other types of home visit programs? A number of other home visit programs have been implemented and tested, sometimes on a fairly large scale. Home visit programs usually follow one of two general models: a model that aims primarily to educate or train parents; little or no contact is made with children other than screening or assessment. A good example of this type of program is Parents as Teachers, which began as a state program in Missouri but since has spread to over 2000 sites in nearly all states. This is the least intensive and, accordingly, perhaps the least expensive type of early childhood intervention. The other model combines parent education services with some instruction to children during the home visits. A good example of this model is the Comprehensive Child Development Program (CCDP), a demonstration project sponsored by the federal government. The main difference between this model and an Abecedarian-type program is that the child instructional services are far less intensive and much shorter in duration.

The Future of Children evaluated six large home visit programs that had a considerable amount of information concerning program effectiveness.[39] Basically, while some of these programs produced some changes in parenting attitudes and skills, and some reduction of child abuse, none of the models "produced large or consistent benefits in child development." The evaluation noted that there was considerable variation in results, such that "benefits cannot be generalized from one home visiting program model to another."[40] The evaluation also noted that most programs had a difficult time delivering all of the intended services to families in the program, and attrition rates were high. On average, families received only about half of the services intended by the program. This may be one reason why benefits were small and inconsistent.

The evaluation results for the CCDP program are especially instructive, not only because it was a large federal demonstration program, but also because it utilized a reasonably rigorous evaluation design. More than 4400 low-income families at twenty-one sites participated in the demonstration program and evaluation, which is the largest sample size of all the single program evaluations. Half of the eligible families were randomly assigned to a treatment group, the other half to a control group. The treatment group parents were visited approximately twice a month for thirty minutes each visit, during which time parents were trained in a specific parenting skill. After the training session, the parent was then asked to demonstrate the parenting activity for a child in the presence of the trainer. The parents and children received these services from birth to age five, although about half of the group entered a Head Start program starting at age four (the home visits continued regardless of getting in Head Start).

Despite the five-year duration of home visit services, the CCDP evaluation found no significant impact on children's cognitive development, and in fact there were no effects on any major outcome for children or parents. In the words of the evaluation authors,

> "The evaluation...found no statistically significant impact of CCDP on program families when they were compared with control families in any of the assessed domains.... The authors conclude that the results of this evaluation do not support home visiting as an effective means...of parenting education...."[41]

Like the Project CARE study, the CCDP study found that home visits without reasonably intensive child instruction are not sufficient to cause consistent, measurable benefits for children's cognitive development.

The largest early childhood program is now the Early Head Start (EHS) program started by the federal government in 1996. By 2002 it had grown to 175 local programs serving 55,000 infants and toddlers from low-income families.[42] It seems fairly clear that this program is motivated by a belief that the most effective interventions for disadvantaged children must come very early in the life of a child. One of the most interesting features of EHS is the diversity of program modes. Rather than a single program model, EHS supports three major modes of service delivery to parents and children at the local level. Some local programs follow the home visit model: they deliver education and training services primarily through weekly and biweekly home visits with parents and their children. The intensity of services is generally greater than that of the CCDP home visit programs described above.

A second group of programs is organized according to the center-based model, where services are delivered primarily at all-day childcare centers. Infants and toddlers receive both instructional and nurturing care in small groups (e.g., child-staff ratios of three to one), and parents also receive special training in parenting skills, health practices, and a variety of other useful topics. Finally, a third set of local programs utilize a mixture of service modes, where some families are offered home-based services, some center-based, and some a combination of the two. Moreover, under the mixed-mode approach families can be shifted from one service mode to another as the needs of the parents and children change over time.

Early Head Start is being evaluated by Mathematica Policy Research (MPR) using a rigorous experimental research design. A purposeful sample of seventeen local program sites was selected to ensure geographic and programmatic representation. To be eligible for the EHS program a family has to be below the poverty line, and to be eligible for the research study a mother had to be pregnant or have a child under twelve months. As eligible families were recruited for the study, their names were sent to MPR for randomized assignment to treatment programs and control groups by a computer program. A total of 3000 families were ultimately included in the evaluation, about evenly divided between program and control. Control group families could receive other types of child development services available in the community, but the study determined that program families on average received much greater levels of service than the control group. For example, nearly 74 percent of the program families received the required intensity of services for at least one follow-up period (about one year) compared to only 14 percent of the control group. The most recent evaluation has been completed for children who have reached age three, which is considered the age of completion for EHS services.

Table 5.5 shows the impact of EHS programs on verbal IQ (PPVT) for the total sample as well as for two important groupings of families. Over all centers and demographic groups, the EHS program has raised children's verbal IQ scores by 2 points, which is an effect size of about .13 standard deviations (statistically significant). Perhaps more important, effects of the EHS program were considerably stronger for one particular type of program and for racial and ethnic minorities. The mixed-mode approach raised verbal IQ nearly 4 points (.23 sds), and verbal IQ scores were raised by just over 6 points for Hispanic children (.38 sds) and nearly 4 points for African American children (.23 sds). Perhaps due to the success of the flexible mixed-mode approach, most of the home-based centers had switched to the mixed-mode approach by the end of the evaluation period.

It should be emphasized that raising children's intelligence is not the only goal of the EHS; it also aims to improve a whole range of child and parent outcomes, including socio-emotional development, parenting skills, and parent's physical and mental health. Nevertheless, the impact of EHS on other outcomes seldom exceeds the magnitudes for verbal IQ shown in Table 5.5. Given the scope and intensity of the EHS program, the overall effects are quite modest. However, the larger effects for the more flexible mixed-mode programs and for minority families is the same order of magnitude observed for some of the exemplary interventions shown in Table 5.4.

Program Costs. What about the costs of early childhood interventions? Unfortunately, not all early childhood intervention projects produce detailed cost estimates, particularly for some of the experimental studies like those shown in Table 5.4, and program costs are not yet available for the Early Start Program. It is possible to make reasonable estimates, however, based on inter-

Table 5.5
Effects of Early Head Start Programs on Verbal IQ at Age 3

	Experimental IQ	Control IQ	Difference	Effect Size (sd's)
ALL PROGRAMS AND GROUPS	83.3	81.1	2.1*	.13
TYPE OF PROGRAM				
Home Based	84.6	83.1	1.5	.09
Center Based	83.2	81.8	1.5	.09
Mixed Approach	82.2	78.5	3.7*	.23
RACE/ETHNICITY				
White	87.7	86.9	.8	.05
Hispanic	77.4	71.2	6.2*	.38
African American	82.6	78.8	3.8*	.23

Tables I, VI.1, and VII.11, adapted from Mathematica report, pages 14, 270, and 381 (see note 42)
* Significant at p <.05

ventions for which cost figures are available. For example, the average costs for Head Start programs during Fiscal Year 2000 was approximately $6000 per child, which is similar to the average per pupil costs for general elementary education.[43] Since Head Start operates as a nine-month school year program for four-year-olds, one would expect higher costs for year-round educational childcare centers that serve very young children. Aside from a longer school year, infants and very young children require much lower child-teacher ratios. Thus the annual costs for the Abecedarian Project was about $11,000 per child in current dollars, or a total of over $50,000 for the full five years.[44] As another example, the Perry Preschool project provided a regular center-based preschool program but also included weekly home visits for parent education and training. The home visits and a low child-teacher ratio of 6-to-1 increased costs to about $12,000 per child per year in 1996 dollars.[45]

Programs that provide only home visits can be less expensive, but then their cognitive benefits are not as large as programs with full-time childcare centers or the mixed-mode approach of EHS. The CCDP cost is quite high for a home visit program, being over $10,000 per child annually in 1994 dollars.[46] Other home visit programs cost about the same as Head Start, or about $6000 per child.[47] Since most of the home visit programs, including the home visit mode for EHS, did not have significant effects on cognitive development, their somewhat lower costs are irrelevant for the purpose of evaluating their potential for raising IQ scores.

Can the relatively high costs of the more successful early childhood interventions be justified in terms of monetary savings to the government? No one has carried out cost-benefit analyses for the programs listed in Table 5.4, but the 1998 Rand study of early intervention carried out a reasonably careful cost-benefit study for the Perry Preschool project. Although the Perry program had no lasting effects on IQ levels (and fairly small effects on achievement), it did have positive impacts on educational attainment and various other socio-economic outcomes such as employment and criminal behavior. The Rand study concluded that the Perry Preschool program generated a net savings to the government of about $13,000 per child through reduced education costs, higher employment and hence higher tax collection, and reduced criminal justice costs.[48] If higher IQ and achievement test scores can generate even larger savings than the Perry Preschool program, it is possible that even the high costs of $50,000 per child for an Abecedarian-type project can be justified ultimately by savings (or additional income) for governments at all levels. To date, however, no such study has been carried out.

Two caveats are in order here about policy feasibility. The cost-benefit study for the Perry Preschool program makes it clear that most of the cost savings accrue later in a person's adult life, such as reduced criminal justice costs and increased tax revenues. If early childhood interventions are government projects, then the government has to advance the funds twenty years before any net savings are realized. It may be hard to sell voters on putting so much money up front, especially if the cost benefit evidence is based on only a few of these programs. A second problem may be one of convincing parents that they should let others become, in effect, "surrogate" parents who provide the type of care that the parents should be providing. It is quite possible that even disadvantaged parents, once they learn about the risk factors, would want to provide these benefits directly to their own children rather than letting others take over their job. This brings us to approaches that make parents the major agents of change.

Whole Family Approaches

For the purpose of maximizing a child's IQ, even the best early childhood interventions generally try to change only the post-birth risk factors, especially the parenting behaviors of cognitive stimulation (instruction) and emotional support. Some programs such as EHS also include pregnant mothers, so prenatal risk factors such as nutrition and low birth weight might also be covered. As important as these activities may be, they constitute only three of the eight environmental risk factors for a child's IQ. Five other environmental factors are not the usual focus of early childhood interventions, including family structure, number of children, age of mother, income, and education.[49] As shown in chapter 3, optimizing all of the environmental risk factors simultaneously might lead to an increase in IQ of as much as 10 points, and if the changes could be implemented by the families themselves, the monetary costs could be much smaller.

Most middle class and affluent parents-to-be already have the type of so-cioeconomic and behavioral characteristics necessary for promoting their children's intellectual performance, and on average these children usually do quite well in school. But what about parents-to-be who come from the lower socioeconomic ranks? Is it possible for them to change all of these factors at once—to finish as much schooling as possible, to marry before having a child, to limit the number children, and to acquire sufficient parenting skills to be above-average on the cognitive and emotional scales? From a theoretical stand-point, it is clearly *possible*, since all of these conditions are subject to deci-sions made by young people. But from a practical standpoint the situation is not so simple. The information about risk factors may not be readily available to low-income youth, and if it is made available, they might not act on it. Indeed, the reason that so many home visit programs have failed to raise IQ, apparently, is that parents did not use the parenting skill information that was provided to them during the home visits. Or, if they did try, they were not able to change their parenting behaviors sufficiently to affect their child's cogni-tive development.

It may be necessary to have more comprehensive policies that offer greater incentives to young families for changing all of these behaviors at once. For the past thirty years, social policies and customs have evolved with diminishing penalties for young women who drop out of high school or who have children outside marriage, and with fewer incentives for get-ting married before starting a family. On the contrary, for a very long time national welfare rewarded single mothers with policies that did not require employment, that paid more benefits for more children, and that penalized marriage. Basically, social welfare provided greater economic security for an unemployed, unmarried mother of three than the job market provided for a married mother of one whose unskilled husband worked for minimum wages.

I am not questioning the basic value or propriety of welfare under these circumstances of disadvantage, but only that welfare may have had unin-tended consequences in increasing the number of children living in poor, single-parent families with limited resources and inadequate parenting skills. This argument was made most forcefully by Charles Murray in his classic analysis of welfare, *Losing Ground*.[50] Moreover, little attention has been paid to the consequences of poor single parenthood on children's cognitive devel-opment, and indeed the plethora of special educational programs such as Head Start and Title 1 may send just the opposite message, convincing at-risk youth that special government programs will be able to fix their child's intellectual deficits regardless of a family's condition.

Of course, national welfare is not the only modern event that contributed to the expansion of single-parent families. Changes in sexual mores and prohibi-tions starting in the late 1950s also contributed to this trend. As discussed by

Francis Fukuyama in *The Great Disruption*, the sexual revolution changed attitudes about sexual freedom, marriage, and fathering responsibilities. Feminists have portrayed this revolution as liberating, but for many women at the bottom of the socioeconomic ladder it might be called oppressing.[51] Premarital sex is as old as the Bible, but the changing standards for male responsibility for children, including the demise of the "shotgun" wedding, was new, and it left increasing numbers of impoverished women with the full responsibility of raising children. It may be more accurate to say that men, not women, were liberated; under the new mores, a man could have as many sexual liaisons as desired without ever having to take responsibility for his children, as long as his mate of the moment did not protest. While many low-income women have gone along with this arrangement, assisted by a welfare program that until recently nullified the advantages of marriage, the real losers are children who are deprived of the benefits of having two parents and the enhanced parenting resources they bring.

There are some social critics who do not mourn the passing of the two-parent family, particularly activists in the liberal feminist movement. Quoting from a recent news commentary from the National Organization of Women (NOW), "It's a patriarchal sexist mentality to say that the cure for a poor mother's poverty is a father's income." And "...writing new laws to promote marriage may push women who don't want to be married into dysfunctional unions..."[52] The viewpoint of many liberal feminists is that a single-mother home should not be seen as deficient, and that government welfare should ensure that the single-parent family has as much financial resources as needed. Given the findings presented in chapter 3, these sentiments are overly narrow and pessimistic. It is not merely a father's income, but all the other contributions a father can make to parenting resources (interaction, nurturing, and instruction) that benefits a child and especially a child's intellectual development.

Also, it is simply unreasonable to imply that the rise of single-parent families, especially among African Americans, is due the inability of black women and men to create functional unions. Clearly, marriages go bad for a wide variety of reasons, including incompatibility and sexual promiscuity. But it is hard to explain the extraordinarily high rate of single-parent families among blacks—and especially the rate of never-married mothers—by arguing that two thirds of black fathers cannot be good husbands. Even in the case of white families, where the rate of single-parent families has risen to about 26 percent, it is unlikely that the main reason is unworkable marriages. Rather, it reflects a conscious choice of many black women and men and increasing numbers of white men and women to have children outside of marriage and raise them in a single-parent home.

I am not arguing for two-parent families here on religious or moral grounds, although such a defense would be reasonable in many quarters. Nor am I defending marriages in which one spouse abuses or mistreats the other spouse.

Rather, I raise the issue of two-parent families as another risk factor for a child's intelligence. Chapter 3 shows that never-married mothers with many children are more likely to live in poverty and have fewer parenting resources, which in turn adversely affects children's intellectual development.

How does one go about restoring the institution of marriage and parenting to its original status in America, especially for black and low-income families, where it seems to be in disfavor? There is no simple solution, but the general approach is to find ways to increase incentives and reduce penalties for marriage and smaller families among low-income populations. At first glance such an approach may seem harsh, but it is really no different than what social welfare did for many years—in reverse. For decades social welfare rewarded low-income single mothers with large families while offering few incentives for low-income married families. If Americans support government financial aid to single mothers with children, why not offer even greater financial aid for low-income married parents, as an incentive to initiate or maintain marriage? It comes down to whether and to what extent American society values the institution of marriage, and more importantly the extent to which it believes that having two parents significantly benefits a child's mental and social development. If the social and behavioral science communities agree that low-income families comprised of never-wed mothers with many children can be detrimental to a child's cognitive and social development, then it is not unreasonable to have policies that try to reverse the upward trends in single-parent families.

The federal government has already taken some initial steps in this direction with the passage of the 1996 Personal Responsibility and Work Opportunity Reconciliation Act, which supplemented the 1995 law creating a new welfare program called Temporary Assistance for Needy Families (TANF). These two laws, more popularly known as "Welfare Reform," replaced the decades-old Aid to Families with Dependent Children with a more restrictive welfare policy whose operation is delegated mainly to the states. Welfare reform limits financial support to five years (with certain exceptions) and has a variety of features that require employment and self-sufficiency. The act also has other mechanisms that encourage or require states to create innovative programs that reward marriage, reduce teen births, limit the number of children born to single mothers, and encourages unmarried biological fathers to become involved in raising their children. For example, there is a bonus program that awards $20 million (each) to five states with the largest percentage reductions in out-of-wedlock births; Alabama, Arizona, Illinois, Michigan, and the District of Columbia won the bonuses in 2000. States are also required to operate a Child Support Enforcement Program, which is designed to locate biological fathers, determine paternity if necessary, and require them to support their children financially regardless of marital status.

Some of the initiatives used by states to increase two-parent families and responsible parenting include requiring welfare clients to participate in child support programs, having a benefit cap when additional children are born, and having new parents enroll in parenting classes. In the case of parents who are minors, many states require that, as a condition of receiving welfare, they remain in high school until they graduate (or get a GED) and, if unmarried, live with a parent or guardian. There are also educational programs that encourage sexual abstinence until marriage.

Some states have been more aggressive than others in experimenting with various family policies as part of their welfare reform packages. The New Jersey Work First program, for example, has several requirements for welfare services that relate directly to family risk factors: (1) Welfare mothers who give birth to additional children are not eligible for additional assistance (family cap); (2) teen mothers under eighteen must live with their parents or other relatives; and (3) mothers under twenty who have not graduated from high school must remain in high school, enroll in a GED program, or enroll in other education/training programs.[53] The Minnesota Family Investment Program changed welfare eligibility rules to put two-parent families on the same footing as single-parent families and reduced the penalties and deductions for earned income. The Delaware "A Better Chance" (ABC) program imposes penalties for failure to meet parenting requirements, has a family cap like New Jersey, puts one-parent and two-parent families on same footing, and requires attendance at parenting education classes. Oklahoma has begun a Marriage Initiative that offers education and training seminars that encourage marriage and discourage divorce.

Since the welfare reform act is relatively new, and many of the pro-family initiatives are even newer, there is not a great deal of information yet about how these new programs are affecting family structure and stability, much less what impacts might be occurring for children. It is already known, however, that welfare rolls dropped dramatically by about half nationally between 1995 and 2000, indicating that the welfare-to-work component is having considerable success in transferring adults from welfare to jobs.[54] As far as impacts on family structure and size, one review concluded that the New Jersey family cap program might have reduced birth rates but a similar program in Arkansas did not; both studies suffered from methodological problems.[55] The Delaware ABC program increased marriage rates and favorable attitudes about marriage among younger single mothers without high school diplomas but not among older or more educated women; the former group clearly has the most to gain.[56] The Minnesota Family Investment Program increased marriage rates slightly among low-income single mothers (about 4 percent), but it had a large impact on maintaining marriage rates among two-parent welfare families (nearly 20 percent). A major research synthesis by the Rand Corporation found that welfare reform had strong and consistent positive effects on employment and earnings, but "the

Figure 5.2
Percentage of Children under 18 in Two-Parent Families
(Source: Current Population Surveys)

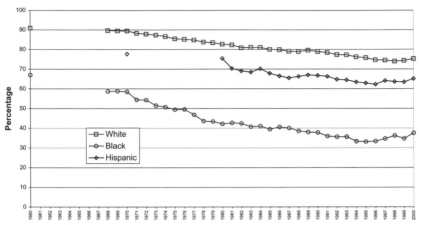

evidence...is insufficient to draw any firm conclusions about the effects of welfare reform on marriage or fertility."[57]

While the research on specific program effects is equivocal, it may not be coincidental that, starting in 1995, the proportion of black children living in two-parent families began rising for the first time since 1960 (when statistics first became available). Figure 5.2 shows the percentage of children under eighteen living in two-parent families by race. The rate of black children with two parents fell steadily between 1960 and 1995, and then it actually turned around and began increasing, gaining more than 4 percentage points between 1995 and 2000. A similar turnaround occurred for Hispanic children in 1996, and there is a suggestion of a turnaround for white children starting in 1998. It is quite possible that welfare reform and associated family initiatives are responsible, at least in part, for this turnaround.

The fact that Congress passed welfare reform in the first place may be a reflection of changes already underway in societal attitudes about marriage, divorce, and parenting responsibilities. Indeed, teenage birth rates were declining even before passage of the welfare reform package. It may be that young people have already started making changes in their family planning without the external incentives provided by welfare reform, although knowledge of how welfare programs now treat single parents and out-of-wedlock children undoubtedly reinforce these changes.

Whatever caused the increase in two-parent families among African Americans, their rate is still low (38 percent) compared to white families (75 percent) and even Hispanic families (65 percent). It is quite possible that, while improved education and income helped reduce the black-white achievement gap between 1970 and 1990, the very large gap in family structure contributes significantly to the stagnation of black achievement between 1990 and 1999. It follows that black children may have the most to gain from policies and programs that encourage and reward two-parent families and good parenting skills.

Summary

In summary, this chapter has presented three major findings about alternative strategies for maximizing a child's IQ and achievement. First, school policies aimed at disadvantaged children, whether special compensatory programs or extra resources such as smaller class sizes, seem to have limited effects on raising IQ and academic achievement. This is not to say that educational interventions during the regular school years have no effect, but that their effects are usually small and inconsistent compared to family influences. One reason is because they may happen too late, and another reason is that their level of intensity is lower than family and parenting behaviors. In terms of a child's waking hours over a one-year period, less than one-fourth of those hours are spent in school. In addition, regular preschool programs likewise have little lasting effects on IQ and achievement, but they do appear to have significant effects on other behaviors and motivation that can reduce dropout rates and ameliorate antisocial behavior in general.

Second, very early intervention programs such as Early Head Start and other full-time educational childcare programs do appear to raise the IQs of disadvantaged children, and therefore this approach represents a distinct policy option. On the downside, this type of early intervention is very costly in the short-run, and if it was expanded on a very large scale it might meet resistance from parents or groups who object to very young children being in full-time childcare for such a long period of time.

Finally, whole family policies that aim to restore two-parent families, reduce the number of children born outside marriage, emphasize the role of fathers, and improve parenting skills may be especially promising because they have the potential to optimize all of the environmental risk factors at once. Demonstration projects developed by states as part of welfare reform have some but not all of these characteristics. While welfare reform has succeeded in reducing welfare dependence and increasing labor force participation, it remains to be seen what kind of impact these policies will have on family structure and other parenting characteristics. If the family characteristics and parenting behaviors of disadvantaged children improve as a result of whole family policies, then these children's IQ and achievement scores should benefit in turn.

Notes

1. James Coleman et al., *Equality of Educational Opportunity*, op cit.
2. The term comes from a famous study by industrial psychologists in a Western Electric plant in Hawthorne, California that found increased productivity no matter what type of work-setting change was tried, and they eventually concluded that it was the attention from the experiment, not the work-setting improvement, that was responsible for increased production.
3. S. J. Ceci and W. M. Williams, "Schooling, Intelligence, and Income," *American Psychologist* 52:1051-1058, 1997.
4. S. Cahan and N. Cohen, "Age versus Schooling Effects on Intelligence Development," *Child Development* 60: 1239-1249, 1989.
5. See note 21.
6. See Marshal Smith, "The Basic Findings Reconsidered," in F. Mosteller and D. P. Moynihan, eds., *On the Equality of Educational Opportunity*, New York: Basic Books, 1972.
7. Coleman, op cit, p. 21-22.
8. F. Mosteller and D. P. Moynihan, eds., *On the Equality of Educational Opportunity*, New York: Basic Books, 1972; Christopher Jencks et al., *Inequality*, New York: Basic Books, 1972.
9. See E. Hanushek, "The Impact of Differential Expenditures on School Performance," *Educational Researcher*, 18(4): 45-65; L. V. Hedges, R. D. Laine, and R. Greenwald, "Does Money Matter?" *Educational Researcher* 23(3): 5-14 for the original meta-analyses.
10. E. Hanushek, "School Resources and Student Performance," in Gary Burtless, ed., *Does Money Matter?* Washington, DC: Brookings Institution Press, 1996. It should be noted that student performance can include either achievement levels or amount of post-high school education.
11. E. Hanushek, 1996, op cit., p. 56.
12. Ibid., p. 57.
13. L. V. Hedges et al., 1994, p. 10.
14. L. V. Hedges and R. Greenwood, "Have Times Changed?" in Burtless, op cit., p. 89.
15. D. Grissmer and A. Flanagan, "Exploring Rapid Achievement Gains in North Carolina and Texas," Washington, DC: National Education Goals Panel, 1998.
16. D. Grissmer et al., *Improving Student Achievement: What State NAEP Test Scores Tell Us*, Santa Monica, CA: The Rand Corporation, MR-924-EDU, 2000, p. 97.
17. This point has been made by Eric A. Hanushek, "Have We Learned Anything New? The RAND Study of NAEP Performance," *Education Next*, Spring 2001 (also www.educationnext.org/unabridged/2001sp/hanushek.html).
18. A similar pattern is observed for black students only.
19. The findings discussed here are from Jeremy D. Finn and C. M. Achilles, "Tennessee's Class Size Study: Findings, Implications, Misconceptions," *Educational Evaluation and Policy Analysis*, 21:97-109.
20. For a comprehensive critique, see E. Hanushek, "Some Findings from an Independent Investigation of the Tennessee STAR Experiment," *Educational Evaluation and Policy Analysis*, 21:143-164.
21. See Brian Stecher and G. Bohrnstedt, *Class-Size Reduction in California: The 1998-99 Evaluation Findings*, Sacramento, CA: California Department of Education, 2000.
22. Ruth H. McKey et al. (CSR, Incorporated), *The Impact of Head Start on Children, Families, and Communities*, Washington, DC: U.S. Government Printing Office,

1985. It should be noted that the Early Start Program did not begin until 1995, so the results of this study apply to three- and four-year-olds.

23. Lawrence J. Schweinhart et al., *Significant Benefits*, Ypsilante, MI: High Scope Press, 1993.

24. Michael Puma et al., *Prospects: Final Report on Student Outcomes*, Cambridge, MA: Abt Associates, April 1997.

25. Other cohorts included a group followed from grades three to five, and another from grade seven to grade ten.

26. Ibid., p. vi.

27. Sam Stringfield et al., *Special Strategies for Educating Disadvantaged Children, Final Report*, Washington, DC: Planning and Evaluation Service, U.S. Department of Education, February 1997.

28. Ibid., Tables 13-19 (pp. 13-94) and 14-10 (p. 54) show summaries of the gains and significance tests.

29. The Detroit enrollment is about seven times larger than the next largest school district, and it is also missing race on about 2/3 of its students in the MEAP data base. The analysis uses what are called "scaled scores" in the MEAP testing program.

30. Percent of children five to nineteen in single-parent families below poverty level and with parent who is a high school dropout.

31. The sds for reading and math are 18 and 28, respectively; the standard deviation of expenditures is $475, and the sd of % on free lunch is 22 percent.

32. Regressions run using teacher salary in 424 or 392 districts (with or without NYC) showed inverse coefficients when SES variables were entered, with or without other resource variables included, meaning that higher salaries are associated with lower achievement when SES is taken into account.

33. See Table C.2 in Appendix C for the raw coefficient for teachers with college math.

34. For this comparison, high SES students are those who are not on free lunch, whose parents have college degrees, and who have four types of reading materials in the home. Low SES students are those who are in poverty, whose parents are high school graduates, and who have two or less types of reading materials in the home.

35. Center for the Future of Children, "Long-Term Outcomes of Early Childhood Programs," *Future of Children* 5(3), 1995 and "Home Visiting: Recent Program Evaluations," *Future of Children* 9(1), 1999, and Lynn A. Karoly et al., *Investing in Our Children: What We Know and Don't Know about the Costs and Benefits of Early Childhood Interventions*, Santa Monica, CA: Rand Corporation, RB-5014, 1998.

36. The seven interventions were the NC Abecedarian project, the Housten Parent Child Development Center (IQ not measured), the Florida Parent Education Project, the Milwaukee Project, the Syracuse Family Development Research Program (achievement not measured), the Harlem Training Project, and the Verbal Interaction Project.

37. Karoly et al., op cit.

38. Karoly et al., op cit.

39. The home visit programs evaluated were Hawaii Healthy Start, Healthy Families America, Nurse Home Visitation Program, Parents as Teachers, Home Instruction Program for Preschool Youngsters, and Comprehensive Child Development Program.

40. "Home Visiting: Recent Program Evaluations," *Future of Children*, op cit., Executive Summary.

41. St. Pierre, Robert G. and J. I. Layzer, "Using Home Visits for Multiple Purposes" in *Future of Children*, op cit, 1999, Abstract.

42. Mathematica Policy Research, *Making a Difference in the Lives of Infants and Toddlers and Their Families: The Impacts of Early Head Start*, Head Start Bureau, U.S. Department of Health and Human Services, June 2002.

43.   Head Start Bureau, "2001 Head Start Fact Sheet," Washington, DC, 2001.
44.   Communication from Elizabeth Pungello, Frank Porter Graham Center, University of North Carolina.
45.   Karoly et al., op cit., Table 3.6 (p. 92).
46.   St. Pierre and J. I. Layzer, op cit., p. 144.
47.   An example is a nurse home visit program in Elmira, New York; see Lynne A. Karoly et al., 1998, Table 3.3 (p. 86).
48.   Karoly et al., op cit., Table 3.6 (p. 92).
49.   The EHS programs have added special initiatives to increase involvement of non-resident fathers in the parental education and training aspects of the programs.
50.   Charles Murray, *Losing Ground: American Social Policy, 1950-1980*, New York: Basic Books, 1984.
51.   Francis Fukuyama, *The Great Disruption*, New York: Free Press, 1999, pp. 120-122.
52.   Sarah S. Taylor, "Heated Debate on Welfare May Focus on Marriage," Washington, DC: NOW Women's Enews.
53.   Information from the web site of the New Jersey Department of Human Services: www.state.nj.us/humanservices/dfd/eligibility.html.
54.   Rebecca M. Blank, "Declining Caseloads/Increased Work: What Can We Conclude about the Effects of Welfare Reform?" *Economic Policy Review* 7(2):25-36, September 2001.
55.   David J. Fein, Rebecca A. London, and Jane Mauldon, "Welfare Reform and Family Formation: Assessing the Effects," research brief #1 from the Welfare Reform and Family Formation Project, Apt Associates, June 2002 (www.abtassociates.com/wrffproject).
56.   David J. Fein, "Will Welfare Reform Influence Marriage and Fertility? Early Evidence from the ABC Demonstration," *Evaluation and Program Planning* 24:2001, 427-444.
57.   Jeffrey Grogger, Lynn A. Karoly, and Jacob Alex Kerman, *Consequences of Welfare Reform: A Research Synthesis*, Santa Monica: Rand Corporation, 2002, p. xiv.

6

The Outlook for Maximizing Intelligence

This book started with four propositions about a child's intelligence and how it might be maximized. The propositions cover the importance and malleability of intelligence, the timing of change, the major risk factors that influence intelligence, and the family as the major agent for changing the risk factors. The previous four chapters evaluated these assertions by reviewing a substantial body of research evidence that bears directly on each proposition.

Having tested and validated the four propositions, this concluding chapter has three objectives. First, the propositions will be stated as an integrated theory of intelligence that embodies the conditions under which intelligence can be maximized. This statement also summarizes the key findings and conclusions from chapters 2 through 5, discussing their interconnections and implications for policy as appropriate.

Second, this chapter discusses an ethical question not yet raised, which is how public policy sets priorities for maximizing intelligence. Should it be concerned only with high-risk children such as those below the poverty line, or should moderate risk groups also be targeted? Current government policies clearly favor the first group, and while this may be a defensible option, other groups of children at risk should not be dismissed without discussion.

Finally, based on the findings and conclusions of chapter 5, this chapter discusses the feasibility of various public policy approaches for improving children's intelligence. Some of these approaches have already been tested and implemented, some have been tested but not implemented fully, and others have yet to be tested.

An Integrated Theory of Intelligence

The theory of intelligence offered in this book can be stated simply. Intelligence is an important human attribute; it can be changed but malleability declines with age; there are ten major risk factors for intelligence, all of which involve family conditions and parent behavior; therefore the family is potentially the best agent of change.

Importance of Intelligence

The first tenet in the theory is that a person's intelligence, as measured by IQ and academic achievement tests, is an important human attribute. First, it is important for everyone because of its strong influence on academic success and educational attainment, which in turn impacts heavily on job and career choices. Second, persons with high intelligence are essential for the fields of science, mathematics, and other professions that require very high levels of reasoning skills.

This proposition was tested by considering the relationships between IQ, academic achievement, and other outcomes as a child develops from the pre-school years, passes through the early and later school ages, and finally reaches young adulthood. Perhaps the most decisive relationship is that found between the IQ scores of high school students and their ultimate educational attainment. The prediction here is very strong. Three-fourths of youth with IQs in the top fifth graduated from college compared to only 3 percent of those in the bottom fifth. The relationship between IQ and income is somewhat weaker, but nevertheless each increase of 20 percentile points in youth IQ is associated with $20,000 higher annual income. Of course, the relationship between IQ and education explains a good portion of the IQ-income relationship, since most higher-paying jobs require at least a Bachelor's degree.

The importance of IQ is also supported by the very high correlations between IQ and achievement scores during the early elementary and the later secondary years, which indicates very little real change in the relative rankings of student IQ and achievement over the school career. This phenomenon is often called the "stability" of IQ.

There are several caveats to this conclusion. First, the correlation between IQ and educational outcomes is not so high as to exclude the importance of other human factors in the attainment of social and economic success. Motivation, creative talents, and interpersonal skills certainly play significant roles in educational and career success, and these other human attributes explain why the correlation between IQ and educational attainment is less than perfect. But the fact that human abilities other than IQ help shape a person's success is no reason to diminish the importance of cognitive abilities.

Second, to say that children's early IQ determines their later IQ does not mean that children are not learning throughout their school years. All children, with the exception of the severely mentally impaired, accumulate considerable knowledge and skills during their school years. Rather, the research evidence says that there is not much change in the *relative* ranking of children's cognitive skills, compared to one another, as they move through the school years. A child whose IQ is 15 points higher than average near the beginning of the school years is most likely to finish school 15 points above average.

Finally, the increasing stability of IQ as a child grows older has an upside that is helpful for the purpose of this book. If the stability of IQ increases with a child's age, then the other side of the coin is that the younger a child, the lower the stability—which means that real change is occuring. This finding suggests that IQ development is taking place during these very early years, which leads to the issue of the malleability.

Malleability and Timing

The second tenet of the theory, that IQ is malleable during early childhood, is intertwined with the nature of IQ, the extent to which IQ might be dependent on genetic factors, and the nature of cognitive development. Of course, the fact that a human characteristic has a genetic basis does not rule out the possibility of intentional environmental modifications, providing the characteristic and its causes are understood. Although basic skin color is an inherited trait, it can be further modified by sun exposure and by certain chemical substances. Therefore, the reason some psychologists believe that the environment does not influence IQ is not just because of its heritability, but also because it has proven quite stable during the school years and quite resistant to change.

This purpose of this book is not to show the exact portion of IQ ascribable to genetic factors, except to say that genes clearly play some role. What is more important is whether IQ and achievement can change after a child's birth, and whether known environmental conditions can influence those changes. For this reason, the question of malleability of IQ is more important than the question of heritability.

Two types of evidence help establish the malleability of IQ, one of which is useful for the purpose of maximizing IQ and one of which is less helpful. First, several studies show that IQ is increasing for societies as a whole, the so-called "Flynn" effect. They show improved absolute levels of cognitive skills for everyone, but they do not explain the mechanisms or causes of the improvement. Hypotheses range from better nutrition, the growth of information technology, more widespread schooling, or other cultural factors not yet understood (or some combination thereof). These studies do not show *relative* gains in IQ for some children, relative to other children.

More helpful are studies showing substantial improvement in the achievement of black and Hispanic students between 1970 and 1990 in comparison to white students. This type of change not only helps to establish the malleability of IQ and achievement, but the *relative* improvement of minority test scores in comparison to whites demonstrates that some type of environmental change occurred that benefited black and Hispanic children but not white children. While there is no consensus about the specific environmental influences that led to these gains, the discussions in chapters 4 and 5 point to improved socioeconomic conditions for minority families.

Equally helpful are the studies that show lower stability (and hence higher malleability) of test scores for younger children. IQ cannot be reliably measured under age three, since cognitive skills are not sufficiently developed for testing until about age three. Starting at age three or four, the pattern of IQ correlations are quite suggestive. The correlations between two IQ tests (say, four years apart) are lower at earlier ages than at later ages. While even the earliest correlations are still quite high, indicating that early IQ is a good predictor of later IQ, the fact that the magnitude of correlation diminishes at younger ages suggests that real developmental changes in IQ are occurring during these early ages. This opens the door to environment influences.

If IQ (or some precursor) could be measured at earlier ages, one might find even lower correlations, which would further diminish the importance of genetic influences. Indeed, if IQ is mostly genetically determined, and environmental influences are weak, there is no reason why IQ correlations should be smaller at younger ages. This assumes, of course, that the reliability of IQ tests is constant over time, which is a major caveat for this discussion. Another explanation for decreasing correlations at younger ages would be increasing unreliability of the IQ test at these earlier ages.

Fortunately, this book does not have to rely on diminishing correlations to decide about the possibility of early environmental influences on IQ. There are two separate pieces of evidence that are more definitive. One comes from the educational interventions for very young children reviewed in chapter 5. Long-term educational interventions for very young children have significant impacts on IQ while interventions for older children like Head Start and Title 1 do not, therefore indicating that environmental influences are stronger at younger ages. While Head Start programs have had other beneficial impacts on child development, such as improved behavioral outcomes (lower dropout rates, less crime, lower divorce rates), only the earliest interventions have been able to produce significant and lasting effects on IQ.

The other piece of evidence comes from examining the relationship between various risk factors and early IQ scores. The fact that environmental risk factors have strong correlations with intelligence test scores by the age of four or five (independent of parent IQ) is perhaps the most telling evidence about influence of the family environment on a child's intelligence.

The Risk Factors for Intelligence

As this book uses the term, a risk factor for a child's intelligence is a characteristic or condition that has a significant predictive correlation with a child's IQ in a longitudinal study. The usage here is similar to risk factors in medical research, for example in longitudinal studies of diseases. In medical research, a risk factor is a human characteristic measured at one point in time that is correlated with disease symptoms at a later point in time. Similarly, a risk factor for IQ is a characteristic at one point in time that has a significant correlation with children's IQs at a later point in time. An environmental risk factor is one that has a correlation after removing the effect of parent IQ.

There are several reasons why the ten most important risk factors for IQ focus on family and parent characteristics rather than environments outside the family, especially the school. First, the research that supports the correlations between these family characteristics and a child's IQ is very extensive. This book relies heavily on data from the Children of the National Longitudinal Study of Youth (Youth Study), primarily because it is one of the few national longitudinal studies that include measures of mother's IQ. But most of the correlations shown in the Youth Study have been replicated in hundreds of studies in the last thirty years, some based on national samples and some based on local samples.

Second, in the Youth Study the correlations between risk factors and a child's IQ are established when children are only four or five years old, before formal schooling has had any substantial impact. Thus family and parent characteristics impact on a child's IQ long before school effects even occur. Finally, when the effect of specific school policies are considered, the correlations between school factors and IQ or achievement are much weaker and less consistent than the correlations with family factors. Indeed, in many studies the correlations between most school factors and IQ or achievement are small and statistically insignificant.

What are the ten most important risk factors? The first and the strongest single factor is parent IQ: the higher parent IQ, the higher the child's IQ. Two additional risk factors are comprised of the familiar socioeconomic cluster: parent's education and parent's income (which also includes poverty). Next are three family characteristics of one versus two parents, number of children, and mother's age when the children were born. Then comes birth weight, which is partly physiological in origin but might also depend on a mother's behavior, particularly nutrition. The last three are the parenting behaviors of nutrition, instruction (cognitive stimulation), and nurturing (emotional support).

All of these risk factors have significant correlations with a child's IQ at age five and math achievement age nine. However, no single factor has effects completely independent of the other factors; they all interact in various ways, some simple and some complex. One of the more straightforward interactions is between parent IQ and education. Alone, mother's education has a very strong correlation with a child's IQ, but when the effect of mother's IQ is removed, mother's education has a much diminished correlation with a child's IQ.

The situation for each risk factor becomes much more complex when their interactions and interdependence are taken into account by means of multivariate analysis. For example, although mother's IQ is the single most important predictor of a child's IQ at age five, when the environmental factors are removed the effect of mother's IQ is reduced by half. The effects of education and family structure appear to operate through income, and income has a stronger independent effect on IQ than education after removing the effect of mother's IQ. The direct effect of two-parent families on IQ is small when controlling for all other risk factors, but the indirect effect of two-parent families is significant given its large effect on income and parenting behaviors.

After carrying out the appropriate multivariate analyses, the list of the most important environmental risk factors is reduced somewhat. Considering both direct and indirect effects, the most important environmental risk factors for a child's IQ are having a two-parent family, the number of children (especially in a low-income, one-parent family), breast-feeding (nutrition), and the parenting behaviors of instruction and nurturing. Parent education is less important because of its high correlation with mother's IQ, and mother's age and low birth weight also diminish in importance after controlling for other family characteristics. If these five factors could be optimized for a family, it is possible that a child's IQ could be raised by up to 10 points, regardless of what the mother's IQ might be.

Parent IQ is not in this list for two reasons. First, parent IQ likely embodies genetic effects, although there may be an environmental component as well— more intelligent parents may have better parenting skills, particularly in the areas of instruction. From a policy perspective, however, a more important reason is that a person's IQ is mostly determined by the time of parenthood, and therefore changing parent IQ before it impacts on a child is not a feasible policy alternative.

It should be clear from this discussion that the environmental risk factors have their major influence on IQ at early ages, a conclusion consistent with the discussion of malleability. The best evidence from the risk factor study are the high correlations between environmental risk factors and a child's IQ when children are four or five years old (after removing the effect of parent IQ). Assuming it takes some time for the correlations to develop, it is clear that the influence of the risk factors takes place at very young ages.

The major caveat for the conclusions about risk factors concerns the complexity of their interactions. While there is little doubt that each of these family or parent characteristics is sufficiently correlated with a child's IQ to be classified as a risk factor, the precise causal relationships and interactions among all ten are less well understood. I have carried out multivariate analyses to help decide which of the environmental factors have the largest direct and indirect effects, but the fact remains that these particular results are based on a single national longitudinal sample. There is no other national longitudinal database with all of these family variables, so it is not possible to replicate all of these findings with another national sample at this time. Nonetheless, because there is a large independent research literature on the importance of these environmental conditions for a child's healthy cognitive development, I am comfortable making policy recommendations based on what is known at this time.

Families as Agents of Change

Assuming the validity of the risk factors, why is it necessary to have another proposition about families as the best potential agents of change? Since all of the environmental risk factors operate primarily through parental decisions and behaviors, and since their influence is strongest during a child's earliest years, it might seem obvious that families would be the best agents of change for maximizing IQ. The situation is more complex, however, than simply identifying risk factors.

For example, the fact that smoking and obesity are risk factors for heart attacks does not tell us how to get people to stop smoking and lose weight in order to lower the risk of heart disease. Likewise, the fact that parent behaviors create most of the risk factors does not tell us the most feasible ways to change these behaviors. At least three of the risk factors—nutrition, cognitive stimulation, and emotional support—can be supplemented by persons other than parents, such as by trained staff at early child care centers. In addition, many educators sincerely believe that regardless of the skill differences that children bring to school, well designed and adequately funded school programs should be able to overcome cognitive skill deficiencies brought by disadvantaged children.

Chapter 5 reviewed three major strategies for raising children's IQ and academic achievement. The first strategy employs special programs for low-IQ children during the regular school and preschool years. The second strategy involves very early childhood interventions that offer intensive instruction and other services from infancy to preschool. The third strategy, called the whole family approach, aims to change all or most of the environmental risk factors simultaneously.

The evidence on compensatory and regular preschool programs generally indicate weak and inconsistent effects on IQ and achievement, particularly when they are compared to the impact of family characteristics. Smaller class sizes and teachers with greater subject mastery seem to be the most promising of the school approaches, but their impact on raising IQ and academic achievement is on the order of only 2 points or so (assuming a test score standard deviation of 15 points). These findings are consistent with the thesis that intelligence is most malleable at very young ages and that malleability is very low after the first two or three years of elementary school.

The promising results of the very early intervention projects like the Abecedarian project and Early Head Start are also consistent with the early age thesis. These programs require intensive educational and family services when a child is very young, some starting as early as a mother's pregnancy. No less intensive interventions (such as home visits alone) or later programs (such as Head Start) have had as large and long-lasting effects on children's IQ as the very early educational interventions discussed in chapter 5. The disadvantages of these early interventions are cost and potential ethical and practical problems. Their total cost can run at least ten times that of regular pre-school programs like Head Start (since they operate for five years), and many parents might object to having their infants and toddlers away from home for such long periods of time. Of course, for those at-risk children whose parents cannot or will not improve the home environment, early childhood interventions may represent the only option.

Finally, whole family approaches have the greatest potential to optimize the risk factors because they aim to modify all of the strongest environmental risk factors: two-parent families, a smaller number of children (for low income families), greater income, and increased parenting resources and skills. Even without changing the level of parenting skills, the presence of two parents with two children versus one parent with three children reduces the parent-child ratio from 1-to-3 to 1-to-1—a three-fold increase in parenting resources per child. If parenting skills could also be improved at the same time, all of the most important environmental risk factors could be changed by a whole family approach.

There is no comprehensive whole family policy in effect today, but some of the pro-family initiatives adopted by states because of welfare reform come close to this approach. For many decades welfare policies were structured so that single mothers with many children received greater financial rewards than two-parent families with fewer children. Some of the family policy approaches embodied in the 1996 welfare reform are turning this around so that two-parent families who work get greater rewards than single mothers who do not. In addition to welfare payments, some states have started other pro-family policies that encourage marriage, involve nonresident fathers in child rearing, eliminate benefits for children born after a mother starts welfare, discourage teenage pregnancy, and many other initiatives.

Research on the specific effects of whole family policies is just beginning and there is no substantial body of evidence on how effective these policies can become. It may not be coincidental that, for the first time since family statistics have been gathered by the U.S. Census, the rate of two-parent families among blacks began rising in 1996, and the rate increased 4 percentage points by the year 2000. Although welfare reform is not aimed specifically at raising children's intelligence, such a result is likely if it continues to improve the risk factors among American families.

While whole family policies are still in their infancy, the theory of intelligence proposed here still points to families as having the greatest potential as agents of change. Since parents are the only persons having control over all of the environmental risk factors, and since they have more contact during early childhood than anyone else, they are in the best position to optimize the risk factors and thereby maximize their children's intelligence. The policy challenge is to inform parents of their unique position and motivate them to improve the risk factors to the extent feasible.

Maximizing Whose Intelligence?

There is one broad policy issue that should be raised before addressing specific policies for improving intelligence. Is it appropriate to focus mainly on those children who are at risk of having low IQs, such as children from lower socioeconomic groups, should a society be concerned about raising the IQs of all children, or should there be some other set of priorities? This raises difficult issues of fairness and practicality, not unlike the debates in economic policy about whether the standard of living should be improved for everyone or primarily the poor.

As far as federal policy is concerned, the question of whose intelligence should be raised is probably settled, since the greatest portion of federal support for public education goes to Title 1 and Head Start programs. These compensatory programs target children below the poverty line who also have low achievement test scores, and given the correlation between poverty and low test scores, this means that most children from poor families are eligible for these special interventions. Recent Title 1 policies recognize school-wide Title 1 programs, which means that after the eligibility rate reaches a certain point, an entire school can receive special Title 1 services, including a small proportion of students who may not have low test scores.

Unfortunately, these programs have not been very effective in raising IQ or achievement levels, and more effective policies will require different strategies. Some new strategies may be more expensive, and most new strategies will be more intrusive because they impact family structure and very young children. Nonetheless, I see no reason to change the priority of state and federal programs being aimed primarily at those children most at risk of having low IQs, which means those children from single-parent families who are living below the poverty line.

This does not mean that the needs of other groups of children should be ignored. Given the nature of risk factors, most children from middle class and affluent families already have low risk environments, such as two parents who are college educated, greater income, better parenting skills, and so forth. There are, of course, middle class families with less favorable risk factors, such as those in which the parents divorce when their children are young, or perhaps those lacking good parenting skills. Because of their education levels, parents in these conditions may be able to improve the risk factors simply by becoming aware of their importance, perhaps through reading popularized accounts of the risk factors and how they might be changed.

Of greater concern are children from "moderate risk " families: parents who are above the poverty line but who have low incomes, less education, are divorced, and have poor parenting skills. These moderate risk families are certainly deserving of some type of prevention effort, perhaps educational programs, that inform them of the steps they can take to improve their family risk factors. This group might also benefit from various incentive policies and programs designed to promote two-parent families and improve parenting skills.

Policy Approaches for Maximizing Intelligence

What types of public policy approaches might offer the best opportunity to help maximize intelligence and academic achievement, particularly for high and moderate risk populations? The challenge to public policy lies in the nature of the theory: maximizing a child's IQ requires action at very early ages, and the risk factors that need to be changed involve family and parent characteristics that are not usually targeted by public policy.

Another difficulty is that some of the risk factors that need to be changed involve family practices that have evolved in our modern culture: shifts in values about marriage, changes in sexual mores, acceptance of single parents, and so forth. Indeed, changes in modern culture may account for a worsening state of several key risk factors, especially the decline in two-parent families and the increase in teenage pregnancy rates. Changes in culture and values are very difficult to counter, since their causes are diffuse and pervasive.

Rather than developing detailed programmatic policies for maximizing intelligence, I will discuss several policy approaches that appear feasible and cost-effective based on current knowledge and experience. Each approach has various strengths and weaknesses that will be mentioned, and some approaches may be more appropriate for certain target groups than others.

The principal targets for these approaches are the two groups of children with greatest need. One of these groups consists of children whose family condition puts them at high risk of low IQ; these children are from families below the poverty line, a high proportion of whom are minority families. The other group is children from "moderate risk" families who are above the poverty line but still disadvantaged with respect to several of the risk factors, including single parents and lower education levels.

Several approaches build on the research evidence reviewed in chapter 5. One utilizes the more promising policies and special programs that can be implemented by regular schools and preschools. A second approach is based on intensive educational childcare for very young children, such as the Early Head Start program. A third looks at pro-family initiatives that have been adopted in a number of states in connection with welfare reform; I will sketch how these might become whole family strategies that attempt to improve all risk factors simultaneously.

A final approach is somewhat broader and is based on general education and prevention strategies that have been applied in many public health campaigns, such as the anti-smoking campaign. General education and prevention campaigns have the potential to benefit any parent or parent-to-be who is interested in learning more about the risk factors and how they might optimize risk factors so as to maximize their children's IQ. Unlike certain other approaches that target only high risk populations, public education campaigns also have the potential for challenging the culture and changing values by pointing out the serious consequences of risky behaviors, in this case decisions and behaviors that might lower their children's IQ.

Policies for Regular Schools and Preschools

Special programs during regular school, such as Title 1 compensatory programs, have not had significant and consistent impact on raising the academic achievement of at-risk children. This is not to say they never have an impact, because one can find some schools where a Title 1 program has had an impact, but the effects are usually small. Moreover, it has never been demonstrated that the occasional successful program can be implemented for a whole school system while preserving the same magnitude of effects. This is because the success of individual schools may be due to idiosyncratic conditions, like a very enthusiastic principal, some very dedicated teachers, or some highly motivated students and parents. These special conditions usually cannot be exported to other schools at will.

To the extent that special policies might raise test scores of low-achieving students, the existing evidence tends to favor smaller class sizes in the early grades and teachers with good mastery of the subjects they teach. Teachers' subject-area mastery can be improved by more rigorous certification methods, especially mandatory skill tests. Even under optimal conditions, however, it is unlikely that improving these types of school and teacher resources will have large effects on academic achievement, for the simple fact that they occur too late in the cognitive development of children. At-risk children enter kindergarten with fewer cognitive skills than middle class children, and it is very difficult to overcome the initial deficit despite extra resources.

Recognition of skill deficits at the beginning of school led to the growth of preschools whose goals are to improve school readiness. Head Start is the largest preschool program in operation, aimed primarily at four-year-olds. The most rigorous long-term evaluations of Head Start for four-year-olds show some initial gains in IQ and achievement scores, but the gains are temporary and usually disappear after two or three years.

Head Start programs have been shown to improve student motivation and certain other outcomes, and some long-term studies show lower dropout rates, less criminal behavior, and higher rates of employment and marriage for Head Start children. But these improved social outcomes are not accompanied by significant cognitive gains, which was among the original goals of Head Start. The reason may be similar to the lack of Title 1 benefits: cognitive skills develop at very young ages, and at-risk children enter preschools with skill deficits that are hard to overcome.

Very Early Childhood Interventions

The belief that regular preschool programs like Head Start might be too late to raise a child's IQ inspired some early experiments using very early childhood intervention strategies for high risk children, of which the Abecedarian project is among the best known. These interventions offer intensive educational childcare and family services—center-based or home-based or both—starting when children are infants and continuing for at least three years. The success of some of these early experiments led to the development of the Early Head Start program, which now offers early childhood education and parent training to over 50,000 children and their families. A rigorous evaluation of Early Head Start shows a modest improvement of about 2 IQ points for all centers and families, but certain subgroups of centers and children (such as African American and Hispanic children) showed IQ gains of 4 to 6 points. Of course, Early Head Start has goals other than improving cognitive outcomes, but other outcomes show the same modest levels of improvement.

Do these results justify making Early Head Start the primary strategy for maximizing children's intelligence, at least for high risk children below the poverty line? Before answering this question, there are at least two considerations. First, the average cost of Early Head Start programs is about $15,000 per year per child, which is more than twice the cost of regular Head Start. Moreover, while regular Head Start lasts only a year, Early Head Start lasts three years, which means a total cost on the order of $45,000 per child. Since there are about 2 million children age three and under who live below the poverty line, Early Head Start for all eligible children could cost up to $90 billion every three years. It is not clear whether Congress would authorize expansion of Early Head Start if the overall impacts remain at the very modest levels seen to date. A stronger case can be made for using the program for those subgroups where the average IQ gains are 4 to 6 points.

Another consideration is the ethical and practical costs of early childcare programs, which means separating mothers from their infant and toddler children for substantial periods of time, at least in the center-based approaches. Although this issue is not addressed directly in the Early Head Start evaluation, it might be one reason why many families did not receive the full intensity of services over the three years of the program. At the very least, those parents concerned about the separation issue will have to be convinced that the gains for their children are substantial enough to justify the personal cost of "sharing" their children with other caregivers.

Since the Early Head Start program is a reality at this time, at least for 55,000 children, the major policy question is whether to expand it for more children below the poverty line. Since research and evaluation is still ongoing, especially a follow-up study to determine how children fare after leaving the program, it is perhaps too early to make specific recommendations about expansion. If the current results hold up, it may be appropriate to recommend Early Head Start for those demographic subgroups that show the greatest benefit from the program.

Whole Family Approaches

An "ideal" whole family approach should try to improve all of the risk factors for a child's intelligence. The ideal program would begin with young people before they become parents, which means targeting teenagers, or even the parents of teenagers. The program would first encourage completion of as much education as possible, minimally completing high school. A major goal for prospective parents would be to delay childbirth until all education is completed, and another major goal would to maximize the rate of marriage before couples have children. Higher marriage rates should result in greater income, but supplemental income from welfare may still be required for low-income families. Other major goals would be to ensure that both parents are involved in raising their children, even if the parents are not married, and to discourage large numbers of children when income and education levels are low. Finally, the program would offer training in parenting skills, including nutrition (e.g., breast-feeding), cognitive stimulation or instruction (e.g., reading to the child), and emotional support or nurturing (e.g., avoiding excessive physical punishment).

At this time there is no single program that corresponds to the ideal whole family approach just described. Under welfare reform, however, many states are developing aspects of the whole family approach. While the primary goal of welfare reform is to move families off welfare and into jobs that will ultimately provide for economic self-sufficiency, the new welfare legislation also provides incentives for various pro-family initiatives. Existing state initiatives include raising welfare benefits for two-parent households, offering programs that encourage marriage, requiring biological fathers to support and help raise their children, stopping benefits for additional children in welfare families, discouraging births to single teenagers, and requiring completion of high school as a condition for welfare benefits.

While most of these state initiatives are commendable, they do not constitute a national whole family policy as yet. Few states have all of the components of a whole family approach, and many states have very few components.

It might be worthwhile to take all the components that have worked reasonably well in one or more states and combine them into a "model" program which could then be proposed as a comprehensive prototype for a whole family policy. States could be given further monetary incentives for implementing the comprehensive prototype. At the same time, each of the components might be strengthened in various ways. For example, there might be larger monetary incentives for two-parent families and reduced benefits for out-of-wedlock births. Parenting skills should always be a key component of any whole family program; young parents—both mothers and fathers—on welfare should be required to attend education and training seminars to enhance the parenting skills of nutrition, instruction, and nurturing.

It goes without saying that there should be a strong federal role in monitoring and evaluating state programs that implement whole family approaches. An excellent evaluation model is that carried out by Mathematica for the Early Head Start program. All evaluations of pro-family initiatives need to include outcomes for children as well as parents in order to discover which initiatives do the most for improving children's cognitive development.

Education and Prevention

While welfare reform offers opportunities to reach disadvantaged children and hopefully improve their risk factors, there are two limitations of welfare reform as the primary focus of a whole family policy. First, most new welfare initiatives do not challenge the culture that has led to the decline in the family (Oklahoma's marriage initiative is an exception). Welfare reform attempts to fix problems that the culture has created, rather than preventing problems by challenging the culture and values that created them. Second, welfare reform does little for the moderate risk families who are above the poverty line but who have low income, divorced parents, and inadequate parenting skills. Although most moderate risk families are working class, there may be many middle class families who have unfavorable risk factors because of certain family characteristics, especially family structure, family size, and parenting skills. Few of these families would receive welfare benefits, and therefore few would gain from whole family policies that are imbedded in welfare reform.

I would suggest a national education and prevention program that promotes the whole family concept similar to the public health campaigns waged against smoking and other behaviors that increase health risks. The Surgeon General's campaign against smoking comes to mind. Great strides were made in reducing smoking by publicizing its serious consequences for lung cancer and other diseases. Although family environments affect many child outcomes, adverse impacts on intelligence—especially for young children—might generate greater motivation for change than other outcomes, especially since IQ influences education and other long-term outcomes.

In addition to a national prevention campaign, perhaps the best way to reach moderate risk families would be through education and prevention programs in junior highs and high schools. Many states already promote school programs for preventing teenage pregnancy that include encouraging delay of sexual activity, promoting marriage, and so forth. These existing programs could be expanded to cover the whole family approach with major stress on how all of the risk factors can have adverse effects on children's intelligence. By disseminating information about IQ risk factors to all young people in school, such programs have the potential of reaching most future parents, and convincing them of the decisions and behaviors they need to maximize their children's IQ. For young parents, high schools and community colleges could also develop classes that offer education and training in parenting skills, again with the main message that good parenting skills are essential for maximizing children's intelligence.

Like all education programs for preventing or changing certain behaviors, effectiveness is determined by the perceived consequences of the behavior and the credibility of the source. If family researchers and policy groups could agree on the importance of the family risk factors for a child's IQ, and the Surgeon General or the Secretary of HHS made a strong endorsement of whole family policy by starting a national campaign supplemented by local education programs in schools, it is quite possible that young people would start thinking about the consequences of their choices regarding education, sexual activity, marriage, and children. Ultimately, the best way to maximize intelligence for the greatest number of children may be to convince parents-to-be that their children's intelligence depends strongly on their own decisions and behaviors, and then give them information and support for choosing the best decisions and behaviors.

Appendix A

Multivariate Analysis of the Risk Factors

The discussion of risk factors in chapter 3 was based primarily on looking at each risk factor separately, both with and without adjustments for mother's IQ. Some of the discussion near the end of the chapter was based on multivariate analyses of the risk factors using the Youth Study (CNLSY) data. This technical appendix presents the regression and path analyses that form the basis of the multivariate discussions in chapter 3, and especially the effect estimates shown in Table 3.8.

Some of the variables used in the multivariate analyses differ from the univariate analyses in chapter 3. First, in order to maximize the number of children included in the analysis and the reliability of test scores, all verbal IQ test score data is used. In chapter 3 only verbal IQ scores from ages three to five were used, so that IQ would be assessed before the onset of formal schooling (and each child had only one IQ score). In this appendix, all IQ scores available in the 1996 NLSY data were used; if more than one was available for a child, they were averaged (about one third had one score, a third had two, and a third had three scores). The average age of the children when tested was about seven.

Second, age of mother when her children are born is confounded with the number of children she has, because mothers of large families will be older for each successive child. For this reason the multivariate analysis uses age of mother at her first birth rather than her age at each child's birth. Another variable utilized in the multivariate analysis but not in the univariate analysis is father's education, which is used here as a proxy for father's IQ. Father's education as of 1994 is used unless missing, and if so the 1992 measure is used. This might lead to some overestimate of potential genetic effects (and underestimate of environmental effects), but it is necessary because leaving it out would almost certainly underestimate the potential genetic effects of parent IQs. Father education is not available for about one-fourth of the weighted sample, in which case mother's education is used instead to prevent loss of cases (mother's education has only a small effect on IQ when mother's IQ is controlled; see chapter 3).

Several other risk factor measures need to be described. Family structure is scored so that a two-parent family receives a score of two, a single mother with

Table A.1
Regressions Used for Risk Factor Effects in Table 3.8

DIRECT EFFECTS	Coefficient	Std. Error	t-test	Probability	Standardized Coefficient	Mean	Standard Deviation
Child's IQ (dep)						100.0	15.00
Mother's IQ	0.332	0.014	23.210	<.001	0.348	100.0	15.00
Father's Education (yrs.)	0.306	0.086	3.550	<.001	0.049	12.6	2.37
Cognitive Stimulation	0.175	0.016	11.270	<.001	0.155	99.9	13.30
Emotional Support	0.132	0.016	8.360	<.001	0.113	100.0	12.66
No. of Children	-1.806	0.179	-10.110	<.001	-0.125	2.7	1.03
Breast-fed (1=yes)	1.654	0.365	4.530	<.001	0.057	0.5	0.50
Birth Weight (lbs.)	0.414	0.131	3.170	0.002	0.037	7.4	1.30
Family Structure[a]	0.936	0.316	2.960	0.003	0.042	1.4	0.66
Family Income ($000)	0.027	0.013	2.080	0.037	0.031	29.9	16.85
Mother's Age at 1st Birth	-0.055	0.057	-0.960	0.336	-0.014	21.1	3.60
N = 4779	R^2 = .37						
Math Achievement (dep)						100.0	15.00
Mother's IQ	0.294	0.015	19.560	<.001	0.315		
Father's Education (yrs.)	0.549	0.091	6.060	<.001	0.089		
Cognitive Stimulation	0.130	0.016	7.900	<.001	0.117		
Emotional Support	0.092	0.017	5.550	<.001	0.081		
No. of Children	-0.500	0.188	-2.660	0.008	-0.035		
Breast-fed (1=yes)	0.482	0.384	1.250	0.210	0.017		
Birth Weight (lbs.)	0.685	0.138	4.950	<.001	0.062		
Family Structure[a]	-0.206	0.333	-0.620	0.535	-0.009		
Family Income ($000)	0.022	0.014	1.640	0.101	0.026		
Mother's Age at 1st Birth	0.230	0.061	3.790	<.001	0.058		
N = 4711	R^2 = .29						

[a] Two parents=2; one parent married=1; one parent never married=0

the father not at home (for whatever reason) is scored as one, and a never married mother is scored 0. Family income is averaged across all years for which there is data and is scored in $5,000 increments (in thousands), and values over $70,000 are collapsed into this category because the relationship with IQ levels out at higher incomes. Number of children is coded from 1 to 5 or higher, again because the relationship with IQ levels levels out after five children. The cognitive stimulation and emotional support scores are averaged over the 1986, 1988, and 1990 administrations to have parenting behaviors during the children's younger ages.

Table A.1 shows the estimated effects for the risk factors on verbal IQ and math achievement using OLS regression. For verbal IQ all risk factors have statistically significant direct effects except mother's age at first birth. For math achievement breast-feeding, family structure, and income do not have statistically significant direct effects. However, family structure and income do have significant indirect effects on math achievement operating through cognitive stimulation and emotional support (see Table A.2).

Table A.2 shows the regressions used for calculating indirect effects of selected risk factors operating through cognitive stimulation and emotional support. Indirect effects are assumed 0 for factors with non-significant effects on cognitive stimulation or emotional support (e.g., father's education on emotional support). The formula for each indirect effect is the beta coefficient for

Table A.2
Selected Indirect Effects on IQ and Math Achievement

	Coefficient	Std. Error	t-test	Probability	Standardized Coefficient
Regression for Cognitive Stimulation					
Mother's IQ	0.193	0.014	14.240	<.001	0.227
Father's Education (yrs.)	0.782	0.082	9.550	<.001	0.142
No. of Children	-1.888	0.171	-11.050	<.001	-0.147
Breast-fed (1=yes)	1.776	0.351	5.050	<.001	0.068
Birth Weight (lbs.)	0.132	0.126	1.050	0.294	0.013
Family Structure[a]	1.274	0.298	4.270	<.001	0.064
Family Income ($000)	0.104	0.012	8.440	<.001	0.136
Mother's Age at 1st Birth	-0.145	0.055	-2.660	0.008	-0.041
Indirect Effects through Cognitive Stimulation:				IQ	Math
Mother's IQ				0.352	0.266
Father's education (yrs.)				0.280	0.211
Family Structure				0.445	0.336
No. of Children				-0.341	-0.258
Family Income ($000)				0.188	0.142
Regression for Emotional Support					
Mother's IQ	0.133	0.013	10.010	<.001	0.163
Father's Education (yrs.)	0.110	0.081	1.350	0.176	0.021
No. of Children	-1.248	0.168	-7.420	<.001	-0.101
Breast-fed (1=yes)	0.952	0.348	2.740	0.006	0.038
Birth Weight (lbs.)	0.015	0.125	0.120	0.905	0.002
Family structure[a]	4.733	0.294	16.110	<.001	0.247
Family Income ($000)	0.107	0.012	8.770	<.001	0.145
Mother's Age at 1st Birth	-0.164	0.055	-3.000	0.003	-0.047
Indirect Effects through Emotional Support:				IQ	Math
Mother's IQ				0.185	0.191
Father's Education (yrs.)				0.000	0.000
Family Structure				1.255	1.302
No. of Children				-0.171	-0.177
Family Income ($000)				0.146	0.151

[a] Two parents=2; one parent married=1; one parent never married=0

the parenting behavior on IQ or math achievement times the beta for the risk factor on the parenting behavior, times the fraction or number of standard deviations that the risk factor is changed (see Table 3.8) times 15 (the standard deviation of the test scores). Thus the indirect effect of mother's IQ on her child's IQ, operating through cognitive stimulation, would be .155 x .227 x (10/15) x 15 = .352.

The path model for the relationships among the various risk factors and child's IQ is illustrated in Figure A.1. For the sake of clarity, this figure shows only the causal arrows for significant direct effects on IQ. Mother's IQ and father's education (surrogate for father's IQ) are assumed to be the only exogenous variables, and both cognitive stimulation and emotional support are the latest in the causal chain—that is, they are influenced by the remaining eight risk factors. The other risk factors are assumed to occupy various intermediate causal positions.

Figure A.1
Path Model of the Risk Factors for a Child's IQ (direct effects only)

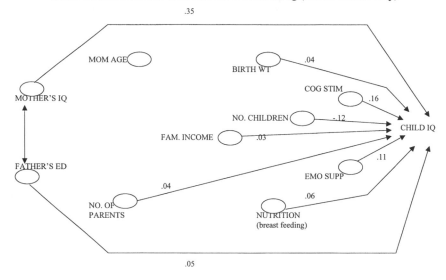

Figure A.2 shows the sub-path models for cognitive stimulation and emotional support, and in this case all significant causal arrows are shown along with effect estimates. Together with the direct effects in Figure A.1, this enables calculation of indirect effects along any causal path. Missing arrows between factors mean that the estimated effect is not statistically significant. For example, the significant predictors for number of children are mother's IQ and family structure when controlling for mother's IQ, father's education, family structure, mother's age, and income.

The largest indirect effects operate through the parenting behaviors of cognitive stimulation and emotional support, partly because they have sizable direct effects on child's IQ (second only to mother's IQ) and partly because six of the remaining eight risk factors also have sizable direct effects upon these parenting behaviors. Number of children also has a large direct effect on child's IQ, but only two risk factors—mother's age and family structure—have significant effects on number of children (notably, mother's IQ and father's education do not). Mother's IQ has large indirect effects on child's IQ because it has significant effects on all but one of the other risk factors and because most of the effects are sizable. Among the environmental risk factors, family structure is the most important because of the number and size of its indirect effects—on mother's age, number of children, and emotional support.

Figure A.2
Indirect Effects through Cognitive Stimulation and Emotional Support

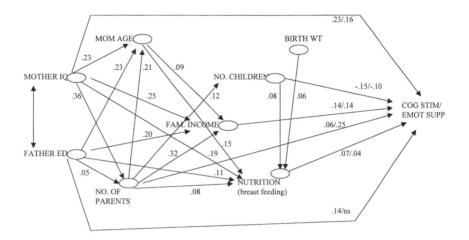

Appendix B

Analysis of Risk Factors for African American Children

Chapter 4 discusses the risk factors for the IQ and achievement scores of African American children taken as a group, including results from multivariate analyses. This appendix discusses and explains the regression and path analyses that form the basis of those discussions.

The multivariate analysis for black children parallels the multivariate analysis of all children presented in chapter 3 and explained in more detail in Appendix A. The primary differences in the analyses of black children is driven by the smaller number of cases, since black children comprised only 16 percent of the weighted CNLSY sample (28 percent of the unweighted sample of mothers and children). The variables used for the multivariate analysis of black children are the same as those described in Appendix A for the total sample, with the exception of the parenting behaviors of cognitive stimulation and emotional support. To prevent loss of cases in this smaller sample, the parenting behaviors were averaged across all scores available from the 1986 to 1994 administrations.

Table B.1 presents the multiple regressions and path analyses that form the basis of the simplified model of black IQ illustrated in Figure 4.20. This reduced model does not include all of the risk factors in the full model, so the estimated effects will differ from the full model shown in Table B.2. In particular, the standardized effects (betas) are all larger in this simplified model than in the full model.

Table B.1
Regressions Used for Path Analysis in Figure 4.20

	Coefficient	Robust Std. Error	t-test	Probability	Standardized Coefficient	Mean	Standard Deviation
Child's IQ (dep)						88.13	13.53
Mother's IQ	0.321	0.022	14.720	<.001	0.296	86.91	12.63
Cognitive Stimulation	0.213	0.021	10.170	<.001	0.209	92.95	13.37
No. of Children	-1.642	0.248	-6.630	<.001	-0.133	2.84	1.11
Cognitive Stimulation (dep)							
Mother's IQ	0.259	0.022	11.960	<.001	0.244		
No. of Children	-2.956	0.246	-12.010	<.001	-0.245		
No. of Children (dep)							
Mother's IQ	-0.020	0.002	-11.140	<.001	-0.232		
N black children = 2174							

203

Table B.2
Regressions Used for Risk Factor Effects in Table 4.1

DIRECT EFFECTS	Coefficient	Std. Error	t-test	Probability	Standardized Coefficient	Mean	Standard Deviation
Child's IQ (dep)						88.13	13.53
Mother's IQ	0.219	0.026	8.450	<.001	0.205	86.91	12.63
Father's Ed. (yrs.)	0.602	0.164	3.670	<.001	0.091	12.24	2.03
Cognitive Stimulation	0.122	0.026	4.730	<.001	0.122	92.95	13.37
Emotional Support	0.077	0.027	2.860	0.004	0.071	91.40	12.33
Birth Weight (lbs.)	0.369	0.199	1.860	0.064	0.037	6.92	1.35
Breast-fed (1=yes)	1.725	0.691	2.500	0.013	0.051	0.21	0.40
No. of Children	-1.396	0.257	-5.430	<.001	-0.115	2.84	1.11
Family Income ($000)	0.073	0.024	3.090	0.002	0.072	20.21	13.24

N black children = 1997 R^2 = .23

INDIRECT EFFECTS FOR TWO PARENTS VS. NEVER MARRIED

	Coefficient	Std. Error	t-test	Probability	Standardized Coefficient	Mean	Standard Deviation
Through Cognitive Stimulation						0.50	
Mother's IQ	0.094	0.026	3.690	<.001	0.088		
Father's Ed. (yrs)	0.969	0.160	6.050	<.001	0.146		
Birth Weight (lbs.)	-0.237	0.195	-1.210	0.225	0.024		
Breast-fed (1=yes)	1.741	0.675	2.580	0.010	0.052		
No. of Children	-2.530	0.252	-10.020	<.001	-0.206		
Family Income ($000)	0.142	0.024	5.900	<.001	0.144		
Family Structure[a]	2.031	0.394	5.150	<.001	0.112	0.87	0.74
Through Emotional Support						0.57	
Mother's IQ	0.103	0.024	4.240	<.001	0.103		
Father's Ed. (yrs.)	0.423	0.152	2.790	0.005	0.069		
Birth Weight (lbs.)	0.023	0.185	0.120	0.901	0.002		
Breast-fed (1=yes)	1.600	0.640	2.500	0.012	0.052		
No. of Children	-1.281	0.239	-5.360	<.001	-0.113		
Family Income ($000)	0.123	0.023	5.360	<.001	0.134		
Family Structure[a]	3.743	0.374	10.010	<.001	0.222		
Through Family Income						0.85	
Mother's IQ	0.253	0.022	11.430	<.001	0.227		
Father's Ed. (yrs.)	1.562	0.138	11.310	<.001	0.230		
M. Age at 1st Birth	0.470	0.066	7.110	<.001	0.129	19.62	3.46
Family Structure[a]	5.942	0.323	18.410	<.001	0.320		
Total indirect effect of two parents vs. never married						1.92	

[a] Two parents=2; mother with father absent=1; mother never married=0

Table B.2 shows the multiple regressions and path analyses that form the basis of the risk factors for African American children's IQ scores that were presented in Table 4.1. It should be noted that the pattern of standardized coefficients is similar to that in the analysis for all children shown in Table A.1. One major difference is that family structure does not have a significant direct effect for black children; another is that family income has a much larger effect for black children than for all children. Like the path model for all children, family structure has large indirect effects for black children operating through its effects on income and parenting behaviors.

The first panel shows the direct effects for child's IQ when it is the dependent variable. Mother's IQ still has the largest single effect, although it is smaller than the coefficient shown in Table A.1. But the effect of father's education is larger, so the potential genetic effect of parent IQ on child IQ is about the same—3.4 points for black children versus 3.9 points for all children. The coefficients for cognitive stimulation and emotional support are also somewhat smaller, but the coefficients for birth weight, breast-feeding, and number of children are about the same magnitude as the regression for all children.

The second two panels show the regressions for indirect effects operating through the parenting behaviors of cognitive stimulation and emotional support. Again, mother's IQ has smaller effects but father's education has larger effects. Generally, number of children and family structure have larger effects for the parenting behaviors in the black subsample than the full sample, but the effects of breast-feeding and income are similar. As in the full model, birth weight does not have an effect on the parenting behaviors.

Finally, the last panel shows the regression for indirect effects operating through family income. These indirect effects are more important than for the full sample because income has a much stronger direct effect on black children's IQ. A 10-point increase in mother's IQ is associated with a $2500 higher annual income, while a two-year increase in father's education is associated with a $3000 higher income. But even after controlling for parent IQ and education, black families with both parents in the home average nearly $12,000 higher than families headed by never married mothers. The indirect effect of two parents (versus never married mothers) operating through the two parenting behaviors leads to a gain in black children's IQ of just over a point, while the indirect effect of two parents operating through income leads to another gain of nearly a point.

Appendix C

Regression Analysis of 1996 NAEP Data

This appendix presents the detailed regression analyses that formed the basis of Table 5.3 in chapter 5. The regression study uses math scores from the 1996 National Assessment of Educational Progress (NAEP) for students aged thirteen (generally eighth grade). The weighted sample size consists of approximately 6800 students with math scores (weighted). The student background measures include race (black, Hispanic vs. white; Asians omitted); free lunch status; parent education (for parent with highest education); reading items in the home (scored from 1 to 4 items, where 1 = 0 or 1 item); two parents at home (vs. none) and one parent at home (vs. none).

The student data was merged with the characteristics of teachers who teach the student's math class. The teacher and school resource measures include years of experience teaching math; having a masters degree or higher; certified for teaching junior high math; either majoring or minoring in mathematics during undergraduate or graduate work; size of the math class as provided by the teacher; and instructional expenditures per student (equipment, textbooks, computers, etc.). About 6000 students had data on their math teacher characteristics, but only 3500-3800 students had associated data on class size and expenditures. Accordingly, the regressions for class size and expenditures were run separately.

The simple correlations among all of the measures are shown in Table C.1. The correlations are based on about 5300 students, except for class size and expenditures; these latter correlations are based on approximately 3500 and 3800 students, respectively.

The multiple regression results are shown in Table C.2. The first two panels show the regressions for student and teacher characteristics only. The next panel shows the regression results for teacher characteristics plus class size; the student background coefficients were very similar. The last panel shows the regression results for teacher characteristics plus expenditures; again the student background coefficients were similar to the first regression.

Table C.1
Correlation Coefficients for Table 5.3

	Math	Black	Hispanic	Free Lunch	Parent Ed.	Two Parent	One Parent	Read. Items	Math Exp.	MA Degree	Certified	Coll. Math
Black (vs. White)	-0.37											
Hispanic (vs. White)	-0.18	-0.13										
Free Lunch	-0.34	0.32	0.17									
Parent Education	0.29	-0.03	-0.16	-0.28								
Two Parents (vs. none)	0.22	-0.23	-0.08	-0.24	0.13							
One Parent (vs. none)	-0.17	0.20	0.04	0.21	-0.09	-0.90						
Reading Items	0.28	-0.13	-0.18	-0.26	0.28	0.22	-0.19					
Math Experience (yrs.)	0.09	-0.01	-0.05	-0.01	0.04	0.03	-0.02	0.03				
Masters Degree (%)	0.00	0.07	-0.02	0.01	0.05	0.00	0.01	0.02	0.32			
Certified for JH Math	0.11	-0.06	-0.07	-0.05	0.01	0.03	-0.03	0.02	0.08	0.09		
Math in College	0.16	-0.07	-0.08	-0.08	0.03	0.05	-0.03	0.04	0.12	0.02	0.56	
Math Class Size[a]	0.01	0.03	-0.02	0.10	-0.01	-0.01	0.00	0.03	0.11	0.06	0.10	0.05
Instructional Expend.[b]	-0.05	0.04	0.07	-0.03	0.01	0.01	-0.02	-0.01	-0.10	0.01	0.01	0.02

[a] N=3510 [b] N=3845

Table C.2
Regression Results for Table 5.3 (NAEP 8th Grade Math Scores, 1996)

Variable	Coefficient	Robust Std. Error	t-test	Probability	Standardized Coefficient	Mean	Standard Deviation
STUDENT							
Math Scores (dep)						273.76	34.01
Black (vs. White)	-30.994	2.638	-11.750	<.001	-0.314	0.14	0.35
Hispanic (vs. White)	-14.911	2.049	-7.280	<.001	-0.135	0.12	0.33
Free Lunch	-9.037	1.422	-6.350	<.001	-0.114	0.27	0.44
Parent Education	6.288	0.553	11.380	<.001	0.187	14.15	2.01
Two Parents (vs. none)	9.139	2.806	3.260	0.001	0.116	0.74	0.44
One Parent (vs. none)	6.242	2.919	2.140	0.033	0.074	0.21	0.41
Reading Items	4.636	0.639	7.250	<.001	0.119	3.21	0.93
TEACHER							
Math Experience (yrs.)	0.206	0.110	1.880	0.060	0.051	13.05	8.20
Masters Degree (%)	-0.247	1.856	-0.130	0.894	-0.004	0.40	0.49
Certified for JH Math	1.255	2.050	0.610	0.541	0.016	0.73	0.44
Math in College	6.880	2.280	3.020	0.003	0.089	0.75	0.43
N = 5285	$R^2 = .30$						
TEACHER							
Math Experience (yrs.)	0.159	0.127	1.250	0.211	0.041		
Masters Degree (%)	-1.764	2.207	-0.800	0.424	-0.027		
Certified for JH Math	3.302	2.334	1.410	0.158	0.040		
Math in College	1.948	2.522	0.770	0.440	0.025		
Math Class Size	-0.124	0.165	-0.750	0.454	-0.025	24.64	6.57
N = 3510	$R^2 = .28$						
TEACHER							
Math Experience (yrs.)	0.269	0.114	2.360	0.019	0.065		
Masters Degree (%)	-1.281	1.939	-0.660	0.509	-0.019		
Certified for JH Math	0.690	2.216	0.310	0.756	0.008		
Math in College	6.208	2.674	2.320	0.021	0.073		
Instructional Expend.	0.002	0.003	0.720	0.471	0.019	575.69	256.53
N = 3845	$R^2 = .31$						

Index